THE CHINA THREAT

THE CHINA THREAT

How the People's Republic Targets America

Bill Gertz

Since 1947
REGNERY PUBLISHING, INC.
An Eagle Publishing Company • Washington, DC

To my family

First paperback printing 2002

Gertz, Bill.
The China threat: how the People's Republic targets America / Bill Gertz
p. cm.
Includes index.
ISBN 0-89526-187-1
1. United States—Foreign relations—China. 2. China—Foreign relations—United States.
3. United States—Foreign relations—1993- I. Title: How the People's Republic targets America. II. Title.

E183.8.C5 G47 2000
327.73051—dc21

00-047920

Published in the United States by
Regnery Publishing, Inc.
An Eagle Publishing Company
One Massachusetts Avenue, NW
Washington, DC 20001

Visit us at www.regnery.com

Distributed to the trade by
National Book Network
4720-A Boston Way
Lanham, MD 20706

Printed on acid-free paper
Manufactured in the United States of America

10 9 8 7 6 5 4 3 2 1

Books are available in quantity for promotional or premium use. Write to Director of Special Sales, Regnery Publishing, Inc., One Massachusetts Avenue, NW, Washington, DC 20001, for information on discounts and terms or call (202) 216-0600.

CONTENTS

"The flames kindled on the Fourth of July, 1776, have spread over too much of the globe to be extinguished by the feeble engines of despotism; on the contrary, they will consume these engines and all who work them."

—Thomas Jefferson, 1821

INTRODUCTION TO THE PAPERBACK EDITION

The devastating terrorist attacks on the World Trade Center and the Pentagon and America's first domestic bioterrorism mail attacks have shifted America's attention and resources to the immediate threat of international terrorism. But we shouldn't be fooled. Since the publication of the hardcover edition of *The China Threat* in November 2000, one thing remains very much the same: the People's Republic of China is the most serious long-term national security challenge to the United States. In fact, after the events of September 11, the China threat should seem all the more real, for Communist China is one of the most important backers of states that support international terrorism.

Across a broad front, Beijing is continuing its covert battle against the United States, while carefully avoiding direct confrontation.

The Chinese government has appeared to support the United States in the war on terrorism. Yet statements by Chinese officials have shown Beijing's support to be questionable and its paranoia to be increasing.

Two days after the September 11 terrorist attacks, senior Chinese colonels Qiao Liang and Wang Xiangsui announced that the attacks could be "favorable to China." Interviewed by *Ta Kung Pao*, a Communist Party–owned newspaper, on September 13, Qiao and Wang gloated about how predictions they had made about the future of warfare had come true. In their 1999 book *Unrestricted Warfare*, in which the colonels urged China's weaker military forces to adopt all forms of warfare to defeat its main enemy—the United States—Qiao and Wang had said that future warfare would combine traditional military and non-military means with the terror tactics of Osama bin Laden, the chief suspect in the September 11 attacks. In the interview with *Ta Kung Pao*, the colonels also stated that the thousands of Americans killed were "victims of U.S. foreign policy" and that the United States should "learn a lesson" from it.

Later, the same Chinese communist newspaper claimed that the deployment of American military forces to a new base in the central Asian nation of Uzbekistan was part of a plan for a future "strategic pincer attack on China."

U.S. intelligence officials also disclosed to me that two Chinese companies secretly assisted the ruling Taliban militia in Afghanistan for two-and-a-half years by installing a telephone switching network in the capital of Kabul. The telephone network was destroyed in U.S. bombing raids during the first two weeks of the campaign on terrorist training camps and Taliban military targets.

China is continuing its irresponsible support for the main state sponsors of international terrorism, including Iran and Iraq. Chinese companies built a fiber-optic communications network in Iraq that was used by the Iraqi military air defense network. It too was bombed by U.S. warplanes. China also continued sales of military equipment and missile goods to Iran and North Korea.

In addition, the strategic marriage of Russia and China grew closer with the signing of a new cooperative agreement in the summer of 2001. U.S. intelligence agencies had earlier detected an alarming scenario during a Russian strategic nuclear war game. In a mock conflict, Russian bombers intervened with nuclear weapons against U.S. forces that had aided Taiwan during a war between China and the island nation. The exercise showed the depth of the strategic union between Moscow and Beijing.

The election of George W. Bush as president marked the beginning of a more realistic approach to China. Within weeks of moving into the Oval Office, the new president was tested by a crisis with China that hardened the administration's policy toward Beijing. On April 1, 2001, an aggressive Chinese F-8 interceptor jet harassed a U.S. EP-3 surveillance plane by flying too close. It sideswiped the aircraft over the South China Sea, and the collision sent the plane into a dive and nearly killed all twenty-four American crew members. The Chinese pilot was sent to a watery grave. The Chinese military then held the Americans on Hainan island for a full eleven days, until after the U.S. government had sent a carefully worded letter of regret over the death of the Chinese pilot. China held on to the EP-3 for months before forcing the United States to remove it in pieces aboard a chartered foreign transport aircraft.

The incident was the clearest example of how China is working to gain dominance over Asia and to drive the United States out of the region.

The U.S. government responded by increasing arms sales to Taiwan to address a dangerous military imbalance caused by the Clinton administration's pro-China policies. And the Pentagon's five-year strategic Quadrennial Defense Review report called for shifting forces toward China. The navy was directed to increase its aircraft carrier battle group presence in Asia, along with adding warships and submarines in the region. The air force was tasked to increase contingency basing in the Pacific and Indian Oceans to support future operations.

Events since the publication of *The China Threat* show that the danger from the nuclear-armed communist dictatorship in China is growing. A chapter-by-chapter review makes clear that the threat from Communist China has not abated and requires attention even as we face the immediate threat of terrorism.

The China Threat: Sean Garland, president of Ireland's communist Workers' Party, confirmed his meeting with Chinese Communist Party official Cao Xiaobing and said his discussions were "political" in nature. In a major speech, General Henry H. Shelton, the chairman of the Joint Chiefs of Staff, warned that China could well become a "twenty-first-century version of the Soviet bear."

The Plan: The Senate Intelligence Committee reaffirmed that China launched a secret plan to influence the 1996 U.S. elections, focusing on candidates who were sympathetic to China's concerns. The committee's report, made public in August 2000 and based on intelligence information, stated that the Chinese used political donations and other means to buy influence. Did China influence the elections? "The answer to that question, the committee concluded, was: Yes," the report said. "The existence of this plan is substantiated by the body of evidence reviewed by the committee, including intelligence reports.... There is intelligence information indicating [Chinese] officials provided funds to U.S. political campaigns."

China Wars: The ideological battle over China policy continues. Months after taking office, the Bush administration dropped its designation of China as a "strategic competitor." National Security Adviser Condoleezza Rice dismissed the term as merely a useful presidential campaign slogan.

The CIA came under fire for its weak analysis on China. The secret conclusions of a group of experts from outside the agency who examined CIA analyses on China are that analysts have done poor work. The panel of experts found an "institutional predisposition" to play down the threat from China, according to one member of the panel. Publicly, the CIA denied that "politicization" or bias tainted its analyses of China.

Satellites to Missiles: The federal criminal case against two U.S. satellite makers who were charged with selling strategic missile technology to China still had not been concluded at the time of this writing. The case was close to being resolved before it was pushed aside by the events of September 11. One reported solution is to dispose of the case by imposing a civil penalty of some $10 million on Loral and Hughes. If carried out, the penalty would be little more than a slap on the wrist for helping improve the reliability of Chinese missiles aimed at U.S. cities.

Panama Red: A declassified State Department report from 1999 sheds more light on Li Kashing, the Hong Kong billionaire whose companies can control the Panama Canal. The State Department document states that Li "is reputed to have a close business relationship with key figures in Beijing and he has a number of real estate and infrastructure projects in the mainland." The report identified him as a "tycoon who is no democrat." The report said Li's companies have investments in seventeen ports around the world that together handle nearly 10 percent of the world's traffic in shipping containers. The document identified Li's other port investments, including holdings in Britain's Felixstone port and ports in the Bahamas, Indonesia, and Burma.

Intelligence officials also disclosed a secret study done in the late 1990s by the U.S. Southern Command, in charge of military forces in

South America, that warned that China is seeking to control international "chokepoints" around the world as part of a global strategy.

Meanwhile, intelligence officials revealed that China had begun shipping military goods, including explosives, to Cuba in ships of the state-owned China Ocean Shipping Company.

And in May 2001, China announced a new "strategic partnership" with the leftist government of Venezuelan President Hugo Chavez. Russia surprised the United States by announcing it would pull out of its electronic listening post at Lourdes, Cuba, opening the way for the Chinese military to take it over.

Proliferation Subversion: True to its pro-Beijing policies, the Clinton administration in November 2000 waived economic sanctions against China for missile sales to Iran and Pakistan, in exchange for another hollow Beijing promise. This time China promised not to export any goods that could assist foreign nuclear missile programs.

Within months, U.S. intelligence agencies identified clear violations of the pledge, with shipments of missile components for Pakistan's nuclear-capable Shaheen 1 and Shaheen 2 missiles.

The Bush administration acted in September 2001 with sanctions on both nations, despite opposition from within the administration by pro-China officials left over from the Clinton administration and by some new political appointees.

In other proliferation activities, federal authorities in Florida uncovered a major Chinese technology transfer program to illegally purchase thousands of radiation-hardened computer chips—components for China's missiles and satellites.

Kindred Spirit: Fired Los Alamos nuclear weapons designer Wen Ho Lee completed debriefings with U.S. intelligence officials about his activities and little information about them was made public. The Justice Department, after promising to release information about the case, has so far released only a scant few pages of material. Portions of an eight-hundred-page report revealed that the Justice Department's failure to approve a wiretap for Lee was one of several mistakes that left the espionage case in tatters. Other officials said pro-China officials in the Clinton administration deliberately sabotaged the Lee investigation because the FBI did not want to upset Beijing at a time when it was seeking permission to open an FBI field office in Beijing.

Paul Moore, a former FBI intelligence analyst and specialist on Chinese spying, summed up the case saying that the Justice Department's report missed the point. "The problem with Wen Ho Lee is that he is like flypaper," Moore told me. "He was doing things that were suspicious and lying while doing them. Either you become more suspicious when you encounter that, or you get out of the counterintelligence business."

"'What are the odds?' is the question you should ask," Moore said. "What are the odds that you run across somebody who is propositioned in a hotel room in China to commit espionage and he has not reported it [to security officials]?" Moore said the same Chinese nuclear officials who met Lee in China during visits there in 1986 and 1988 later came to the United States and met with Lee.

"When you are doing odds, you have to multiply, not add," Moore said. "You get all these different things, and he's lying to you. And all these things happened before he made copies of the nuclear codes. The record is very clear: Wen Ho Lee is a liar and a thief. The question is: Is he taking the information he's stolen and giving it to a foreign country? I don't see any proof that he did so. But he may have been preparing to do so."

The nuclear codes that Lee stole were never found. The culprit who gave China secrets about every deployed U.S. nuclear warhead remains unidentified and unprosecuted.

Flashpoint Taiwan: China's relentless missile buildup opposite Taiwan has continued. Up to 350 short-range missiles, new CSS-6s and CSS-7s, are now in place and represent a clear and present danger to Taiwan's twenty-three million people. In an interview with me in the summer of 2001, Taiwan President Chen Shui-bian compared China's growing missile threats against the island to the 1962 Cuban missile crisis. But he noted a clear difference: the Cuban crisis ended. "For the twenty-three million Taiwanese people," Chen said, "our missile threat is not only a thirteen-day threat. Rather, we have lived for a very long time under a missile threat on a daily basis." The Taiwanese president highlighted the severity of the problem: "The PRC threat is directed not only against Taiwan. It is at the same time also a threat to the United States and Japan."

Chen called on the United States, Japan, and Taiwan to jointly develop missile defenses against Chinese short-range missiles, a call that for the most part fell on deaf ears in Tokyo and Washington.

A Pentagon report made public in December 2000 stated that China's use of force against Taiwan could come in three forms: an invasion of Taiwan or an offshore island, a blockade aimed at crippling Taiwan's economy, or air and missile attacks on Taiwan's people, military, and economic infrastructure.

But the report by the Pentagon's Office of Net Assessment, a kind of internal think tank, made a startling statement. Because of "gaps" in the U.S. government's knowledge of Chinese Communist Party and military intentions, "we cannot expect to predict confidently the outcome of a military conflict," the report stated. It was a stunning indictment of U.S. intelligence deficiencies.

The most important statements on Taiwan, however, came from President George W. Bush. Bush shocked the Chinese communists and their sympathizers in the United States with a statement he made on ABC's *Good Morning America* in April 2001. Asked if the United States has an obligation to defend Taiwan from a Chinese attack on Taiwan, Bush said, "Yes, we do, and the Chinese must understand that." He added that the United States would do "whatever it took to help Taiwan defend herself."

Around the same time, however, the president turned down a Taiwanese request to buy advanced U.S. warships, notably guided-missile destroyers equipped with Aegis combat control systems, which could provide future missile defenses. The Bush administration did sharply increase its weapons offered for sale to Taiwan, including diesel-powered submarines, but balked at offering the advanced Aegis-equipped warships, hoping to use future sales of the Aegis ships to pressure Beijing into reducing its missiles opposite the island, an unlikely prospect.

The weapons offer paled in comparison to the president's "whatever it took" statement of support, a position interpreted by officials in

Beijing as a warning that the United States would use even nuclear weapons to defend the island.

The publication in January 2001 of *The Tiananmen Papers* deserves mention. The book, by Liang Zhang (a pseudonym), and edited by academics Andrew J. Nathan, Perry Link, and Orville Schell, is a collection of smuggled, top secret Chinese Communist Party documents related to the 1989 massacre of students in Tiananmen Square. Its stark revelation is that democracy in China was further along in 1989 than the world suspected.

The papers, which U.S. government officials judged to be authentic, reveal that the debate on political reform inside the ruling Politburo was fierce. One group, led by two top Communist Party leaders, Zhao Ziyang and Hu Qili, sounded like Russia's Boris Yeltsin calling for true democracy. The hard-liners, led by Premier Li Peng, won out, but only after the Politburo deadlocked and was unable to vote for the use of force to oust the protester from the square. An "illegal" committee of Party elders made the telephone call to the Chinese military to clear the square, proving that the People's Liberation Army could not get written orders to kill the students, only phone calls.

My recommendation for reducing the China threat still stands. U.S. military strength and democracy for China are the key ingredients for continued peace and prosperity in Asia. Trade is not enough. There needs to be a movement to pressure the communist rulers in Beijing into democratizing. In Taipei, Taiwan's government is investigating ways of implementing my recommendation of creating an Asia-Pacific Democracy Community to counteract Beijing's exploitation of the so-called overseas Chinese community to toe the Beijing line.

We know that trade and international economic integration are not sufficient to achieve democratic political reform in China, any more than they have been sufficient to achieve political reform in the Islamic world or Africa. Chinese Premier Li Peng stated in March 2001 that China will never adopt Western-style democracy. "We will not copy the experience of letting two parties take shifts in running the affairs of the state or introduce a two-chamber congress," Li said.

Creating a noncommunist China that is prosperous and free remains the hope for the future. It will require dispelling illusions that trade alone will reduce the China threat. Only sustained leadership from the United States, a recommitment to a large American military presence in the Pacific, and a determination to bring democratic reforms to Communist China can make the China threat a thing of the past.

Bill Gertz
November 2001
Washington, D.C.

INTRODUCTION

Afundamental lesson of the twentieth century is that democracies cannot coexist indefinitely with powerful and ambitious totalitarian regimes. Sooner or later the competing goals and ideologies bring conflict, whether hot war or cold, until one or the other side prevails. This central lesson must be learned before we can even begin to understand the China threat. Unfortunately, President Bill Clinton and his advisers have proved to be slow learners.

Nazism and Soviet-style communism guided the past century's dictatorships. Fascism was discredited only after its brutal regimes were destroyed at fearful cost in human life and material wealth. Western resolve choked Soviet communism so captive peoples could free themselves. The great threat of the twenty-first century—to the United States and the world—is the nuclear-armed communist dictatorship in the People's Republic of China. Its rulers oppress 1.3 billion people under "socialism with Chinese characteristics."

This book is an examination of the recent history of the China threat and how it grew stronger through the misguided policies of the Clinton-Gore administration. While Bill Clinton's predecessors in the Oval Office share the blame, the magnitude of the Clinton-Gore administration's missteps, fumbling, and outright appeasement is in a class by itself. The result has been that the United States has actually helped create a new superpower threat to world peace and stability in the decades to come.

While the China threat is not yet in the same league as that posed by the nuclear-armed Soviet Union during the Cold War, Beijing is a serious danger nonetheless. As a dictatorship with no regard for human life and no input from outside its small circle of Communist Party policymakers, it has repeatedly shown itself to be prone to miscalculations on a staggering scale—miscalculations that have cost tens of millions of its own people's lives. In light of this record of massive blunders and the continuing insularity of its ruling clique, there exists the very real possibility that China's rulers could make the same kind of catastrophic miscalculation that Japan's dictators did in attacking Pearl Harbor. Serious internal problems—widespread corruption, social unrest, and economic instability—might combine with their long-standing ambition to dominate the Pacific region and tempt Beijing into the dictator's historic strategy: military aggression.

Another danger, somewhat ironically, is that China will collapse and fragment, Soviet-style. The country is not unified; it could easily separate into several nation-states. While this could eventually reduce the threat of a Chinese Communist superpower, it would throw into question the central government's control over a small but growing strategic nuclear arsenal.

The great unknowns about the almost opaque Chinese Communist system also hold many dangers. For American intelligence agencies, China is a "hard target"—a euphemism betraying our ignorance about the inner workings of the last remaining nuclear-armed communist state. Not knowing or understanding the true nature of Chinese communism, China's government, and its military poses the most serious internal threat to the United States today. Communist governments have never responded favorably to concessions; they pocket them and demand more. But they do respond to pressure. Before pressure can be applied, however, a strategy is needed, and the crucial requirement for a strategy is solid intelligence.

Those who insist, ignorantly or deliberately, that China is not a threat put great faith in the supposedly democratizing effect of increased trade with the West. Unhappily, there is little evidence that the Beijing dictatorship has been undermined by such trade. The growth of prosperous coastal cities has not alleviated the poverty of rural China. The levers of power that keep the Party in control remain unchanged and unreformed. The permanent normal trade status granted to China in 2000 by Clinton and Congress will do little to liberate the Chinese people or lessen Beijing's threat to the West. To the contrary, the Clinton policy of conciliation has only increased the danger.

Perhaps the greatest failure of the Clinton appeasement policy was a moral one: It betrayed the long-suffering Chinese people. Their true aspirations emerged with tragic results in the Tiananmen Square demonstrations. The protesters looked to the United States as the beacon of freedom and hope. We learned from survivors of the Soviet Empire that it was the United States, by its very existence, that kept their hopes of freedom alive. Thus, while the Beijing regime is a threat to the United States, our nation by its very existence is a threat to Beijing. Any strategy designed to counter the China threat must include persistent exploitation of America's status as a model of democracy and a symbol of hope for the oppressed Chinese people.

The frightful human toll of the Chinese Communist regime is almost beyond imagination, despite attempts by some academics and other apologists to ignore or minimize the slaughter. As long ago as 1971 in a study done for Congress, Professor Richard L. Walker, in "The Human Cost of Communism in China," noted that Beijing was responsible for the deaths of between 34.3 million and 63.8 million people. The figures can no longer be dismissed as those of a Cold War anticommunist. A 1999 estimate by European historian Jean-Louis Margolin confirms Walker's figures. Margolin stated that Chinese communism took the lives of 44.5 million to 72 million people—through repression, famine, executions, and forced labor.

Since the fall of Eastern European communism in 1989 and the collapse of the Soviet Union in 1991, China's rulers have survived by rejecting the central economic tenets of Marx, Lenin, and Mao Zedong. But they have kept communism's brutal totalitarian structure, which is so aptly captured in Mao's famous nostrum: "Political power grows out of the barrel of a gun."

The central question underlying the China threat is whether the Beijing regime, direct heirs of those who sacrificed so many millions of their countrymen at the altar of a false god, could be reformed by exposure to the civilizing influence of the West. Bill Clinton believed it could. His biggest mistake was treating the Beijing government as just another foreign government, no different from or worse than a noncommunist dictatorship. The problem is that China's patient communist rulers have a strategy that stretches over the next several decades. They rightly regard the United States as their main enemy and the primary obstacle to China's goal of achieving world status and Pacific domination.

Bill Clinton was elected in 1992 as a critic of George Bush's friendly policies toward China, having lambasted Bush for "coddling" dictators from Baghdad to Beijing. But the new president soon became a key facilitator of China's march to world superpower status. Clinton criticized China's human rights record, but only because polls showed it would gain political points. There was never a serious effort to bring about changes in Beijing's behavior. The idea of pressure—using leverage to force changes—was specifically rejected by the Clinton administration as counterproductive. The central theme of Clinton's policy was that China is a "normal," nonthreatening power. That is the same theme that has been advanced by China's communist rulers from its first premier, Chou Enlai, to its current president, Jiang Zemin.

China's always pragmatic rulers know well that decisions made today by U.S. defense planners, under the mistaken notion that China poses no threat in the future, will prevent the United States from preparing for the challenge from China in the crucial decades up to 2030. Weapons systems being designed and researched today must anticipate the threats of tomorrow.

Business groups have played a key role in playing down the China threat. Their argument is that free trade will not only help China evolve peacefully but will even undermine the communist system. But the evidence from trade with Beijing over the past two decades shows that China today is less free and more threatening than it was before the United States established formal government-to-government relations in 1979. Free trade has not worked. A prosperous middle class in China is emerging, but there is no sign it will lead the government toward democratic reform.

The China threat is real and growing. The solution is not trade but democracy. But as China's rulers have made clear, their current program of modernization leaves out democratic reform. Resolving the China threat will require patience and clearheaded strategy. It will require studying the People's Republic of China, understanding its strategy and tactics, and forming alliances with democratic states that share democratic values.

Most important of all, the United States must maintain and build up its military power, following the same strategy adopted by President Ronald Reagan that left the Soviet Union in ruins: peace through strength.

CHAPTER ONE

The China Threat

> *"Every communist must grasp the truth:*
> *Political power grows out of the barrel of a gun."*
>
> —Mao Zedong

The B-2 stealth bombers took off from Whiteman Air Force Base, Missouri, around 9:00 AM. It was Friday, May 7, 1999. Flying nonstop and refueling in midflight over the Atlantic Ocean near Britain, the aircraft were nearly invisible to Serbian air defense radar as they approached the Balkans. One of the aircraft reached the skies over the capital of Belgrade around midnight and launched five Joint Direct Attack Munitions, or JDAM, bombs. The 2,000-pound high-explosive weapons are among the most advanced precision-guided bombs in the U.S. conventional arsenal. The JDAMs maneuvered precisely to their targets with the help of signals sent by satellites that are part of the Global Positioning System, the navigation system used by boaters and military alike. Three of the bombs slammed into a building in downtown Belgrade that U.S. and NATO targeters believed was a key Yugoslav army weapons-buying facility.

In fact, the bombs rocked the embassy of the People's Republic of China.

Ten days later, a top secret report was completed by the Defense Intelligence Agency (DIA). The report was based on intelligence from the headquarters of the Ministry of State Security, China's civilian intelligence service, and was sent to what remained of the Belgrade embassy's intelligence station. "Chinese embassy personnel in Belgrade were instructed... to collect missile fragments from the bombed embassy building and send them back to China, probably aboard the aircraft chartered to evacuate injured embassy personnel," the report said. Three Chinese nationals were killed in the bombing, and about twenty-seven others were injured.

The DIA report went on to state: "Separately, an internal Chinese ministry level document revealed that the secure communications area and the defense attaché office within the Chinese embassy received the most damage from the NATO attack.... [The Chinese] also believed that NATO had intentionally hit the embassy as part of a larger conspiracy to drag China into the crisis."

The report also indicated that a Chinese news organization "relayed guidance for reporting on the situation relating to the bombing."

"The guidance, probably sent nationwide, instructed reporters not to report that NATO's attack was accidental and to focus on the U.S. government, citizens and investors," the report said. "Reporters are forbidden from covering demonstrations targeting any NATO countries except the United States." The intelligence exposed how China's communist leaders were using the state-controlled news media to focus public anger on the United States, which China views as the "world hegemon" to be stopped by less powerful states led by China. Riots by Chinese were orchestrated by government officials, and the American ambassador, James Sasser, was forced to remain holed up in the embassy while mobs of people stoned the consulate building.

This was just a small, visible part of a new Cold War against the United States on the part of the communist government in Beijing.

A day after the bombing, an official Chinese Foreign Ministry spokesman issued a statement condemning the blast: "This act by NATO is a gross violation of China's sovereignty and a willful trampling on the Vienna Convention on Diplomatic Relations as well as the basic norms governing international relations. This is rarely seen in the history of diplomacy."

The statement also included a not-so-subtle threat that received virtually no attention from the U.S. news media. "The U.S.-led NATO must bear all responsibilities arising therefrom. The Chinese Government reserves the right to take further actions on the matter." In essence, the communist government in Beijing viewed the attack as deliberate and tantamount to an act of war. The reference to "further action" was a sign that Beijing would not allow the action to go unanswered.

Inside the Pentagon, military planners working on the Kosovo operations around the clock had to consider the worst possible outcome of the errant bombing: retaliation. China's options ranged from providing diplomatic support to Yugoslav leader Slobodan Milosevic all the way to conventional and possibly even nuclear conflict with the United States. Vociferous and repeated public apologies by Bill Clinton and other high-ranking administration officials appeared to be enough to mollify China's communist rulers temporarily. No troop movements or preparations for launching long-range nuclear missiles were ever detected. It was unlikely that China even contemplated the action, but under the circumstances no one could be certain, especially given the portrait of an aggressive China that was emerging from top secret intelligence intercepts.

COMMUNIST CHINA'S PLAN

Three years earlier, in May 1997, a U.S. Air Force RC-135 intelligence-gathering jet took off from Kadena Air Base, Japan. The reconnaissance aircraft bristled with electronic spying equipment sensitive enough to pick out individual telephone conversations from the millions of signals in the airwaves over China. The jet flew along a flight path parallel to the coast of China about fifty miles offshore. The ultrasensitive electronic eavesdropping equipment on the militarized Boeing aircraft swept the airwaves during the nine-hour flight. In secret reports, the flights are given code names like "Bachelor Warrior," "Beggar Hawk," and "Distant Wind." The plane's electronic ears can hear as far away as western China, into the remote Xinjiang region, where Beijing conducts nuclear testing. This spring mission produced a rare intelligence gem. No Chinese interceptor jets diverted the plane, and a wealth of intelligence was recorded and passed on to analysts at the Pentagon.

The analysts began the task of separating the valuable material from mundane military information. The intelligence was polished and given a code word that assigned it a rank within the "Top Secret" designation.

"Moray" is the first level of Top Secret. Then comes "Umbra." The most sensitive data is "Gamma."

Within a few days, the intelligence analysts had discovered that a senior Chinese Communist official had had a secret meeting with Sean Garland, managing director of a Dublin, Ireland, company identified in the intelligence report as GKG Comms International Ltd. But Garland is more than a businessman. He is well known to American and British intelligence.

A summary of the report was distributed to the highest-ranking officials in the Clinton-Gore administration in early June 1997. Among the items it contained were details of North Korea's first launch of a new antiship cruise missile, Russia's launch of a new generation spy satellite, and a warning from a Mexican drug lord about an upcoming raid by Mexican troops on a farm suspected of housing drug production equipment.

But it was the following passage that caught the eye of senior intelligence officials:

Suspected Supernote Distributor Meets with Chinese to Discuss Undisclosed Business Deal (TSC OC)

(TSC OC) Sean Garland, Managing Director of GKG Comms International Ltd., in Dublin, met recently with Cao Xiaobing, Bureau Director-General within the Central Committee, to discuss unidentified business opportunities according to late May 1997 information. (COMMENT: Garland is suspected of being involved with counterfeiting U.S. currency, specifically, the Supernote, a high quality counterfeit $100 bill.) (W9B2, 3/00/18224-97, ILC)

Aside from his business interests, Garland was secretary general of the Workers' Party in Ireland. A telling document obtained from Soviet archives revealed that Garland wrote to the secretary of the Communist Party of the Soviet Union on September 15, 1986. In the "dear comrade" letter, Garland stated that the Workers' Party of Ireland had developed a five-year program and asked Moscow to provide one million pounds to help. The cash would be "of benefit to the world struggle for Peace, Freedom and Socialism." The document was posted on the Internet by Vladimir Bukovsky, the well-known Russian dissident who spent years in the Gulag Archipelago.

The meeting between Cao and Garland in 1997 showed how China had become the ideological leader of what was left of the world communist movement. U.S. intelligence officials saw Communist China clandestinely supporting international communists, including those involved in international criminal activities—even those suspected of developing counterfeit $100 bills.

The intelligence was unwelcome news for the Clinton-Gore administration and was suppressed, as so many reports exposing the Chinese threat have been suppressed under Bill Clinton's pro-China foreign policy. The reports have always been handled the same way. The standard procedure has been to dismiss such secret intelligence as "unconfirmed." When it could not be dismissed, it was simply hidden or ignored. Among those covering up for China were White House National Security Adviser Samuel "Sandy" Berger, a former trade lawyer who worked to establish joint ventures in China for U.S. corporations, and Secretary of State Madeleine Albright, a liberal Georgetown University professor whose views of Communist China are extremely favorable. The Pentagon intelligence report and others like it contradicted the political line laid down by President Clinton: China is not a threat, and China must be "engaged" at all costs—even if U.S. national security and interests are harmed.

The reality today is that China is a major threat to the United States, and a growing one. China's rulers—from its president to the general in charge of the all-powerful Central Military Commission—remain communists, and the fifty years of communist rule are replete with brutal repression, mass murder, and border wars with China's neighbors. But communism seeks to change not only external political conditions but also the internal nature of human beings—hence its emphasis on mass indoctrination and its hatred for anything that might offer a contrary view of man. It is this feature of communism that accounts for its most dangerous characteristic: its failure to value human life. In the twentieth century, tens of millions perished under communist persecution.

Harry Wu, a Chinese democracy activist, has documented Chinese Communist excesses at their worst. Wu, now a scholar at the Hoover Institution on War, Revolution, and Peace at Stanford University in California, obtained documents that reveal how the rulers in Beijing allow the body organs of executed prisoners to be sold for medical transplantation. Outside of a few international human rights groups, this ugly practice has drawn little outrage.

Many American political leaders have sought to downplay or ignore the ideology behind Communist China. An observer listening to the opinions of American government officials, business leaders, academics, and many in the news media would find it hard to discern that China's rulers today are communists at all. The pervasive view is that China's leaders have embraced capitalism, that communism in China is dead. Even many intelligence officials deny a "China threat." A senior Pentagon military intelligence officer who requested anonymity told me that "statements" by China's leaders belied any threat from China. "We aren't trying to portray China as an enemy," he said. "We are within the context of our professional work trying to portray our concern over the direction China may go in future years." The official said there was a penchant among some in the press, government, and the private sector to portray China in "the most contentious terms." Relations could become confrontational, he acknowledged, but they are not now. "It's hopeful, positive, productive," he added. "I visited there, met a number of my counterparts. I think we have the beginnings of a positive relationship."

The assertion showed how deeply China is misunderstood, even—or perhaps especially—at high levels of the U.S. government. In the military, the threat a foreign country poses is based on that nation's power and capabilities: its hardware and weapons systems. Statements by leaders, especially communist leaders, are what intelligence analysts term "intentions"; because these can change, they should never be used as the basis for threat assessments. As President Ronald Reagan said years ago, to much ridicule from his critics, communists will do anything, including lie and cheat, to accomplish their goals. So it is in the case of China.

But the prevailing political orthodoxy in the Clinton-Gore administration was a continuation of the "anti-anticommunism" of the Cold War Left that sees McCarthyism, not communism, as the central problem, something that should be discredited, marginalized, or dismissed as extremist, part of what Hillary Rodham Clinton denounced as the "vast right-wing conspiracy." The Clinton-Gore policy on China was called "engagement" and held that China's transformation was inevitable and could be impeded only by critics of "engagement" and Communist China.

If President George Bush envisioned a New World Order, President Clinton had in mind an even newer world order, such as saying that the conflict in Kosovo was not a mere regional conflict but rather was fought by NATO for "the future of the world." The young people of America, he said, "are likely to live in a world where the biggest threats are not from other countries." Cold War visions of communists clashing with Western supporters were outdated, he insisted. The real threats to world peace would come from racial, ethnic, and religious fighting, organized crime, drug traffickers, and terrorists armed with weapons of mass destruction.

In reality, pro-China policies of earlier administrations were based on realpolitik and Chinese concessions, such as China's permitting the United States to use electronic eavesdropping posts near its borders, which allowed U.S. intelligence agencies to spy on Moscow's strategic nuclear weapons.

By contrast, the pro-China policies of the Clinton-Gore administration were a disaster for America's national security interests, which were not even considered in the rush to enhance China.

Quite the opposite: The Clinton-Gore administration's loosening of trade restrictions with China vastly improved China's military power with transfers of strategic high technology. All the while the administration insisted it was doing nothing to enhance China's military power. Some Clinton officials even went so far as to state, privately of course, that it was a good thing that China had obtained nuclear weapons secrets from the United States. After all, they said, why should the United States be the only nation with advanced warheads and

missiles? With that astonishing rationale, the Clinton-Gore administration brushed aside all worries about the Chinese gaining information
on *every* deployed nuclear weapon in the U.S. arsenal and improving
their own nuclear weapons.

THE GROWING THREAT

In 1998 I visited the PLA museum in Beijing. Entering the huge, fortress-
like hall, visitors are greeted by thirty-foot statues of such communists
as Marx, Engels, Lenin, and Stalin. Stalin, let it be remembered, is cred-
ited by historians with causing the deaths of millions of people through
repression, execution, forced labor, and government-induced famine.

Michael Pillsbury, a senior Pentagon planner during the Reagan
administration who specializes in Chinese affairs, revealed much of the
continuing hostile nature of China and its national strategy against the
United States in his book *China Debates the Future Security Environment*. Using original-language sources, Pillsbury discovered a deep hostility toward the United States on the part of Chinese Communist Party
leaders and military officers. One confidential Chinese government
report leaked to the Hong Kong press in 1997 predicted a future war
between China and the United States over Taiwan:

> With the return of Hong Kong and Macao to Chinese rule, the Taiwan
> issue will inevitably become China's major event around 2010. If the
> United States uses force to meddle in China's sovereignty and internal
> affairs, China will certainly fight a war against aggression, thus leading
> to a limited Sino-U.S. war. China must be prepared for this. With the
> change in the international situation, the United States will make use of
> islands, maritime space, and resources and will encourage and support
> Japanese militarists in provoking a war against China.... China is the
> U.S. number one political adversary at the turn of this century. China
> must make systematic preparations against the invasive war and mili-
> tary attacks unleashed by the United States under any pretext.

Examples of official Chinese government hostility can be found in the *People's Daily*, the official Communist Party newspaper. On June 22, 1999, for example, the newspaper, which is strictly controlled by top Party leaders, stated that the United States and Nazi Germany are "exactly the same" in "their self-centeredness and ambition to seek hegemony." According to China, the United States engages in mass extermination on the same scale as the Nazis. Written a month and a half after the bombing of the Chinese embassy in Belgrade, the article noted that the "utilization of advanced technology to slaughter peaceful citizens is by no means less barbaric.... Hitler not only used in war what were considered to be the most advanced weapons of the time, such as airplanes, tanks, and long-range artillery, to massacre peaceful citizens in anti-Fascist countries, but also built concentration camps in Auschwitz and in other areas to slaughter Jews and prisoners of war with 'advanced' technology. Executioners drove hundreds and thousands of people into gas chambers and poured cyanide through air holes in the roof, killing them all. Today, the U.S. hegemonists use high-tech weapons to attack FRY [Federal Republic of Yugoslavia] civilian facilities several hundred miles away from the battlefield, or, with laser and global position systems several thousand meters above the sky, treated innocent and peaceful citizens as live targets. The flagrant use of missiles by the U.S.-led NATO to attack the Chinese Embassy in Yugoslavia was a barbaric atrocity that the then-Nazi Germany had not dared to commit."

Such comments were almost never refuted by the Clinton-Gore administration, which simply tried to ignore them. Defense Secretary William S. Cohen, the only Republican in the Clinton cabinet, mildly chastised the Chinese during a visit to China's National Defense University in July 2000. He said Chinese media characterizations of the United States as a hegemon seeking to dominate the world were "not only unhelpful, but... untrue." The vitriol against America in the Chinese press continues unabated, however.

The Chinese government is not shy about its communist, anti-American ideology. In a December 1999 speech during Beijing's takeover of the Portuguese colony of Macao, Chinese leader Jiang Zemin said:

"We must assess the trends in the world and envisage our country's destiny with Marxism-Leninism, Mao Zedong Thought, and Deng Xiaoping Theory in particular, never deviate from the reality of China, unswervingly keep to our own road and carry the socialist reform and socialist modernization through to the end so as to constantly open up new spheres for China's development and prosperity. The bell is ringing for the advent of the 21st century. Political multipolarity and economic globalization are the two major trends in the future world." "Multipolarity" means knocking the United States off its perch as the world's sole superpower.

Many Chinese government statements and reports can be viewed through the CIA's Foreign Broadcast Information Service, which produces scores of translations every day. The People's Republic of China makes official statements available from the Chinese Foreign Ministry's Internet site (http://www.fmprc.gov.cn/english/dhtml). Read enough of these statements and you will know that China is not a friendly power.

China's communists believe world socialism is inevitable. As Pillsbury says, China asserts that "the new Chinese-style world system of the Five Principles will be much better than systems of the past and present, because there will be harmony, no 'power politics,' and no more 'hegemony.' This harmonious world requires a transition away from capitalism in the major powers toward some type of 'socialist market economy.' Just as China has modified the doctrines of Marx, Engels, Lenin, and Stalin to produce what Deng Xiaoping called 'Socialism with Chinese Characteristics,' so will the United States, Germany, Japan, and Russia ultimately develop their own socialist characteristics." When Chinese tanks rolled through Beijing's Tiananmen Square to crush democratic protests, they did so under the watchful gaze of a large portrait of Mao Zedong above the main building in the square. It is Mao's communism that justifies, sustains, and guides China's government even as it enriches itself with Western investment.

In a December 1998 speech, Jiang Zemin affirmed that "without Comrade Mao Zedong's leadership, there would not be New China; and without Comrade Deng Xiaoping's leadership, there would not be the path of building socialism with Chinese characteristics!"

Such socialism "with Chinese characteristics" means a communism that fulfills China's sense of its own superiority. China considers its culture to be the oldest in the world. It refers to itself as the Middle Kingdom—the place between heaven and earth. And to restore its former grandeur through modernizing communism, it will pay any human price.

The editor of 1999's *Black Book of Communism*, scholar Stephane Courtois, notes that the total number of people killed under communism is 100 million. Of these, between 44.5 million and 72 million deaths resulted from communism *in China alone*.

The worst communist slaughter of the Chinese people was in the "Great Leap Forward," when between twenty million and forty-three million people died, mostly due to the government-induced famine.

Another factor is labor camps, known as the Laogai, that have claimed as many as twenty million Chinese lives and continue to operate today. But under the Clinton-Gore administration's policy of "engagement," public discussion of this repression is frowned upon in the United States.

French historian Jean-Louis Margolin, who wrote the *Black Book*'s chapter on China, notes that "whatever happens to 'real socialism' now depends on the development of Communism in China" because it is by far the leading communist power.

Margolin says Beijing has become "a second Rome for Marxism-Leninism," and it is in this context that the secret meeting between Sean Garland and Cao Xiaobing should be viewed.

Veteran China watcher Willy Wo-Lap Lam, whose columns for the *South China Morning Post* are often based on inside information from Beijing, says that China's communist rulers are clinging to the idea that "the great renaissance of the Chinese race is only possible under the party's leadership." So they have created a new propaganda campaign saying that the Communist Party is the institution that will advance China's economy and culture, as well as the interests of "the people."

Lam writes, "Under the pretext of concentrating the nation's energy and resources on enhancing patriotism and gearing up 'military preparedness,' the leadership has dragged its feet on real liberalization measures such as expanding village-level elections."

Much also is made of China's shift toward a market economy. The reality remains that China permits no political freedom and even its tolerance of capitalism is limited. Jiang Zemin, the Chinese president, announced in May 2000 that the Chinese Communist Party would increase its control over businesses by installing party "cells" within every enterprise. Party commissars in the cells were directed to "work hard to unite and educate entrepreneurs to advocate various policies of the party, run businesses according to law, and protect the employees' interests." The new directive contradicts the claims of the Clinton-Gore administration that economic liberalization will lead to democratization in China.

During his eight years in office, Clinton rarely if ever called for democracy in China, despite the official policy of his administration outlined in the annual National Security Strategy report that called for enlarging democracy throughout the world.

For those who think China is not a threat to the United States, General Chi Haotian, vice chairman of the Communist Party Central Military Commission, is proof they are wrong. In December 1999 General Chi gave this chilling assessment of China's future relations with the United States:

> Seen from the changes in the world situation and the United States' hegemonic strategy for creating monopolarity, war is inevitable. We cannot avoid it. The issue is that the Chinese armed forces must control the initiative in this war. We must make sure that we win this local high-tech war against aggression and interference; win this modern high-tech war that [the] military bloc, headed by U.S. hegemonists, may launch to interfere in our affairs militarily; and win this war ignited by aggressor countries' sudden offensives against China. We must be prepared to fight for one year, two years, three years, or even longer.

To the Communist Chinese, we are the enemy, the one barrier to Chinese greatness. With that understanding, Beijing devised its strategy that became known as "the Plan," which, as we'll see, had catastrophic results for American security during the Clinton-Gore administration.

CHAPTER TWO

The Plan

*"There are several incidents that suggest
that the President and senior White House officials knew
or had reason to know that foreign funds were being
funneled into the DNC and the reelection effort."*

—Interim Report for Attorney General Janet Reno and FBI Director
Louis Freeh from Charles LaBella, supervising attorney,
Campaign Financing Task Force, July 16, 1998

Senior FBI officials working in the National Security Division knew something was wrong after reading the first intercepts. China is generally a "hard target" for U.S. spy agencies. That is, it is one of the most difficult nations for the alphabet soup of U.S. intelligence agencies to gather vital information about. But in this case, a "technical penetration" of the Chinese embassy in Washington obtained detailed intelligence. A technical penetration is spy talk for an electronic eavesdropping bug that snoops on conversations or data in machines and transmits the information to U.S. intelligence technicians.

It was early 1996, and these intercepts began arriving in special pouches hand-delivered by couriers from the National Security Agency (whose work is so secret that its acronym, NSA, is wryly said to mean "No Such Agency"). They went to a special room inside the upper floors of the J. Edgar Hoover Building, the FBI's sprawling headquarters on Washington's Pennsylvania Avenue. The agents in this special section, known as the National Security Division, are cleared to see the most sensitive U.S. intelligence. What the intercepts revealed was that the People's Republic of China (PRC) had launched a major program to influence American politics, including Congress and the White House.

The Chinese like to quantify things, and their espionage and influence campaign is part of a strategic plan to revive China through the "Four Modernizations," which are directed at industry, agriculture, science and technology, and defense.

China's most threatening modernization, from the American point of view, is its plan to build the People's Liberation Army (PLA) into a world-class military force with the most modern strategic nuclear missiles and a navy capable of projecting power far from Chinese shores. China's modernization goal is to defeat the United States whenever it stands against Chinese strategic or political objectives—thus the need to conduct political warfare. To quote Mao, "The mind of the enemy and the will of his leaders is a target of far more importance than the bodies of his troops."

China's changing views of warfare are outlined in the 1999 book *Unrestricted Warfare* by two PLA colonels, Qiao Liang and Wang Xiangsui, who advocate expanding combat beyond the battlefield to include computer warfare, international terrorism, biological and chemical warfare, economic and financial warfare, and more: "Warfare no longer is an exclusive imperial garden where professional soldiers alone can mingle." On cyber, techno-warfare, the authors conclude: "Clearly, it is precisely the diversity of the means employed that has enlarged the concept of warfare. Moreover, the enlargement of the concept of warfare has, in turn, resulted in enlargement of the realm of war-related activities.... The battlefield is next to you and the enemy is on the network. Only there is no smell of gunpowder or the odor of blood." To Qiao and Wang, the modern warrior will be a combination of traditional military commander, modern computer hacker, international financier, and global terrorist. "Obviously," they continue, "warfare is in the process of transcending the domains of soldiers, military units, and military affairs, and is increasingly becoming a matter for politicians, scientists, and even bankers."

Political warfare can take many forms, and, when carried out efficiently and with secrecy, using intermediaries and "deniability," it is extremely difficult to detect. But by any measure, the Chinese in these political operations during the Clinton-Gore administration were hugely successful. Bill Clinton and Al Gore secretly helped China make great strides in building up not just its military forces but its economic and political power as well. The deception reached all the way to the top of the U.S. government. On March 7, 1997, Clinton, in what aides later rushed to say was a misstatement, went so far as to describe China as no longer run by communist rulers. But in truth, at a White House press conference, reflecting on the question of how the world would appear in thirty to forty years, the president said, "One of those great questions is how will Russia and China, the two great former communist powers, define their greatness in the next century."

Congressman Dana Rohrabacher, California Republican, was one of the few members of Congress to recognize the growing threat from China and the U.S. government's misguided assistance to it. He put it this way: "With the wealth of technology that Bill Clinton and the corporate power brokers are transferring, China is steadily building a state-of-the-art army, navy, and air force, and strategic missile force. This is a power that will threaten anyone who gets in their way. And we are financing it. We are subsidizing it. We are facilitating it. And this administration is celebrating it. And when the party is over, as I say, a very few rich Americans are going to be better off, and a multitude of our own working people will be displaced by low-tariff imports.... Our military personnel will be in grave danger and our country vulnerable to nuclear attack and high-tech warfare attack. All of this from this nonsensical policy."

The key figures in the Clinton-Gore Chinese fund-raising scandals are well known, and all of them—John Huang, Johnnie Chung, Charlie Trie, Maria Hsia—were used by the Chinese, indirectly and directly, to influence the 1996 Clinton-Gore reelection campaign and gain access to top officials in the administration. They funneled Chinese government cash to the Democratic Party to the tune of some $1.2 million. Of that money, hundreds of thousands of dollars were illegal foreign contributions. Investigators in Congress exposed key funding transfers, and the Justice Department succeeded in prosecuting some of the players. The three major bagmen were given light sentences in exchange for agreeing to cooperate with authorities.

Against a mass of evidence, the Clinton-Gore administration, perhaps the most skilled at public and media manipulation in American history, succeeded in downplaying the campaign scandal as nothing more than a few zealous fund-raisers who overstepped a few relatively unimportant laws. The administration erected a stone wall against investigators. Some witnesses fled the country, while others refused to testify or suffered memory lapses. The Democrats in Congress defended the administration, the State Department refused to give congressional inquirers any cooperation, and the Beijing government, of course, rejected congressional requests for information from the Bank of China that would have exposed how the cash was transferred.

The full details of the Chinese plan to buy influence in the Clinton-Gore administration remain buried in the computer systems of the National Security Agency. But the information that is public is damning enough.

One clear example of Chinese government influence was the work of agent Ted Sioeng. Sioeng's ties to Beijing were identified in a 1996 communications intercept between Communist China and the Chinese embassy in Washington. His name was mentioned in connection with the plan to increase Chinese political influence with U.S. politicians. Sioeng donated some $400,000 in 1995 and 1996 to the Democratic Party at the urging of John Huang, the former executive of the Indonesian Lippo Group and a senior Commerce Department official who became a top fund-raiser for the Democratic National Committee in the 1996 presidential election. Huang's bank records revealed that his account received wire transfers totaling more than $2 million from two Hong Kong holding companies at the same time Huang was contributing large sums to Bill Clinton's 1996 reelection campaign. The holding companies had business dealings in Communist China.

Maria Hsia also has been identified by the FBI as a Communist Chinese agent. "We had information, both public and classified, that showed she was doing work for the PRC surreptitiously," said Senator Fred Thompson, chairman of the Senate Governmental Affairs Committee that investigated the campaign finance scandal. "That's what we call an agent." The final report of the committee noted, "[T]he FBI, in every sense of the word, approved our delineation of her as an agent."

Hsia, a Taiwan-born U.S. citizen, was convicted by a federal jury on March 2, 2000, of illegal fund-raising. She had been indicted in February 1998, accused of conspiring to defraud the government and making false statements to the Federal Election Commission. Hsia had been working as a fund-raiser for Gore for ten years. But she is remembered for the infamous—and illegal—1996 fund-raising event that Vice President Al Gore attended at the Hsi Lai Buddhist Temple in California. Gore gave conflicting explanations for why he appeared at the clearly illegal fund-raiser, none of them convincing. But all of this is well known. What has not been well reported are the contents of a July 1999 report by the Justice Department's inspector general, Michael Bromwitch.

SUBVERTING THE FBI

In his report, Michael Bromwitch documented how the White House— under the pretext of trying to prepare Secretary of State Madeleine Albright for an official visit to China—sought information on the campaign finance investigation. The FBI balked. According to the report, "Some officials advocated providing only a limited response because they believed that providing investigative information to the White House about the PRC and campaign fund-raising violations was akin to briefing the subject of an investigation about that investigation. Ultimately, the White House counsel only received copies of teletypes concerning the PRC plan to influence Congress that had previously been transmitted to the White House." Bromwitch's report said that both the FBI and the Justice Department tried to "ensure that information that might undermine the criminal investigation was not disseminated to the White House. Senior Justice officials insisted on passing everything to the White House."

FBI Director Louis Freeh was at odds with Deputy Attorney General Jamie Gorelick about sending raw FBI investigative files to the White House. The FBI worried that its probe would be compromised. Freeh eventually agreed to provide the counterintelligence information, "but there was some stuff on the illegal campaign contributions" that he did not want given to the White House counsel, a former FBI official close to the case told me. "There were things that they just could not know about that really we felt at the time didn't really affect what Madeleine might be talking about."

"I was concerned about sensitive sources and methods," the former FBI official said. "And here we sent over all this raw data, and I really wanted these files back because I didn't know where they were. Reno didn't have them and Jamie [Gorelick] didn't have them, well where in the hell were they because they were the only ones [who were] supposed to look at them?" As it turned out, the files were sent to the Office of Intelligence Policy and Review, which had passed them on to the special campaign finance task force. The FBI finally retrieved the files but not until after they had been passed to people without a legitimate need to know. The FBI feared that soon its sources would be compromised by White House leaks.

"There was a lot of stress and strain between the CI [counterintelligence] folks and the criminal prosecutors over there because they would demand to know the identities of sources," the former FBI official said. "We were not averse to doing this. But they've got to understand we didn't want to wipe out our coverage of the Chinese target. That was our problem. We did early on. I think we did pass something to them, and it ended up in the newspaper. It had to do with intercepts, NSA [National Security Agency] stuff."

After the *Washington Post* first revealed the Chinese influence plan on February 13, 1997, in a front-page story by Bob Woodward and Brian Duffy, the Chinese government was alerted to the fact that there was a leak. The scoop revealed that electronic eavesdropping had picked up information showing that the Chinese embassy on Connecticut Avenue in northwest Washington was used for planning foreign contributions to the Democratic National Committee. "We were picking up conversations and things like that," the former official said. After the *Post* story, "the Chinese followed up with sending a search team over, and we knew about that and that clearly sent a chill through all of us. Clearly the Chinese can read a newspaper and see what's going on."

Did the plan work? According to the former FBI official, the Chinese sought and received from the plan "favorable consideration" in U.S. policy. "It's more favorable treatment, favorable outlook. I can't remember any specific instances where they were trying to accomplish a certain goal. By goal I mean a specific issue." The FBI missed a lot about the plan because it was focusing on specific targets of political influence when in fact the Chinese operation was much more subtle, not focused on specific objectives.

It is clear, however, that the influence operations made it easier for the Chinese to conduct espionage against the United States, especially against U.S. nuclear weapons laboratories. Also, the plan to portray China as nonthreatening contributed to China's massive technology collection effort, an effort that allowed U.S. government controls to be loosened and hundreds of advanced supercomputers to be acquired. A top secret National Security Agency report in May 2000 disclosed that the China Academy of Engineering Physics, the PRC's premier nuclear weapons development facility, was using U.S. supercomputers to conduct simulated nuclear detonations. The Clinton-Gore administration completely ignored the intelligence. Instead, it pressed Congress for legislation that would further loosen controls on high-performance computers.

The leaks were damaging. "We lost some coverage, there is no question about that, because every time any iota of information came up, it ended up in the damned newspaper. It was everywhere." One FBI agent retired early after stating that he would resign before giving up the identities of the FBI's intelligence sources to the White House.

Meanwhile, the White House and a Justice Department political appointee without the so-called need to know were hounding FBI headquarters with constant requests for information identifying sources of the intelligence about the Chinese. The requests angered counterintelligence agents. "In all my years [in U.S. counterintelligence] no one had ever asked me for the identity of the source," the former FBI agent said.

"They had only asked me, 'Is the source good? What's the bona fides?' And I was really offended by the fact that people wanted to know.... I mean, that's the keys to the kingdom; you don't do that. But how good is he? That's what you want to know. Is this guy accurate? Well, 90 percent of the time you know."

The investigation was "so politicized and highly politically charged," the former agent said. "There were a lot of problems with that investigation, and it was because you had the Republicans here and the Democrats here and the White House here and everybody here; you know, it was like a feeding frenzy. Trying to protect, find out. Very, very difficult times."

FBI officials said that after the White House was briefed, the campaign finance investigation was suppressed for political reasons, and the question became whether Chinese influence activities were legal or illegal rather than how had a foreign government subverted the American political process and to what ends. But some of the ends nevertheless became public knowledge.

An example of how the Clinton-Gore administration politicized American counterintelligence is Taiwan. A classified memorandum from Attorney General Janet Reno to FBI Director Louis Freeh known as the National Security Threat List shows that the White House classified Taiwan as a "country threat" equal to Russia, China, Cuba, North Korea, and the nations designated as state sponsors of international terrorism. Reno refused to comment when asked why Taiwan was on the list. FBI officials said the island was added for political reasons by the State Department, which insisted Taiwan be included even though Taipei's intelligence services were not in the same league as the other hostile spy services. The Taiwanese have been linked to improper military technology acquisition, but their efforts pale before what China obtained. Asked about the inclusion of Taiwan on the list, Senator Jon Kyl, Arizona Republican and member of the Senate Select Committee on Intelligence, replied, "What threat? It is very strange to me that Taiwan would be on this list especially since other countries that spy on us are not."

The threat list included the top spying threats in order of priority: Russia, People's Republic of China, Cuba, North Korea, Federal Republic of Yugoslavia, Serbian-controlled Bosnia, Vietnam, Syria, Iraq, Iran, Libya, Sudan, and Taiwan.

For the Clinton-Gore administration, it was a perverse exercise in moral equivalence. If China, perhaps the most sophisticated and aggressive spy threat operating today, is on the list, then Taiwan had to be on it too, or so went the thinking of the Clinton national security officials. The addition of Taiwan outraged many FBI officials who insisted that if Taiwan were included, countries such as Israel and France, whose spying is far more aggressive, should be added. The entire document is reproduced in the appendix.

One striking example of attempted Chinese government influence occurred during the Taiwan Strait crisis of March 1996. While Taiwan prepared for its presidential election, China launched large-scale war games that the Pentagon identified as possible preparations for an invasion. The war games included several M-9 missile firings that hit in waters north and south of the island, what military officials called "bracketing," sending a not-so-subtle threat. The United States responded by sending two aircraft carrier battle groups to the region.

In response to the crisis, Charlie Trie, a Chinese-born restaurateur and Little Rock friend of—and fund-raiser for—the president, met with Mark Middleton, a White House aide and Democratic Party fund-raiser.

Trie gave him a letter to be passed on to the White House. One witness told House investigators that Trie had spoken to "people in the White House and National Security Council about the danger of confronting China over Taiwan."

Middleton stated in a cover letter to the White House accompanying the letter, "As you likely know, Charlie is a personal friend of the President from [Little Rock]. He is also a major supporter. The President sat beside Charlie at the big Asian fund-raiser several weeks ago. Thanks for your always good assistance."

Written in Mr. Trie's broken English, the letter to the president stated:

> Regarding the current situation in the Taiwan Strait Crisis and also the
> U.S. aircraft carriers and cruisers involvement, I would like to propose

some important points to you in order not to endanger the U.S. interest based on the followings:

1. Any negative outcomes of the U.S. decision in the China Issue will affect your administration position especially in this campaign year;
2. Why U.S. has to send the aircraft carriers and cruisers to give China a possible excuse of foreign intervention and hence launch a real war? And, if the U.S. recognized "one China" policy, don't such conduct will cause a conflict for "intervening China's internal affairs?" Therefore, won't the recent inconsistent talks by the captains and some governmental officials in the mass media cause problems for the U.S. policy of not interference of China's internal affairs?...

The last two items on Trie's list were the most direct:

7. Once the hard parties of the Chinese military inclined to grasp U.S. involvement as foreign intervention, is U.S. ready to face such challenge?
8. It is highly possible for China to launch real war, based on its past behavior in Sino-Vietnam War and Zhen Bao Tao war with Russia....

The fact that President Clinton had the National Security Council (NSC) respond to a letter from a restaurant owner was an indication that it might have been a back-channel communication from the Chinese government. The NSC's response for the president stated that the aircraft carrier deployment "was intended as a signal to both Taiwan and the PRC that the United States was concerned about maintaining stability in the Taiwan Strait region. It was not intended as a threat to the PRC." The letter was handled by National Security Adviser Anthony Lake and NSC staffer Robert Suettinger.

Trie also was cited in the report by the House Select Committee on U.S. National Security and Military/Commercial Concerns with the People's Republic of China. The panel, headed by Representative Christopher Cox, California Republican, uncovered a tantalizing, but still unexplained, document from federal investigators. A handwritten note in Mandarin found in Trie's Little Rock, Arkansas, office carried sixteen items and was written on the stationery of the Hong Kong

International Hotel. According to the Cox Committee report, the first three items were: "Hughes U.S. Government Export Control Licenses Bribery Problem—Government Official." Investigators said the document linked Trie to U.S. satellite technology transfers to China.

In mid-2000 the extent of Clinton-Gore administration corruption relating to foreign cash was exposed in a secret Justice Department memorandum by Charles LaBella, the chief lawyer in charge of the department's Campaign Financing Task Force. The memorandum, written in 1998, was so devastating that Attorney General Janet Reno refused to release it for nearly two years. When it was made public in June 2000, the reason was clear. The memo stated that Clinton and Gore were desperate to raise campaign funds, regardless of the donor or source. "The intentional conduct and the 'willful ignorance' uncovered by our investigations, when combined with the line blurring, resulted in a situation where abuse was rampant, and indeed the norm," LaBella said. "At some point, the campaign was so corrupted by bloated fundraising and questionable 'contributions' that the system became a caricature of itself."

LaBella disclosed that, had the evidence involved people other than the president, the vice president, and senior White House officials, a criminal probe would have been launched "without hesitation." But the high-level officials' involvement prompted "a heated debate within the Department as to whether to investigate at all," he stated. "The allegations remain unaddressed."

LaBella revealed that among the cash funneled into the presidential election campaign was a $100,000 donation in August 1996 made by Charlie Trie as a "conduit contribution." Investigators viewed this as another example of Trie's "acting as a conduit for PRC money into the Presidential election."

LaBella also wanted to investigate Trie's Taiwan letter and its connection to a contribution of several hundred thousand dollars made at almost the same time to the president's and Hillary Clinton's legal defense fund, the Presidential Legal Expense Trust. He asked: "[W]ere the contributions related to the subject matter contained in Trie's Taiwan Straits letter sent to the White House by Middleton on the day the contributions were tendered by Trie? Were they intended to facilitate the letter finding its way to the President? Were they offered as an incentive to encourage a positive action on the letter?... These are questions that can only be answered following an investigation." But an investigation was never carried out, and the matter was covered up by the Clinton-Gore administration.

LaBella compared the Trie letter on the Taiwan Strait to the timing of campaign contributions made by Bernard Schwartz, the chairman of the satellite maker Loral, who won a waiver for a U.S. satellite export to China even though his company was then under criminal investigation for supplying missile technology to Beijing. "The timing of the Trie 'donations,'" LaBella wrote, "is at least as curious as the timing of contributions of Bernard Schwartz and the waivers sought by Loral in connection with its satellite project in China. The Loral matter is currently the subject of a full criminal investigation."

LaBella, like so many others who didn't follow the political line laid down by the Clinton-Gore White House, was later punished for his harsh assessment, which triggered a call for the appointment of an independent counsel. He was passed over for a key U.S. attorney job.

But his conclusion bears repeating: With so much smoke in the allegations of corruption, there can be little doubt that there is a fire somewhere. "It seems that everyone has been waiting for that single document, witness, or event that will establish, with clarity, action by a covered person (or someone within the discretionary provision) that is violative of a federal law," he stated. "Everyone can understand the implications of a smoking gun. However, these cases have not presented a single event, document, or witness. Rather, there are bits of information (and evidence) which must be pieced together in order to put seemingly innocent actions in perspective. While this may take more work to accomplish, in our view it is no less compelling than the proverbial smoking gun in the end."

FBI Director Louis Freeh, who also was rebuffed in his call for an independent counsel investigation, stated in a November 24, 1997, memorandum to Reno that the FBI's investigation of "Campcon"—campaign contributions—focused on "[e]fforts by the PRC and other countries to gain foreign policy influence by illegally contributing foreign money to U.S. political campaigns and to the DNC through domestic conduits." Freeh stated that the FBI had conflicting duties—to keep the president informed of national security issues and "simultaneously [to] keep from the White House certain national security information that may relate to the ongoing criminal investigation" of Chinese government influence operations. He noted that the Justice Department and the FBI "faced this conflict several times during the course of the investigation, most recently in early November 1997." He was referring to the problems of sharing sensitive intelligence information relevant to Chinese influence operations against the White House.

In China, a key figure in the influence operation has run into serious problems. PLA General Ji Shengde, the official who funneled $300,000 into bank accounts of Democratic Party fund-raiser Johnny Chung, was reported in July 2000 to be facing indictment in Beijing. He was charged with stealing the equivalent of $12.5 million—an amount that was expected to lead to execution, if he were to be found guilty.

After the fund-raising allegations surfaced in 1999, General Ji was removed as director of the PLA Second Department, the military intelligence agency. But it was his role in a major corruption scandal involving smuggling through the southern Chinese port of Xiamen that would lead to his demise. According to U.S. officials, the corruption scandal, which became public in early 2000, provided Chinese leaders with a convenient cover to punish the key figure in China's influence plan while maintaining the official fiction that there never was an influence operation. It was General Ji who told Chung, "We really like your president."

"THE PLAN CONTINUES TODAY"

With evidence like this, it is hard to disagree with Senator Fred Thompson, who wrote that his investigating committee "believes that high level Chinese government officials crafted a plan to increase China's influence over the U.S. political process. The committee has identified specific steps taken in furtherance of the plan. Implementation of the plan has been handled by Chinese government officials and individuals enlisted to assist in the effort. Activities in the furtherance of the plan have occurred both inside and outside of the United States. Our investigations suggest that the plan continues today."

In an interview, Thompson told me, "It's going to be a long time before everything comes out on this. But I've never understood how the president, in light of what we know about these Chinese activities, could so aggressively embrace [the Communist Chinese], place in jeopardy Taiwan, overlook and ignore their proliferation activities, jump through hoops to avoid calling them to task."

The president was willing to criticize China only on its poor human rights record, which recently involved a major crackdown on the Falun Gong meditation group and systematic repression of Buddhist minorities in Tibet, Muslim Uighurs in Xinjiang, and Christians nationwide. The reason, according to Thompson, is that the issue of human rights "polls well" in White House surveys of public opinion.

On the political influence of U.S. campaigns, Chinese government officials were "clearly involving themselves in our processes over here, putting money into his [Clinton's] campaign," Thompson said. "Just from the standpoint of appearances alone you would think the president would be more circumspect. I guess history will tell."

Thompson said political influence activities by the People's Republic of China were only one part of an attack on the United States. "There has been a consistent, pervasive full court press," he said. "It's had to do with industrial espionage. It's had to do with the things that apparently have been going on at Los Alamos [nuclear laboratory]. And there was political influence, not necessarily illegal. A lot of this stuff may not be illegal."

But even if much of it was not, strictly speaking, illegal, the "plan," according to Thompson, was orchestrated "at the highest reaches of the Chinese government." Moreover, plenty of activities obviously *were* illegal. "I have seen people go to jail on much less circumstantial evidence than what we have," Thompson said. "People in this town talk about circumstantial evidence as if it's no evidence. But there are extremely severe consequences in our legal system from a good strong circumstantial evidence case before a jury. And we had half a dozen very significant players, money raisers, in some cases wealthy individuals over here with very strong ties to the PRC."

To illustrate his point, Thompson compared the influence operation to a plan to rob banks in a community; if the local police uncover the robbery plan, and then, six months later, the banks start to be targeted for robberies, "you tend to conclude circumstantially that there is a relationship between the plan and the bank robberies."

"And that's kind of where we stood," he said. "All these things had happened and are consistent with the things we learned."

Since the hearings in 1997, "we learned that the Chinese military, at least from what we were able to pin down... sent some money to the DNC, and I feel quite sure in my own mind that that was a small part of a larger effort."

Thompson explained that the Chinese influence operation was subtle and similar to what domestic political contributors hope to get when they send money to politicians. It may not be the passage of specific legislation but perhaps to influence political leaders on many different issues related to things controlled by Washington. "I think the same thing is true with the Chinese government, whether it's permanent normal trade relations, whether it's Taiwan, whether it's a host of other issues," he said. "There will come a time and place where it will be beneficial to have... people placed. I don't think it's a direct government-to-government thing. I think the purpose of the contributions was to enhance the John Huangs of the world and their credibility so that when the time came they could call on him either for direct information or for their ability to influence the thinking of public officials." Thompson said the U.S. government never really uncovered the total Chinese program. The original Chinese plan was much broader than the 1996 presidential election and involved efforts to recruit people who were pro-Beijing in state and local elections. "We really only got, in all fairness, sketches of it," he said.

Thompson said government secrecy rules were a problem that prohibited discussing in public what the FBI knew about the Chinese influence operations. At the opening day of hearings, June 8, 1997, the chairman bluntly revealed that China spent money on a plan to influence the U.S. political process. Democrats disagreed by claiming there was no evidence that the plan included illegal activities. The spin was very effective in influencing news reports. If nothing was illegal, then it was no big deal—so went the thinking of the Democrats, no doubt influenced by the public relations specialists at the White House.

Senator Thompson explained that he had been reluctant to talk about the sources of his information because "the intelligence community had convinced me that it was very delicate and even stating the source could cause problems. I determined later that that was total baloney."

Would releasing the intelligence to the public have made a difference?

"It would have alleviated the controversy that the White House, in conjunction with Senator [John] Glenn and some others, caused," Thompson said. "There was a lot of pressure brought to bear on me after that. I could feel—but couldn't see—the tremendous orchestration and pressure." The White House, Senate Minority Leader Tom Daschle, and Democrats on the committee "kept this thing controlled and partisan."

The key tactical error was to agree to limit the time of the campaign finance investigation. Once that was set and the committee was limited to nine months and twenty days, the Democratic strategy was easy—delay and stall. When the time ran out, the investigation was over and Clinton and the Democrats had averted a major scandal, as they had on so many occasions in the past.

Thompson said he was frustrated by the effectiveness of the political spin, which was boosted by a news media sympathetic to the Clinton-Gore administration. "You got a guy coming back from China who has close ties to the PRC, he opens up a secret bank account or something and funnels money into the DNC, and you've got a plan out there to do that very thing, and the Washington press corps's response is, 'It's circumstantial. No confession,'" Thompson said.

The committee also discovered that the supposedly independent Justice Department Campaign Financing Task Force investigation was politically wired to the White House. The prosecutors maintained "on a day-to-day operational basis" constant contact with high-level officials in the Justice Department, who in turn were talking to Clinton's political operatives at the White House. "This was not an independent, free-floating, highly-charged prosecutorial fighting machine," said Chris Ford, a Thompson aide who was a key official in the Senate probe. "This was a closely-managed-from-above operation."

Thompson noted that the campaign task force was "totally inept" and would have been unable to "play it straight" even if it had wanted to.

The committee had identified three people as more than just overt friends of China. Ted Sioeng, Maria Hsia, and it linked John Huang to Chinese intelligence. Ford said that "we identified those three in the report as being subject to information to that effect."

"A SERIOUS THREAT TO OUR NATIONAL SECURITY"

The U.S. government's most complete statement about China's secret plan to influence the American political process was released in May 1999. The report by the Senate Intelligence Committee was almost completely ignored by the major news media. And the Clinton-Gore administration, as it had in the past, also did its best to spin the national press into believing there was nothing new in the report.

The Intelligence Committee report put it bluntly: China had a plan to influence the political process in the United States. Chinese leaders put money in it, and it worked. "Direct or indirect funding by foreign governments or entities of American election campaigns are [sic] a grave concern to the United States.... A covert effort to influence the U.S. political process does represent a threat to U.S. national security.... Any time a foreign government or group attempts to covertly influence American policy, or through clandestine means tries to affect U.S. political campaigns on the federal, state or local level, our sovereignty and national security are threatened. The Committee believes this is a serious threat to our national security."

Fred Thompson was one senator who did not ignore the Senate Intelligence Committee report. Regarding the threat from the People's Republic of China, he told me: "We are so behind the curve. We are so of the moment. I keep hearing the Cold War's over. The most liberal

Democrats and the most conservative Republicans [who] are trying to push the merchandise out the door are together in this 'the Cold War's over.' And we're going to have to get a goddamn bomb laid on us in order to get anybody's attention any more. 'Peace and prosperity, let the good times roll.' And we are never ahead of the curve. We're never planning." Unlike China, we have no plan.

CHAPTER THREE
China Wars

> *"Let your plans be dark and impenetrable as night, and when you move, fall like a thunderbolt."*
>
> —Sun Tzu

In the early 1990s, FBI counterintelligence agents came across evidence that was a counterspy's worst nightmare. Classified intelligence reports showed that China's spy service was running several "assets," as spies are called in the vernacular, who were operating clandestinely inside the U.S. government. One, however, was different from the others. He didn't work for just any agency of the government. From the reports, it is was clear this agent had burrowed deep inside the U.S. intelligence community, meaning that Communist China had access to vital U.S. defense and intelligence secrets. The information was revealed to the FBI in highly sensitive communications intercepts between the Chinese embassy in Washington and PRC intelligence in Beijing. The intercepts suggested the agent was supplying Chinese intelligence with classified defense information. The spy even had a code name: "Ma"—Chinese for "horse." Additionally, a Chinese government official who defected to the United States after the Tiananmen massacre of 1989 told U.S. intelligence that China had successfully developed between five and ten clandestine sources of information in the United States. The defector said these agents were known as "Dear Friends" of China. Only one had access to Top Secret-Sensitive Compartmented Information, or SCI—the most sensitive U.S. intelligence data. It was Horse.

FBI counterintelligence agents began searching for the agent. Their search led them to the Defense Intelligence Agency (DIA), the Pentagon's

intelligence arm. A key suspect emerged. His name was Ronald Montaperto. At the time, Montaperto was a senior DIA analyst specializing in
"estimates"—as the agency called its analyses—of matters related to
China and East Asia. The job required making official contacts with Chinese government and military officials. In Washington, that meant
defense attachés posted to the Chinese embassy. Chinese defense
attachés are all intelligence officers working for the military intelligence
department of the PLA General Staff. One of the attachés was People's
Liberation Army Major General Yu Zhenghe. Yu was the air attaché and
had developed a close relationship with Montaperto—close enough to be
invited to Montaperto's wedding in 1990.

The hunt for a Chinese "mole" was rare for the FBI. Most of the other
moles uncovered inside the U.S. government during the 1980s, in what
became known as the Decade of the Spy, were spies for the Soviet Union.
There was one exception. A Chinese intelligence officer who defected to
the United States in 1985 identified a U.S. government Chinese language
specialist as a spy. The defector was Yu Qiangsheng, a senior intelligence
officer in the Ministry of State Security. Yu had great access to information about Chinese intelligence operations and agents. It was Yu who
first put a CIA counterspy on to Larry Wu-Tai Chin, a Chinese language
specialist in the CIA's Foreign Broadcast Information Service, which
publishes translations of foreign news publications and broadcasts. Yu
has been resettled in the United States and remains under federal government protection. He fears for his life from Beijing agents. Chin would
eventually be unmasked. He had burrowed within the CIA for some
thirty years and had provided valuable political intelligence to Beijing.
Chin was a rare catch. But before he could be interrogated thoroughly
for "damage assessment"—to determine the extent of the intelligence
damage—Chin committed suicide in his jail cell.

After the bloody military crackdown of protesters in Beijing's
Tiananmen Square in 1989, several other Chinese intelligence officers
defected to the United States, determined to help America defeat the
communist government. Two of them had worked inside the Chinese
embassy in Washington. The information they provided was extremely
valuable and helped to confirm and update the important information

provided years earlier by Yu. The defectors explained how careful Chinese intelligence is in contacting and servicing its clandestine agents. Chinese intelligence officers never meet their clandestine agents inside the United States. The FBI was considered too good at catching spies, so it was safer to meet abroad, preferably in China. Similarly, Yu had revealed how Chin would often meet Chinese intelligence officers during his annual vacations to Canada.

The new Chinese defectors of the 1989–1990 period—who had had access to intelligence reports sent from the embassy to Ministry of State Security headquarters in China—revealed that Chinese intelligence had recruited several people who were referred to as "Dear Friends" of China. These Dear Friends provided valuable intelligence and were rewarded with paid trips to China, business opportunities in China, and prestige-building access to senior Chinese officials during the visits.

From their knowledge of the embassy intelligence cables, the defectors were able to reveal to U.S. intelligence debriefers some details of the information China was obtaining from the agents known as Dear Friends. To the U.S. counterspies, one of the most troubling signs was that large amounts of extremely sensitive military intelligence information was being provided to China. Based on the defectors' testimony, the FBI launched a major espionage probe and came up with a list of twelve suspects that fit the profile of the special Dear Friend with access to U.S. military secrets. Then the bureau began systematically "interviewing" each one of them. It was during this process that the FBI met Montaperto, in late 1991 or early 1992. At the time he was chief of DIA's estimates branch for China, a position he held from September 1989 until his departure from the agency in February 1992. He had joined DIA as an analyst in October 1981 and worked his way up through the ranks over the following ten years.

Intelligence intercepts of Chinese government communications gathered by the National Security Agency and supplied to the FBI later revealed that one of the most important agents being run by Chinese intelligence was code-named Ma.

The FBI investigation continued, and eventually agents confronted Montaperto. The confrontation took place in what the FBI called "hostile interrogations." FBI agents grilled Montaperto in three separate meetings. They asked him bluntly if he had passed any classified intelligence information to China's intelligence service. He said no. Any contacts that he had with Chinese intelligence were authorized, he claimed. Montaperto did admit to the DIA that he knew General Yu.

Montaperto was cleared by the FBI, though some counterintelligence officials still suspected that Montaperto was Ma. But they couldn't prove it. Montaperto said the matter had been put to rest conclusively. "I can honestly say they looked me in the eye and said, 'We don't think you're a spy,'" he said of the meetings with the FBI.

But soon after the investigation, Montaperto left the DIA. In an interview with me, he denied that the FBI probe had had anything to do with his leaving the DIA. As for his friendship with General Yu, the Chinese intelligence officer, Montaperto said, "One does not have friends with Chinese officials," meaning his contacts were strictly professional.

"Did General Yu attend your wedding?" I asked.

"Yes," Montaperto confirmed. It was a relatively small wedding, he explained, because it was his second marriage. Montaperto said he invited Yu and other Chinese officials because he thought it would be a good experience for them to attend the ceremony.

One other thing: Hanging on the wall inside Montaperto's office was a large scroll of Chinese calligraphy. It contained the characters "horse dragon virtue," which when spoken in Mandarin sounds like Montaperto. A second Chinese character set also was on the scroll. It was Chinese for "war horse." The scroll is signed by another Chinese intelligence officer, who, like Yu Zhenghe, was an attaché at the Chinese embassy in Washington when the scroll was given as a gift to Montaperto. Montaperto insists the scroll was from a student in Shanghai.

The FBI never found the clandestine spy named Ma. Several of the Dear Friends, however, were uncovered, although the bureau never brought them to prosecution. The FBI was hamstrung by the limited details provided by the former Chinese intelligence officers, who had seen the cables but did not have hard copies of them. One of the Chinese agents was a Chinese-American employee at a U.S. defense con tractor in northern Virginia. He was never prosecuted, although his access to classified information was cut off.

Montaperto did not totally leave the government. Instead, after leaving DIA in 1992 he took up residence at the Pentagon's National Defense University located at Fort McNair, a scenic base overlooking the Potomac River in southwest Washington, D.C. Montaperto became a "social science analyst" with the National Defense University's Institute for National Strategic Studies, a think tank for security issues within the university. His biography listed on the National Defense University Internet site contains only four sentences and makes no mention of his DIA experience. It states only that he is a China affairs specialist: "Currently he is defining strategies and policies for managing future U.S. interests in the Asia-Pacific region."

Because the FBI could not prove its suspicions, Montaperto was allowed to retain his top secret security clearance. But he does not have the same access to intelligence information at the National Defense University as he had at DIA. Yu, meanwhile, remains one of China's most important intelligence officers. He works for PLA General Xiong Guangkai, the PLA deputy chief of staff for intelligence. According to one U.S. national security official, Yu returned to the United States during the 1996 Taiwan Strait crisis and tried to meet Montaperto.

Montaperto's primary job at the National Defense University is to oversee the China portion of an annual "Strategic Assessment," to speak on China policy around the world, and to organize an occasional conference on China. In each aspect of his job, he has displayed a pronounced pro-China view that plays down China's military capabilities generally and strategic and conventional force developments specifically. Montaperto denies that he is a "panda hugger," as the soft-liners on China have been called by Pentagon China specialists. But he confesses, "For some people, I will always be considered a 'panda hugger.'"

When Congress ordered the creation of a special National Defense University clearinghouse for intelligence on the People's Liberation Army, it was Montaperto who presented the plan to the Pentagon. It called for hiring thirty-three specialists, opening a large office in southwest Washington, and spending $4.5 million annually. At first the

Pentagon rejected it because it appeared more like a plan to promote military-to-military contacts with the People's Liberation Army than one to provide useful information about the strategy and direction of the Chinese military. The Clinton-Gore administration had already dramatically increased meetings and exchanges with Chinese military leaders, which the Chinese had exploited to develop intelligence. Many in the Pentagon had had enough of that, and senior Pentagon officials objected to Montaperto's appointment as director of the new center. But the university went ahead anyway and made him interim director.

The importance of the China center was highlighted when Clinton opposed the requirement to set it up on signing a $289 billion defense bill in October 1999. Congress's mandating of the Chinese military center and reports on China's military buildup, the president said, assume "an outcome that is far from foreordained—that China is bent on becoming a military threat to the United States."

"I believe we should not make it more likely that China will choose this path by acting as if the decision has already been made," the president said in an official statement accompanying his signing of the defense bill.

Yet the president's policies and those of the soft-liners who refused to recognize the nature of the People's Republic of China had done more to increase the danger from China than any of the China skeptics in Congress who felt more should be done to learn about China's military intentions.

BREAKING THE ENEMY'S RESISTANCE FROM WITHIN

Montaperto's downplaying of the China threat is at one with Communist Chinese military policy, which involves deception—preventing the U.S. "hegemon" from recognizing the emerging power of China until it is greater, at least regionally, than America's. According to the late Chinese leader Deng Xiaoping, China must avoid provoking a conflict with the United States—at least until China builds up sufficient military, economic, and political power to win. In the words of Deng, "Hide brightness; nourish obscurity." Or as the official translation in Beijing put it, "Bide our time and build up our capabilities." Chinese military writings predict that China's "dangerous decade"—when it faces a strategic checkmate—is the period between 2020 and 2030. By 2020, America will not be able to ignore China's growing might, and China's military and strategic planners fear the country will not be powerful enough to take on the United States until 2030. What China wants is three more decades of Clinton-Gore "engagement," which downplays Chinese military capabilities, encourages decreasing American defense spending, and gives China major technical and financial boosts.

Chinese government officials view certain China specialists in the United States as important outlets for Beijing's views. Many of these China specialists are current or former government officials. Unlike the thousands of political scientists who specialize in European and Russian affairs and other geographic specialties, the China experts who specialize on international security and foreign affairs could fit in a large conference room. And most of them communicate via Internet discussion groups, which have become a major target of Chinese government influence efforts.

Take "Chinasec." Every morning a group of about a hundred high-level U.S. policymakers and intelligence officials receives e-mail postings as part of an Internet discussion group. The group goes by the innocuous-sounding name of "Chinasec," for China security. But the informal electronic gathering includes some of the most important China policymakers in the U.S. government, including the Pentagon's desk officer for China matters, Colonel John Corbett. The group is decidedly pro-China and often criticizes news stories that explore Chinese weapons sales to rogue states or espionage against America. Newspaper reports by this author have been a frequent target. For instance, when the *Washington Times* reported on the critical views of China held by Condoleezza Rice, a key foreign policy adviser to Republican presidential candidate George W. Bush, the Chinasec group swung into action. The secret e-mail network adopted the standard Clinton-Gore administration posture—spin. The article was dismissed as exaggerated and the work of a "nonexpert."

The Chinasec online discussion group is secret, but not in the U.S. government classification sense of that term. Most of its participants hold high-level security clearances. At least ten CIA officials are members. It is part of an informal but very powerful network of current and former government officials, academics, and other China experts who exert a major influence on U.S. policies toward China.

The ancient Chinese strategist Sun Tzu wrote that "supreme excellence consists in breaking the enemy's resistance without fighting." The view of China presented by these pro-Beijing specialists is not manufactured by the Chinese Communist Politburo, but it serves the Politburo's strategy. The key theme of all Chinese propaganda directed abroad is simple: China is not a threat. This theme is a key element of Chinese Communist Party overt and covert influence efforts. And it is the litmus test for those experts Beijing labels "Friends of China." "China is not a threat" is a key identifier for this theme and a constant refrain of the Clinton-Gore administration.

CASH-REGISTER FOREIGN POLICY

President Clinton outlined the crux of the Clinton-Gore China policy in a letter to Congress in early 2000 seeking support for legislation granting China permanent normal trade status, a prerequisite for Beijing's entry into the World Trade Organization. The president, as in the past, was rewarding China despite its bad behavior. So he ignored Chinese violations of internationally accepted norms on human rights and weapons sales to terrorist states.

"We will continue to protect our interests with firmness and candor," Clinton stated, "but we must do so without isolating China from the global forces empowering its people to build a better future." In essence, the president was justifying policies that have allowed China to grow stronger, economically, politically, and militarily, based on the unwarranted hope that trade will liberalize the regime.

A. M. Rosenthal, the retired executive editor of the *New York Times*, believes China has scored remarkable successes in manipulating the United States. "Never in American history has this country been so influenced by a foreign dictatorship," Rosenthal told me. "In fact, possibly excluding Britain, never to my memory has any country at all had so much influence in American political, economic, and academic life."

Nazi Germany, by comparison, had only a handful of agents in the United States. "But the Chinese Communists are a powerful influence with the president of the United States, and through him with the White House and various cabinet departments, many members of Congress, universities, down to the state and local levels where economic pressure from within the U.S. moves mayors and governors to support legislation that would help the Chinese economically, like the permanent 'normalization' of trade," Rosenthal said. Trade with China is, of course, avidly supported by American business, which is willing to overlook human rights violations in exchange for access to China's vast market.

"The only country with a real human rights policy, with teeth, is China," says Rosenthal. Foreign corporations are warned that any talk of pressuring the ruling Communist Party to end the inhuman treatment of dissidents will bring official retaliation. The Beijing government knows that its control over foreign companies that seek access to the huge Chinese market is a powerful political tool to keep them in line.

But it's not just businessmen seeking profits who are to blame, though money is a major factor that cuts across from corporations to political fund-raisers. Rosenthal, now a columnist and unabashed defender of freedom and democracy, criticized the U.S. academic community, in particular, for creating illusions about China while ignoring its Soviet-style Laogai concentration camps, where millions of Chinese have been incarcerated, many for alleged political crimes, such as criticizing the Communist Party or practicing meditation as members of the Falun Gong religious group. "In academia, the emphasis of public comment is not on the Laogai but on what are seen as positive developments, such as local elections or a brief period of time when Beijing permits some 'liberal' comments to be published," Rosenthal said. "The end of those 'liberalization' efforts or their perversion gets nothing like the attention that went to their initial announcement."

Rosenthal says China's most important influence has been to change the way people in the United States treat dictatorships hostile to the United States. During the Cold War, American officials would criticize Soviet repression in face-to-face meetings with Soviet representatives. "That does not happen to the Chinese," he says. "Instead, it has been my experience that it is the critics of China who generally meet with annoyance and criticism, certainly in the government and very often in the universities." China's persecution of Christians, too, "has met with a yawn from the heavy majority of American clergy," Rosenthal goes on. "In fact, I have had some clerics tell me they never heard of it. Obviously there are people among the clergy and politicians who do stand up to the Chinese Communists, and there may be some big businessmen who do too. Maybe—but I don't know them."

The key to the Chinese success, according to Rosenthal, has been Americans' desire for cash. "Money is a major reason—the hope that more trade will enrich businesses and some occupations, like farming," he said. "The about-face of Clinton in accepting the cash-register philosophy of foreign affairs is another. But they could not have done it alone, the lobbies and the president. They needed the support of major politicians in both parties. They needed the naiveté or callousness of the American public, who did not understand what was going on, that Clintonian 'engagement' was between U.S. officials and Chinese officials, not between the U.S and the Chinese people, and therefore was a fraud, the classic big lie."

AN AMERICAN POLITICAL BASE

Despite the soft-line approach to China, a 1999 public opinion poll revealed that years of Clinton's foreign policy of engagement toward China had not convinced the majority of the American people that China was a benign power. The results of a *Wall Street Journal*–NBC News poll published in September 1999 found that 60 percent to 80 percent of the American people consider China to be an "adversary," not, as the Clinton-Gore administration would have it, a strategic partner.

China's efforts to influence the United States are not limited to Democrats. Beijing also has its covert allies within Republican Party ranks. The debate over China surfaced during a secret struggle over the party's platform at the presidential nominating convention in Philadelphia in August 2000. Robert Blackwill, a former U.S. government arms control official, was assigned the task of drafting the Republican Party national security platform, and his initial draft had a pro-Beijing slant. Blackwill, a friend of Condoleezza Rice, the national security adviser to George W. Bush, is director of the China Initiative, a program at Harvard University's John F. Kennedy School of Government. The China Initiative—which was funded by a mysterious Hong Kong patron named Nina Kung, who in 1997 provided $1 million to the program—has been described by one Pentagon official as a "training program for Chinese spies." Within the China Initiative is the Kennedy School's Executive Program for Senior Chinese Military Officers, which Blackwill chairs and which has brought to Harvard four groups of twenty-four top People's Liberation Army officers. Numerous Chinese defense and military officials, many of them colonels handpicked by People's Liberation Army intelligence chief Lieutenant General Xiong Guangkai, have attended the China Initiative. According to U.S. intelligence officials, Chinese military intelligence favors the Harvard program over official U.S. government exchange programs because the Chinese believe it is easier to avoid FBI counterintelligence surveillance in Boston than in Washington, D.C.

In an initial draft of the GOP platform, Blackwill, attempting to soften the language, described China as a "competitor," not a "strategic competitor." After objections from conservatives on the platform committee, including Bob Livingston, former congressman from Louisiana, the term "strategic competitor" was restored in the final platform. But in an alarming demonstration of Chinese intelligence-gathering skills, the Chinese government obtained a copy of the unfinished GOP platform document that included Blackwill's softened stance toward Beijing. Moreover, a senior Chinese military intelligence officer, Major General Chen Kaizeng, attended the convention and was present at a private meeting sponsored by the International Republican Institute, a meeting that featured top foreign affairs and defense officials.

The platform differences over China were a sign that the Republicans remain divided on the issue of China, with many of the leading figures adopting the shortsighted view that China poses no threat to the United States and seeing China mainly as a business opportunity.

Among those who keep trying to alter public opinion is former Secretary of State Henry Kissinger, who has used his extensive access to Chinese leaders to help his consulting business flourish. Kissinger played the key role in secret talks during the 1970s that led President Nixon to establish informal ties with China in 1972 and ultimately led to formal diplomatic relations in 1979, which ended the mutual U.S. defense treaty with Taiwan. Kissinger's view is that because China has moved away from socialism economically, it is no longer communist and no longer a threat. "The Chinese Communist Party has claimed relevance only for its own country," he said in one speech. "It is practicing a method of economy that would have been deemed totally heretical by the Soviet leaders of the 1970s. China has claimed no right to intervene in foreign countries on behalf of its ideology. It will no doubt grow in power but as a totally different phenomenon."

From this line of Kissinger, there has developed a pro-Beijing Republican coterie. It includes Alexander Haig, who was Kissinger's deputy in the China gambit before going on to become NATO commander and secretary of state; Kissinger protégé Brent Scowcroft, who was President George Bush's national security adviser; and Lawrence Eagleburger, who was Bush's deputy secretary of state and, in the last year of the administration, secretary of state.

Haig's pro-Beijing views were related in a 1998 conversation about Tiananmen Square. The retired four-star general explained how he traveled to China after the 1989 massacre and was invited by a senior Chinese general to visit his residence. An official car picked him up at the Beijing hotel, and the PLA general told Haig that no one had died in the square during the military operations on the night of June 3–4, 1989. The PLA general explained how the crackdown was necessary for "stability." Haig accepted the explanation uncritically and was convinced in part because of the high level of his source. But official U.S. reports have said at least a thousand people were killed in gunfire or by being run over by PLA tanks. The Clinton-Gore administration and Beijing's Republican fellow travelers give credence to China's belief that America is manipulable and in decline.

"In the picturesque terms of ancient Chinese statecraft," China scholar Michael Pillsbury says, "America is a decaying hegemon whose leaders are as yet unaware that their fate is unavoidable, so the U.S. leadership is pursuing several dangerous but doomed strategies."

One "dangerous but doomed" strategy was U.S. support for Taiwan. But as a result of its aggressive public diplomacy, Communist China has succeeded in causing a fundamental shift in U.S. policy toward Beijing and away from Taipei, the Taiwanese capital.

Former FBI official I. C. Smith, a veteran counterintelligence officer who specialized in Chinese intelligence activities, said the Communist Chinese had no political base of support in the United States in 1979 when formal diplomatic ties were established. Chinese diplomats struggled to figure out the workings of the United States. One diplomat, Cao Guisheng, a first secretary in the embassy political section in Washington, predicted that Jimmy Carter would easily be reelected in 1980. The Chinese government was shocked when Ronald Reagan was elected by a landslide. "They just could not imagine the transfer of power," Smith said.

But if China was bad at understanding American politics in 1980, by the time of the Clinton-Gore administration it had learned the power of money and deception. An unclassified report by the FBI and the CIA sent to Congress in March 2000 concluded that the national security priorities of the People's Republic of China include "monitoring as well as influencing... worldwide perceptions of China." According to the counterintelligence report, China's foreign intelligence collection goals "include gathering information about key players and developments in countries that might affect China's interests. Penetrating the U.S. intelligence community is a key objective of the Chinese."

Only one paragraph of the unclassified version of the report explains Chinese "propaganda and perception management" operations.

"China primarily uses government-owned or government-controlled press to ensure its views on policy issues are heard in the United

States," the report says. "For example, *Wen Wei Po*, which appears as a periodic supplement to Chinese-language newspapers published in the United States, is a favored outlet for reaching ethnic Chinese audiences, whose perspectives in turn can influence the broader public's views of China." *Wen Wei Po* is published in New York and is targeted at what Beijing calls the "overseas Chinese"—the community of ethnic Chinese who are presumed to remain loyal to China and open to the official Chinese Communist Party political line.

RED TEAM, BLUE TEAM

William C. Triplett II, former professional counsel to the Senate Foreign Relations Committee and coauthor of two books on China, sees the battle over China policy in military terms. Triplett coined the term "Red Team" to describe pro-Beijing specialists—a play on the fact that most of them fail to recognize the communist nature of the PLA or go to great lengths to ignore it. The opposing group of China specialists, mainly conservatives, has set up what Triplett calls the "Blue Team"— analysts who consider themselves locked in an ideological struggle with the pro-China experts. The Red/Blue team concept is standard in the military for war gaming and is used to denote the good guys and the bad guys. In the case of the China experts, the colors also represent the struggle of freedom against communist dictatorship, although few in the Red Team would ever admit to being sympathetic to such a thing. White House spokesman David Leavy denied that White House officials responsible for China are "pro-Beijing." However, a senior Pentagon official described the differences over China policy in the late 1990s as "open political warfare" between key White House National Security Council and State Department officials on the one hand and the Pentagon on the other.

Triplett views the Red Team's efforts as nothing short of subversive. "They have subverted American policy to the point that we're unable to reach a consensus on how to deal with the China threat," he said. "They have undermined the consensus-making that is so critical in a democratic society faced with a nondemocratic military threat."

Writing in apparent support of the Red Team, the *Washington Post* leveled a biased attack against the Blue Team, accusing it of exaggerating the threat from China. "Though little noticed, the Blue Team has had considerable success," wrote reporters Robert Kaiser and Steve Mufson in a 3,000-word article. They continued:

> By attaching riders to legislation in Congress, [the Blue Team] has restricted the scope of Chinese-American military relations, forced the Pentagon to report to Congress in detail on the China-Taiwan military balance, and compelled the State Department to take a harder line on China's human rights and religious rights abuses. Some Blue Team allies have promoted public fears of a Chinese takeover of the Panama Canal; several congressional offices report a deluge of mail about Panama's choice of a Hong Kong firm to operate shipping facilities at both ends of the canal, a cause taken up by conservative radio talk show hosts. Allies of the Blue Team have harassed China's biggest oil company, complicating its efforts to sell shares on the New York Stock Exchange. Members of the Blue Team initially drafted and then helped push through the House of Representatives this month [February 2000] the Taiwan Security Enhancement Act, a measure to strengthen U.S. military ties with Taiwan that has angered China.

The article hit all the key themes advanced by both the China experts and Beijing itself. The tone imparted the idea that anyone who is critical of China's communist government is out of the mainstream, to be dismissed as a right-wing zealot, a conspiracy theorist, or worse. The article coincidentally echoed Chinese Foreign Minister Tang Jiaxuan's statement about his talks with Secretary of State Madeleine Albright regarding "anti-China" forces in the United States.

Beijing does not limit its propaganda efforts to China experts. It knows well how to use its power to control the American press. The key, again, is access. For major American newspapers, wire services, and broadcasters, having Chinese government permission to operate in the Chinese capital of Beijing is a top priority. The problem arises when writings or broadcasts are perceived by the Chinese Communist bureaucracy as anti-Chinese or even anticommunist. That can result in stern rebukes from Chinese officials. The warnings can be implicit or explicit: Report things that the Information Ministry dislikes and your reporters will be expelled and your bureaus closed.

In a December 1999 *Washington Times* exclusive, this author revealed information from inside the U.S. intelligence community showing that China was building up its short-range missile forces opposite Taiwan. The buildup was significant, as revealed in DIA reports that secretly concluded that China now possessed the capability to conduct missile attacks against the island with little or no warning. The danger of war had increased. For its aggressive coverage of Chinese military development, the *Washington Times*, which has no bureau in Beijing, drew official Chinese government protests.

Contrast this with China coverage in the *New York Times*. On the same day that the exclusive on the missile buildup appeared, the *New York Times* ran a soft news feature by one of its Beijing-based reporters about how Chinese were taking to "fat farms" to lose weight. Such soft stories come often from the Beijing-based American press, and they do little to illuminate Chinese repression and the looming threat of China's expanding military and its patiently aggressive foreign policy.

Of course, positive pro-China stories not only mollify Beijing, they also maintain a reporter's access to prestigious numbers of the Red Team, which includes Sandy Berger, national security adviser to the president. Berger was a speechwriter with little foreign policy experience who joined Bill Clinton's presidential campaign in 1992. While Clinton was criticizing President George Bush for "coddling" dictators in Beijing over the bloody 1989 Tiananmen massacre, Berger was quietly working behind the scenes as a trade lawyer for the Washington firm Hogan & Hartson. Berger's job included arranging joint ventures between American companies and Chinese firms. It was Berger who persuaded the president to drop any linkage between China's human rights abuses and U.S. trade, a policy also favored by Clinton's first national security adviser, Anthony Lake.

Another key pro-China official is Kenneth Lieberthal, a professor of political science and business at the University of Michigan's Center for

Chinese Studies who became the National Security Council's top China expert in 1998. Lieberthal was on the board of directors of the National Committee on U.S.-China Relations, the New York–based nonprofit organization that is the central connecting point with the government of the People's Republic of China for education and academic exchanges. Until his appointment to the White House, his pro-China views were limited to books, articles, and news interviews. Lieberthal criticized the White House in 1995 for a fragmented China policy that was a "hodge-podge" of competing interests that belittled the Chinese. At the time, the Commerce Department and the U.S. Trade Representative Office were at odds over expanding trade and protecting U.S. companies from intellectual property theft. And the State Department and related bureaus were divided over whether to criticize China's human rights record as well as whether to punish China for it weapons proliferation activities. The Pentagon, too, was divided over the wisdom of its military-to-military exchange program.

A few years later Lieberthal was in charge of National Security Council staff policy at the White House. His solution to the "hodgepodge" was granting more concessions to Beijing without seeking anything in return. And he openly opposed increased U.S. support for Taiwan, a prosperous and thriving democracy that could be used as a model for reforming the communist dictatorship in Beijing.

In a 1993 *New York Times* article Lieberthal wrote, "The U.S. should stop punishing China for the massacre of demonstrators in Tiananmen Square in 1989. China is too important to make this the pivot of our policy." Democracy in China appears to have no place in Lieberthal's policies.

At the State Department, the key players have been Stanley Roth, assistant secretary of state for East Asia, and his deputy for China, Susan Shirk. Shirk left government in early 2000 to return to her post as director of the Institute on Global Conflict and Cooperation at the University of California at San Diego's Graduate School of International Relations and Pacific Studies. She was known in the Pentagon for screaming her opposition to arms sales to Taiwan. The Pentagon brass view such sales as an effective way of keeping U.S. military forces from warring with China. But the Red Team is vehemently opposed to helping Taiwan because it will anger China.

Before leaving office, Shirk undermined American gunboat diplomacy by sending out an e-mail message to a group of academics stating categorically that the U.S. aircraft carrier *Kitty Hawk* would not be used to defend Taiwan. The e-mail surfaced in early March 2000 as Chinese rhetoric and threats against Taiwan were at an unprecedented pitch in the days before Taiwan's presidential elections. The Pentagon had sent the *Kitty Hawk* to exercise in waters off Japan as a subtle signal to the Chinese not to test-fire missiles off Taiwan, as they had done prior to the 1996 elections. Because the academics on the "Chinapol"— China Policy—discussion group were decidedly pro-Beijing, Shirk's e-mail was an unofficial signal that could easily affect Communist Chinese calculations. One Pentagon official compared it to the remarks by April Glaspie, the former U.S. ambassador to Iraq, who told Saddam Hussein in July 1990 that the United States had "no opinion" about Baghdad's border dispute with Kuwait. A month later Iraqi forces invaded, believing they had been given a green light by the United States.

Stanley Roth, Shirk's boss, was a former Democratic congressional staffer. Roth's career until 1992 was as the staff director of the House Foreign Affairs Subcommittee on East Asian and Pacific Affairs. He summarized American policy toward China in a May 2000 speech: "Our objective is a strong, stable, prosperous, and open China, one which respects and builds upon the diverse views and strengths of its own people. Our strategy is to integrate China into regional and global institutions, helping it become a country that plays by the accepted international rules, cooperating and competing peacefully within those rules. 'Engagement' is the coherent set of tactics to accomplish this strategy, working with China at every level and at every available opportunity to manage, if not resolve, specific differences and identify and expand issues on which we take a common approach." Roth's nutshell summation was instructive for what it left out. Democracy and freedom in China are not part of the Clinton team's goals for China. In effect, the Clinton-Gore administration's policy toward China is *China's policy* toward China. Roth claims that the policy will further U.S. interests because a poor and unstable China is more dangerous than a rich dictatorship with modern nuclear and conventional forces.

The pro-China elements of the Clinton-Gore administration faced a few naysayers. One was Kurt Campbell, the deputy assistant defense secretary for East Asia within the Office of International Security Affairs. Campbell, a Soviet specialist by training, got his job through connections at Harvard's John F. Kennedy School of Government. Campbell tried to play the role of honest broker when it came to Taiwan and recognized the common sense of helping Taiwan's defenses as an easy way of preventing a war in the Taiwan Strait that could involve the United States. In 1997 Campbell launched a secret program—secret even to the pro-China acolytes at the White House and State Department—to increase defense relations with Taiwan. The activity was legal under the 1979 Taiwan Relations Act, which outlined semiofficial ties between the United States and Taiwan.

After the secret Taiwan program was revealed in an article by *Los Angeles Times* reporter Jim Mann, the Red Team singled out Campbell as an obstacle to engagement. That was enough for Lieberthal at the National Security Council to hatch a secret plan to replace Campbell in late 1999 with a protégé who had worked under him at the University of Michigan. It was David Shambaugh, a political science professor at Michigan who is now a professor at George Washington University in Washington, D.C. Shambaugh was a graduate student under Lieberthal, and his main credential was his work as editor of the *China Quarterly* from 1991 to 1996. He was to be quietly moved in as a "consultant" to the Pentagon's China shop. Political pressure would then be placed on Campbell to step aside. "The idea is for the NSC and State to plant their guy in the Pentagon and reverse the policies and choke off Campbell initiatives," said one Pentagon official.

After this author's story about the plot appeared in the *Washington Times*, Defense Secretary William Cohen stepped in and downgraded Shambaugh's consultancy. But the damage was done. Though Campbell was coaxed by Cohen into staying on until May 2000, he had already announced that he would leave government service in late 1999, having done his time as point man for the Pentagon on China affairs. After Campbell left the Pentagon to become vice president at the Center for Strategic and International Studies, a Pentagon Near East specialist—not Shambaugh—took the China post. Shambaugh, who was left mostly writing opinion articles for newspapers, also took part in a program to bring visiting Chinese military officers to the United States.

The Chinese thanked Shambaugh for his activities with an article in the official newspaper of the People's Liberation Army. The *Liberation Army Daily* reported on November 11, 1999, that Shambaugh had been a great help for a visiting Chinese colonel who spent several months in Washington. The PLA colonel, Chen Bojiang, praised Shambaugh for providing him with background information on U.S. specialists on China's military. "Professor David Shambaugh not only gave me a detailed briefing on the backgrounds and fields of study of each of the experts, but also strongly recommended that I interview each one," Chen said. "He finally told me that he was very familiar with them all, and that he would write to each of them introducing me, asking them to let me interview them." The Chinese article outraged several Pentagon officials, including one who said such actions came close to assisting Chinese intelligence gathering, since that is exactly how Chinese spies gain access to American officials and "vacuum clean" them for valuable intelligence and information. Shambaugh denied that he had assisted Chinese intelligence in any way.

Another major promoter of the China-is-not-a-threat theory is retired Rear Admiral Eric A. McVadon, who was a naval attaché at the U.S. embassy in Beijing from 1990 to 1992. McVadon, like Montaperto, is a major spokesman for U.S. policy toward China abroad and travels frequently under the sponsorship of the U.S. Information Service, which has a program to promote the benign view of China. McVadon has written that China is not strong enough militarily to invade Taiwan because it lacks the ships for amphibious assault and in general lacks the naval forces for the action. He ridiculed the idea that China would use commercial fishing boats to move troops to Taiwan. Moreover, an operation to seize a port and use it as a staging area for military operations against Taiwan is not within China's power, according to McVadon.

McVadon also consults for the CIA, where his dovish views have influenced that agency's assessments of the Chinese military. In addition, he takes part in the U.S. Navy's annual war games known as Global 2000. Based on his view that China's military is so weak, he has been able to ensure that U.S. forces always win the exercises. His role in the games has caused critics in the Pentagon to charge that he is undermining efforts to deal realistically with the China threat. McVadon declined to be interviewed.

In short, McVadon is one of the most influential voices in U.S. academic and government circles and has one of the most benign views of China. His book, *Crisis in the Taiwan Strait*, contains twelve major points about the situation—all of which were contradicted by the Pentagon's official report to Congress on the cross-Strait confrontation.

McVadon's twelve points include:

- "The PRC has not built an amphibious and logistic force to carry out an invasion of Taiwan."
- "It simply cannot be factually asserted that the PLA Navy has undertaken a major building program to provide the capability to invade a well-defended Taiwan."
- Regarding an assault by commercial boats: "Someone recently suggested that this operation would enter the history books as 'the Million Man Swim.'"
- On taking a port as a base of attack: "An operation of this sort, even if carried out in conjunction with other military operations, would have unacceptably low odds for success."
- On the PLA navy's assurance of controlling the seas in the Strait in a conflict with Taiwan's navy: "The consequence of this situation for PLA Navy leaders is that their doctrine for dealing with Taiwan cannot include assurance of sea control of the Taiwan Strait and adjacent Chinese and Taiwan coastal waters."
- Adding China's large submarine force into the equation: "The five Han class nuclear attack submarines are noisy and unreliable, easily detected and tracked—conceivably even by Taiwan's limited antisubmarine forces."

- On China's ability to attack: "The PLA Navy contends with unacceptable shortcomings in both amphibious assault and sea control capabilities."
- "Put succinctly Beijing does not wish to use its air and navy forces in combat against Taiwan because it is not ready to do so and is profoundly concerned about the outcome if compelled to do so."
- After Defense Secretary William Perry called China's firing of short-range missiles at Taiwan in 1996 reckless: "What it does suggest is that the tactics employed in this tiff with Taiwan, and tangentially with the United States, illustrate that Beijing acted with calculated rationality, recognizing and taking into full account its military capabilities and intentions."
- "For many reasons, including profound uncertainty, it does not wish to use military force against Taiwan."
- "Beijing can be counted on to be obnoxious, but it is far less likely to be stupid."
- "These exercises have not convinced experienced observers that the PRC can mount a major successful operation against Taiwan...."

McVadon's twelve passages are at the heart of the pro-China academics' argument that Communist China is not a threat. Because of this argument, McVaden and the others maintain that the United States should not sell Taiwan the weapons it needs to defend itself, including advanced Aegis battle-management-equipped warships, P-3 surveillance aircraft, diesel submarines, advanced air-to-air missiles, Maverick missiles, and other weapons needed to maintain a balance of force and, thus, stability.

Coincidentally, blocking U.S. weapons sales to Taiwan is one of Beijing's highest foreign policy priorities and is a topic hammered home at every meeting between American and Chinese national security officials.

CHINA BETS ON RED

Communist China has set as one of its supreme national goals the monitoring around the world of what it calls the China Threat Theory.

The goal is not just to monitor anti-China forces but to neutralize them. Since the 1970s, Beijing has sought to develop worldwide networks of pro-Beijing experts and turn them against the "bad" experts, those who in Beijing's eyes are behind promotion of the China Threat Theory. Yu Qiangsheng, the Ministry of State Security intelligence officer who defected in 1985, revealed that much of the information Larry Chin, the most senior Chinese spy ever caught in the United States, had provided his masters in Beijing was intelligence on American China analysts. The information was used to mold a more favorable view of the Chinese Communist government. Beijing's main objective is to push China critics to the fringe of establishment opinion. According to Chinese intelligence defectors, a key issue for the Chinese is manipulating views about China's strength and threat potential around the world.

Defectors from China have revealed that the Chinese government uses access to top Beijing officials as a key lure for American academics and business people in order to get them to promote China's foreign policies. When China experts brag of their meetings with Chinese leaders, it is safe to assume they are being treated to such access for calculated political purposes.

In early 2000 the House of Representatives passed, with wide Republican and Democratic backing, the Taiwan Security Enhancement Act, which was a major setback for Clinton and the pro-China lobby.

Another setback for the Red Team was the disclosure in 1999 that the U.S. Strategic Command—in charge of fighting a nuclear war and maintaining the U.S. nuclear arsenal—is working on a plan to retarget strategic nuclear weapons on China. The strategic war plan dropped China as a target during the 1970s as part of the Nixon administration's China policy. But the targeting plan is currently being worked on in secret at the Strategic Command's military headquarters at Offutt Air Force Base, Nebraska. The effort is controversial because it contradicts the public position announced by President Clinton during a 1998 visit to Beijing that both China and the United States had agreed to "detarget" their nuclear weapons from each other's cities (though missiles can be retargeted in a matter of minutes).

The Chinese and the China lobby express their frustration by finding ways to punish Beijing's critics and Taiwan supporters. "They deny
access to critics as a way to minimize their stature," said one Pentagon
official. Such was the case of Michael Ledeen, a former National Security Council consultant during the Reagan administration, now with
the American Enterprise Institute. In 1999 Ledeen's daughter planned
to travel to China with a friend. But when embassy officials in Washington discovered her father was Michael Ledeen, who had written critical articles about Communist China's arms transfers, the visa was
denied. The not-so-blunt message: If you want to travel to China, say or
write nothing critical about China.

James Lilley, who was born in China and has held numerous U.S.
defense and intelligence posts, has for the same reason been singled out
for criticism by the Chinese government. The communists quietly put
out the false word that this distinguished expert on China, who speaks
Mandarin, does not understand China. By contrast, Charles "Chas"
Freeman, a former Pentagon assistant secretary in the Clinton-Gore
administration, is given easy access to China and is afforded high-level
treatment normally reserved for sitting high government officials.
Freeman's stature was enhanced in a 1995 exchange with the Chinese
military, when PLA Lieutenant General Xiong Guangkai used him as
an unofficial conduit for Beijing's thinly veiled threat to the United
States. Freeman duly reported this message to White House National
Security Adviser Anthony Lake: The Americans risk a Chinese nuclear
strike if they intervene in a conflict between China and Taiwan—and,
as the PLA general put it, Washington cares more about Los Angeles
than about Taipei.

Outside of government, an unofficial sponsor for pro-Beijing policies
and views is the National Committee on U.S.-China Relations, based in
New York City. It is the funnel for all private U.S.-China high-level
exchanges. The committee receives funds from the U.S. government in
addition to private contributions. As a sign of its stature in China, Chinese Premier Zhu Rongji spoke to the committee during a 1999 visit.
During the speech, Zhu said he had met with Vice President Al Gore as
part of a U.S.-China environmental forum. For Gore, there is no other

issue in U.S.-China relations. According to an aide to the vice president, Gore stated during a policy meeting in his office that he would give China "whatever it wanted" if only Beijing would agree to reduce its emissions of carbon dioxide. Zhu, in turn, called China's 1998 investment in environmental improvement "unprecedented."

For China to sign on to Gore's environmental programs, Zhu said, "the prerequisite to all this is that the United States government must adopt an enlightened and progressive attitude and policy and allow American businessmen to go to China to invest in China's environmental sector." He added with a laugh uncharacteristic of Chinese Communists, "I said to Vice President Gore that surely there can be no problem with doing this—after all, there could be nothing of military significance in this area, nor should there be any cases of alleged espionage coming out of this area."

Another key private-sector Red Team member is Michael Swaine, a China analyst at the Rand Corporation in Santa Monica, California. Swaine, under a contract from the air force worth about $2 million, wrote a report on China's grand strategy that one air force general criticized as echoing the Beijing line. "We're paying a million bucks for Chinese propaganda," the general said. The brass were particularly upset with the Swaine report for playing down the threat from China. The air force wants to present realistic assessments in order to boost its new concept of using Air Expeditionary Forces, rapid-response teams of warplanes and support aircraft that could respond quickly to a missile attack on Taiwan or a war on the Korean peninsula. The report will, of course, make it harder to garner support for the new force.

Yet another important Red Team player is Michel Oksenberg, who worked on President Jimmy Carter's National Security Council staff and was a key official in establishing diplomatic relations with Beijing in 1979. He is currently a member of the board of governors of the Smith Richardson Foundation, which once gave Shambaugh a $100,000 grant to promote his views of China. Oksenberg's pro-China leanings were captured in a 1990 book by Stephen W. Mosher, *China Misperceived: American Illusions and Chinese Reality*. Mosher quotes an Oksenberg essay titled "On Learning from China," in which he describes the United States as having a "dreary list of domestic problems: racism, bureaucratism, urban decay, pollution of the environment, depletion of natural resources, inflation and unemployment, inadequate medical care for the poor, the increasing use of narcotics and the accompanying rise in crime." Oksenberg goes on to ask whether "America is doomed to decay until radical, even revolutionary change fundamentally alters the institutions and values."

Oksenberg then offers up a curious model for reform: Communist China. "Of all the nations from which we might borrow, one is particularly intriguing—China.... [T]he Chinese Revolution is an optimistic statement about the capacity of man to solve his problems.... The Chinese dedication to building a more decent just society might also spur us."

As we will see, for the Clinton-Gore administration, part of building "a more decent just society" came to mean helping Communist China make its strategic nuclear missiles more reliable.

CHAPTER FOUR

From Satellites to Missiles

"In 10 years, it will be an era in which strategic nuclear weapons and strategic non-nuclear weapons both exist. Due to rising technology levels, non-nuclear weapons will become conventional strategic weapons... so that certain strategic targets can be reached."

—Huan Xiang, Deng Xiaoping's national security adviser,
Liberation Army Daily, 1985

China's government in 1997 established a large-scale program to steal U.S. technology. It was revealed by a congressional investigation headed by California Representative Christopher Cox. The policy typified the Chinese penchant for quantification. "The Sixteen-Character Policy," as the Chinese call it, is China's blueprint for covert and overt efforts to steal, buy, or otherwise acquire sensitive military technology. As the Cox Committee's report documented, the sixteen characters—which are shown on the following page—mean: "Combine the military and the civil; combine peace and war; give priority to military products; let the civil support the military." The acquisition effort, which has been very effective, is large-scale and centrally directed. China, with the help of the Clinton-Gore administration, acquired from American businesses and defense contractors what previous administrations fought hard to protect from export. Today, China's nuclear missiles, most of whose warheads are targeted on American cities, are more lethal in terms of their warhead-killing power, more accurate in terms of the missile guidance systems, and better designed and crafted than just a few years ago.

The sixteen characters

"In combination, these pose a significant threat to the United States military," Cox said in an interview.

Contributing to the threat, President Clinton removed export controls on high-speed computers, which are now being used to develop China's growing arsenal of advanced nuclear weapons, weapons the Chinese have threatened to use against the United States on several occasions. As Cox says, "Whereas we used to deny the sale of high-performance computers to the PRC, now, increasingly, that is permitted. As a result, high-performance computers from the United States have been obtained by PRC organizations involved in the research and development of missiles, satellites, submarines, military systems components, military aircraft, command-and-control, military communications, microwave and laser sensors."

Bill Clinton's destruction of export controls is one of the most serious national security betrayals committed during the eight years of his administration. Its effects are palpable. The United States government did more than turn a blind eye to China's military development. Its policies actually boosted that effort, all with the misguided aim of promoting U.S. business interests and helping international markets.

OPENING THE FLOODGATES

The disaster began with the dismantling of the Coordinating Committee for Multilateral Export Controls, the Paris-based organization known as COCOM. COCOM was a product of the Cold War and gained strength during the administration of President Ronald Reagan. The Defense Department had a major role, and American businesses objected to the sometimes lengthy reviews imposed on deals involving potentially dangerous military technology. But the controls were needed. A Russian agent code-named "Farewell" exposed how the Soviet Union had successfully obtained vast amounts of its weapons technology from U.S. companies. The danger was not theoretical; the U.S. intelligence community highlighted the acquisition in several reports, both classified and unclassified.

Yet Bill Clinton made removing these controls one of his first actions as president. Along with White House National Security Adviser Sandy Berger, the Clinton-Gore administration stripped away national security export controls with a vengeance. The president revealed his intentions in a 1993 letter to Edward McCracken, chief executive officer for Silicon Graphics, the Mountain View, California, computer maker. Clinton blamed the national security export controls for costing U.S. businesses some $9 billion annually in lost sales. "One reason I ran for president was to tailor export controls to the realities of a post–Cold War world," Clinton stated. He went on to say that "strong controls" were still needed to combat "proliferation" and terrorism. But the words, like so many of the president's, were hollow. In the president's liberal worldview, major world powers like China and Russia should no longer be treated as enemies but as "strategic partners," partners to be "helped" and not "contained." In his letter, the president promised McCracken that he would soon undertake a major liberalization of export controls on goods sent to "free world" destinations. But the main beneficiary was China. "I am also currently engaged in seeking

major reforms to COCOM, which should lead to significant liberalization of controls on computers, telecommunications and machine tools,
while establishing a more effective structure for addressing the changing national security threats we face in the years ahead," the president
stated, calling his plan a "more intelligent" export control policy. "It is
important. It is the right thing to do. And many of these changes are
long overdue," he said.

In reality, it was the wrong thing to do. After dismantling COCOM,
the Clinton-Gore administration never fulfilled its promise to replace
it with a new international export control regime. A structure known
as the "Wassenaar agreement" was supposed to replace COCOM, but
its key feature is that it allows each country to decide whether to permit an export on national security grounds. When the administration
tried to get the Wassenaar members to agree to notify the United States
in advance of its military-related sales, they refused to cooperate. Peter
Leitner, a national trade control specialist with the Pentagon, put it
bluntly: Wassenaar controls are "a handful of weak, ineffectual regimes
which are little more than cardboard cutouts designed to maintain the
facade of an international technology security system." After the election of Clinton and Gore and the demise of COCOM, "the floodgates
opened," said Representative Curt Weldon, Pennsylvania Republican
and member of the House Select Committee on U.S. National Security
and Military/Commercial Concerns with the People's Republic of
China. "Everything and anything was for sale. Our companies got their
way; they got to sell whatever they wanted; foreign countries and companies, the same thing; and China took advantage of it."

Communist China's Commission of Science, Technology, and Industry for National Defense, or COSTIND, is responsible for getting foreign
military technology for the People's Liberation Army. The Clinton-Gore
administration took the extraordinary step of actually seeking to work
with COSTIND to help it acquire high technology. The Pentagon, under
Defense Secretary William Perry, established a joint Pentagon-COSTIND
enterprise to help China "convert" defense industries to commercial
use. The Pentagon defended the program, as one defense official put it,
to get "a better understanding of defense decision making." The official

also said the program is aimed at creating better business opportunities for American companies in China. The official statement of principles for the commission says a key goal of the group is to promote "industrial partnerships, technological relationships and investment by American firms in China, and by Chinese firms in the U.S." The Pentagon claimed the program is an effort to work with the Chinese defense industry and not the People's Liberation Army, but China's defense industry is controlled completely by the People's Liberation Army and the Communist Party.

COSTIND is a tool of Chinese military strategists who believe high-technology weaponry is the key to China's future role as a global power. COSTIND controls a vast conglomerate of research institutes, factories, and government organizations with up to three million people. Its published writings discuss the concept of "three moves on the chess board"—a metaphor for developing advanced weapons in anticipation of how enemies will react to the arms. The COSTIND journal, *Contemporary Military Affairs*, published an article by Chen Huan calling for the rapid development of technology for information warfare, stealth weapons, and long-range precision attack capabilities. According to Chen, "There will be three main forms of long-range strikes in the future: the first is the one in which the air arm independently carries out long-range strikes; the second form is one in which the long-range strike combines with the long-range rapid movement of troops transported by land and sea with the vertical airdrops of airborne forces; and the third form is five-dimensional—air, land, sea, space, and electromagnetic—long-range combat."

COSTIND's goal for cooperating with the United States will be to help develop exotic weapons, including laser weapons, ultrahigh frequency weapons, ultrasonic wave weapons, stealth weapons, and electromagnetic guns. China's new warfare will be "paralysis combat"—attacking the vital point of information and support systems to paralyze the opposing force and collapse its morale with one blow. "In the wars of the past," Chen writes, "the power to inflict casualties mainly depended on the effects of kinetic energy and thermal energy, but the weapon systems produced by the third military revolution mainly use sound, electromagnetism, radiation, and other destructive mechanisms. The main radiation weapons are laser weapons, microwave weapons, particle beam weapons, and subsonic wave weapons; they possess enormous military potential."

Why the Pentagon should be involved in trading with a self-professed enemy of the American "hegemon" was not explained by Defense Department officials, who insisted China would not gain military technology from the exchanges. But the leader of the Chinese joint commission with the Pentagon was Ding Henggao, then-chairman of COSTIND, and Defense Secretary William Perry had known the PLA general. On October 17, 1994, when Perry was asked by the *Los Angeles Times* whether the Pentagon would sell weapons to China, Perry replied negatively but then added, "I never say never."

Officials at the Pentagon in charge of protecting defense technology were astonished. "In China, 'defense conversion' is a subterfuge for defense production," said one official opposed to the program. Nicholas Eftimiades, Defense Intelligence Agency (DIA) analyst and author of a book on China's intelligence services, says, "COSTIND personnel engage in espionage by attempting to steal foreign technology with military applications, primarily from the United States." The joint U.S.-Chinese commission was killed by legislation introduced by Republicans in Congress who feared, justifiably, that the Chinese were not the least bit interested in converting their defense industry and wanted the exchanges with the Pentagon only to gain technology for their military buildup.

In June 1999 China showed it was serious about developing high-tech weapons by creating a task force of weapons scientists and engineers. The force was modeled on China's crash effort in the 1950s to develop its first nuclear weapons. This panel was headed by PLA General Xiong Guangkai, deputy chief of staff for intelligence—the same man who let the United States know it could face a strategic nuclear attack if it tried to defend Taiwan.

The task force also included representatives of COSTIND, the Ministry of Science and Technology, the Ministry of Information Industry, the Ministry of Education, the Chinese Academy of Sciences, and the Chinese Academy of Engineering. In 1996, while Perry was encouraging "engagement" with China, he was investigated by the General Accounting Office for his role in winning Pentagon permission to export advanced fiber optics telecommunications technology as part of a joint venture known as Hua-Mei Telecommunications. The system, according to defense officials, should have been blocked because it was a dual-use technology that would be used vastly to improve not only civilian telecommunications but also the Chinese People's Liberation Army's command, control, communications, and intelligence functions—the "software" of war fighting. All high technology sold to China goes to its military as a matter of course. Not surprisingly, the Cox Committee discovered that China is diverting its U.S. supercomputers for weapons purposes.

CHINESE TRADE FOR CORPORATE CASH

Despite such discoveries—that China was threatening our national security—the Clinton-Gore administration's business-as-usual approach never abated. On March 16, 2000, the U.S. ambassador to China, Joseph Prueher, held a dinner meeting at his official residence in Beijing. Seated with Prueher were seventeen American and Chinese officials and representatives of three U.S. satellite makers, including William Wright, a former Pentagon official who now works for Space Systems/Loral, a company whose chairman was the largest contributor to Bill Clinton's 1996 reelection campaign. At the time of the meeting, Loral and a second company, Hughes Electronics, were under federal investigation on charges of illegally passing technology to China that increased the reliability of China's strategic nuclear missiles.

In 1997 the Justice Department launched an investigation into how Loral and Hughes Electronics provided China with extremely valuable technology to keep China's Long March rocket boosters from blowing up. More reliable boosters meant fewer launch failures and lower insurance rates for Loral and Hughes satellites.

But the improvement did not help U.S. national security. In fact, by speeding up the modernization of China's strategic nuclear forces, it severely threatened the United States. For the Clinton-Gore administration, the fact that American cities had become easier targets for Chinese nuclear strikes was secondary to helping American corporations do business. The Loral/Hughes technology transfer violated U.S. export laws because it was sensitive "dual-use" technology.

But the Chinese were getting used to having American officials bend the rules on their behalf. In a tough Senate battle over his nomination as ambassador to China, Prueher, a retired four-star admiral and former commander in chief of the U.S. Pacific Command, was accused of violating U.S. policy by pressuring Taiwan's defense minister, Tang Fei, into negotiating with China. Prueher was also accused of altering U.S. defense planning in ways that would make it more difficult to defend Taiwan in the event of a mainland attack. Other documents sought by the senators purported to show that Prueher had allowed Chinese military officials to gain access to tour a U.S. nuclear attack submarine and to visit a sensitive U.S. Navy training facility. The Pentagon and the U.S. Pacific Command never produced the documents and claimed they were unable to find them during a search.

And now Prueher was hosting a dinner with American satellite makers that were accused of providing China with the technology to boost the reliability of its strategic missiles.

On the other side of the banquet table sat the heads of China Aerospace Science and Technology Corporation (CASC) and China Telecommunications Broadcast Satellite Corporation, known as ChinaSat. According to Loral spokesman Tom Ross, the company wanted the meeting specifically to discuss the U.S. government's refusal to allow the transfer, though it had initially been approved, of Loral's ChinaSat 8 communications satellite. The satellite deal was worth $124 million, and the company wanted to collect the money. At first the embassy denied that ChinaSat 8 had been discussed. "The ambassador agreed to host the dinner at Loral's request to demonstrate the embassy's support for these three major exporters as well as the U.S. industry and its workers, and to learn more about the business plans of these Chinese companies," embassy spokesman Bill Palmer said. "U.S. satellite exports to China produce millions of dollars in earnings and provide jobs for thousands of U.S. workers." According to Palmer, "The Chinese were contemplating taking their business to a non-U.S. competitor firm." As a result, the embassy—"sensitive to the potential damage to U.S. commercial interests of losing satellite business to competitors"—held the dinner. As for the criminal investigation of the two companies, "the ambassador is well aware of the federal investigations of Hughes and Loral. As a result, there was no discussion of ChinaSat 8." Later, the spokesman said that "when one Chinese guest raised ChinaSat 8 with an embassy officer, that officer did not respond."

Just two months before this dinner, ChinaSat, the state-run satellite maker, had secretly launched the first of a series of military communications satellites called Feng Huo-1. The satellite was never announced in the official Chinese press as a military system. But a secret DIA report noted that Feng Huo-1 is the key component of the Chinese military's first integrated system for combining army, navy, and air forces into a single fighting force.

As one intelligence official put it, "This is a major force multiplier." The satellite was launched atop a Long March rocket—precisely the dual booster and missile launcher that was the beneficiary of improper technology transfers from Loral and Hughes in 1996.

According to the DIA report, the new system, known as Qu Dian (pronounced "choo dee-en"), "will yield an integrated battlefield picture, centralizing data from ground, air and naval platforms for wide dissemination to subordinate units." The intelligence report concluded that, when fully deployed in the next several years, the Qu Dian system "will allow theater commanders to communicate with and share data with all forces under joint command." The system will provide Chinese military leaders with "a high-speed and real-time view of the battlefield which would allow them to direct units under joint command more effectively."

The CIA, however, sought to minimize the importance of the development of the Qu Dian system by claiming, in a "dissent" to the DIA conclusion, that the "rigidity" of the Chinese military command structures will limit the effectiveness of the new Qu Dian system. But the CIA has its own critics. Larry Wortzel, a retired army colonel who spent four and a half years as a military attaché in China, told me he believes it is dangerous for U.S. analysts to play down China's growing military capabilities. The Qu Dian system "improves command and control and when the system is in use and used in exercises, it will help to improve decision making. It took the PLA about four years to learn to use the computer-based war-fighting simulation system it was given by the U.S. Army in 1988, and they'll learn to use this system, too."

A U.S. Army general, Wortzel said, had foolishly decided to help the Chinese military to learn to fight combined arms warfare, utilizing the unique strengths of the various services in unison. To this end, the American general gave a PLA general a series of computer simulations. "After a period of about six to eight years of studying American ways of war, he turned a unidimensional... service, infantry-oriented corps into what we would call a pretty good combined-arms army, with integrated artillery, with integrated missiles, with integrated armor, and with helicopters," Wortzel said.

The satellite meeting at the American embassy in China was remarkable because of its context. Less than a year earlier, Congress had released portions of a classified report from the Pentagon outlining the severe national security damage caused by Loral and Hughes with their "serious export control violation."

The satellite makers must have known the Clinton-Gore administration cared little about U.S. national security. And they were right. Even though Loral and Hughes were facing criminal prosecution for illegal satellite technology transfers, President Clinton signed off on a license for Loral's ChinaSat 8 communications satellite to be launched in China in February 1998. The export required a waiver that determined the satellite sale was in the national security interest. White House National Security Adviser Sandy Berger urged the president to approve the waiver even though he stated in a memorandum that the Justice Department's Criminal Division had concerns. "In any case, we believe that the advantages of this project outweigh this risk, and that we can effectively rebut criticism of the waiver," Berger stated in a

February 12, 1998, memorandum to the president. By allowing Loral to sell yet another satellite to China, while in the middle of a criminal investigation, the Clinton-Gore administration set up Loral's lawyers to ask in court, "If what we did was wrong, why did the president of the United States allow us to sell another satellite?"

In an astonishing miscue, the Pentagon's Defense Security Service, the agency responsible for industrial security, gave Loral an award for its "outstanding" security practices in July 2000. The award was given even though Loral had been under federal indictment over its sensitive rocket technology transfers to China for three years. The Pentagon quickly withdrew the award and called the incident an embarrassment.

Charles LaBella, the Justice Department's top lawyer in charge of the Campaign Financing Task Force, stated in a memorandum released in June 2000 that the president's decision to issue the Loral waiver perhaps betrayed a conflict of interest and that the matter required investigation by a special prosecutor. "One of the areas to be reviewed is whether the contributions of Bernard Schwartz [Loral's chairman] somehow corruptly influenced the president's decision to issue the 1998 waiver to Loral over Justice Department 'concerns' that the waiver may adversely impact the ongoing criminal investigation," he stated. "That is, was the waiver corruptly influenced by the president's desire to help his friend and generous DNC [Democratic National Committee] contributor Schwartz and to impede the ongoing investigation?" LaBella didn't answer. But the answer is clearly yes. Two high-level Justice Department officials are prepared to testify that "the president's decision—*even now*—continues to have the potential to adversely affect an ongoing criminal investigation being conducted by the department." LaBella pointed out that White House counsel Charles Ruff was claiming that department lawyers did not object strongly enough to the waiver in conversations. "At a minimum," LaBella said, "the conversation will likely be spun by the White House."

The sequence appears to show a quid pro quo. Schwartz donated $30,000 to the Democratic National Committee on January 21, 1998. Clinton signed the presidential waiver on February 18, 1998. Schwartz gave another $25,000 to the DNC on March 2, 1998.

"If in fact there is anything to investigate involving the Loral 'allegations,' it is... an investigation of the president," LaBella said. "The president is the one who signed the waiver; the president is the one who has the relationship with Schwartz; and it was the president's media campaign that was the beneficiary of Schwartz' largess by virtue of his own substantial contributions and those which he was able to solicit."

Loral and Hughes weren't the only corporations under suspicion. In early 2000, Lockheed Martin, the nation's largest defense contractor, with annual revenues of more than $25 billion, was charged with thirty violations of U.S. export and munitions control regulations that included illegally supplying China with satellite technology that had direct application for China's strategic nuclear missiles.

China's acquisition of satellite rocket technology from Lockheed began in 1994 when Martin Marietta Astro Space was working for the Hong Kong–based satellite company known as AsiaSat. The company is closely linked to China. The State Department charged in an eleven-page letter to Lockheed Martin Corporation that the company illegally helped develop satellite rockets that can be used for multiple nuclear warheads. Of the 1994 technology transfers, State Department spokesman James Rubin said, "The company made no effort to retrieve the exported information, nor did it inform the U.S. government of the export prior to the disclosure of the facts through a Customs Service investigation." Civil action, he said, not criminal prosecution, was being sought "based on the facts of the case and the gravity of the charges."

"In our view any assistance to Chinese technical capabilities in space launch has the potential to be applied to missile development," Rubin said. Nevertheless, the Clinton-Gore Justice Department decided not to prosecute the company, and Lockheed insisted it had done nothing wrong. The company blamed the Clinton-Gore administration for its confusing export licensing requirements. But by any standard, Lockheed's work with China was a threat to national security.

In September 1994 Lockheed specialists traveled to China and analyzed Chinese test data on solid rocket motor failures. They then put together a detailed assessment of the problems.

Solid rocket technology—like other technical assistance Lockheed supplied the Chinese—is critical in helping the Chinese develop multiple independently-targetable reentry vehicles, or MIRVs. The rockets can be adapted to guide clusters of nuclear warheads launched on a single missile. As the Cox Committee stated, China has threatened to "MIRV" its warheads in response to deployment of U.S. national missile defenses. So far, China has not deployed MIRVs on its current nuclear arsenal but has shown the capability of adding up to three warheads on its new DF-31 truck mobile intercontinental ballistic missile. The DF-31 was flight tested for the first time in 1999 with "penetration aids"—dummy warheads designed to fool missile defenses. These used "kick motors," another technology on which Lockheed provided assistance to the Chinese, which "are terribly important in positioning a bus [satellite carrier] to its final position and are interchangeable with the technology used for pointing warheads to precise points on the ground," said Henry Sokolski, a former Pentagon weapons proliferation specialist, now the executive director of the Non-proliferation Policy Education Center. "That's the reason the technology is controlled. If this stuff didn't have any military value, it wouldn't be licensed."

The State Department said Lockheed failed to notify the government of its meetings in China on the test-firings and violated its munitions license by providing assistance to China Great Wall Industries and by sending copies of the solid rocket motor assessment to another Chinese company, AsiaSat. Lockheed was also charged with unlawfully exporting five documents containing technical data that required a license and improperly providing defense services related to testing and evaluation, hardware design and manufacturing, and "anomaly analysis"—help in fixing problems. In addition, the company failed to reveal the unauthorized exports in license applications to the State Department.

In June 2000 Lockheed Martin agreed to pay a fine of $13 million for violating the rules regarding the sharing of rocket technology with the Chinese.

SELLOUT

The Clinton-Gore administration began its technology giveaway to China at a luncheon meeting in September 1993 between Bill Clinton and Ed McCracken, the head of Silicon Graphics, a huge high-technology firm that was one of the new president's most ardent supporters. The two men discussed how the president planned to approach the issue of America's strongest economic advantage: its unrivaled leadership in the field of high technology. Computers were reshaping the way the United States did business. McCracken was one of many American business leaders who believed that national security expert controls were no longer needed.

McCracken and the other businessmen were wrong, but their cash spoke in the Clinton-Gore White House.

Representative Curt Weldon, a member of the special congressional committee that investigated Chinese weapons technology efforts, put the blame squarely on the Clinton-Gore administration. "The influence that was peddled by these financial people ended up lowering the controls over our regulation of technology being sold abroad," Weldon said. "These people and their money influenced key decision makers in this administration. In my opinion, that lies in terms of fault at the feet of this administration itself. And as much as we would like to totally blame China, I blame our own government.... What occurred here was the elimination in a wholesale way of a legitimate process that was in place under previous administrations to monitor technology and to do it with our allies."

The Cox Committee found that China had acquired through both illegal and legal means military technology that was a danger to U.S. national security. "The Select Committee has discovered evidence of a number of their successes," the report stated. "Given the size and variety of the PRC's overall effort, and the limited U.S. resources and attention devoted to understanding and countering its unlawful and threatening elements, there is clear cause for concern that other serious losses have occurred or could occur in the future."

Weldon noted that the Cox Committee's revelation about spying at U.S. nuclear weapons laboratories tended to distract attention from the exports of U.S. missile technology—the key reason the panel was formed. "While it is true," Weldon said, "the laboratory security was one part of what we looked at, it is only one small part of the bigger picture of the way that we loosened the controls over our technology for the past seven years."

China is to blame for its theft of technology and secrets. But Weldon also noted that "the bulk of the responsibility lies with our own government. It was our government that failed the American people." Weldon produced an elaborate diagram showing the complex network of Chinese government agencies, companies, and front organizations used in the worldwide technology-gathering effort. "We estimate there were hundreds and hundreds of front companies established by the Chinese to acquire technologies, paid for by these entities, to go to the arms of the People's Liberation Army, because that is a desire they had for these specific technologies. A very elaborate scheme, but very simple. The financing through the entities to buy it go back to those entities that wanted to improve their missile systems, their nuclear programs, their computing capabilities, the design of their fighter aircraft, whatever the need might be.... If we are stupid enough to sell sensitive technology, how can we just blame China for buying it in the open market? This was the network."

For Weldon, this is the biggest and most damaging scandal of the Clinton-Gore administration. "This is about the very core of what our country is about. No one, no party official in either party, no elected leader, has the right to allow a wholesale technology faucet to open that we are going to have to pay the price for."

The Senate Intelligence Committee, which oversees U.S. spy agencies, issued another report that received less attention than the Cox panel's report. Based on a review of the most sensitive U.S. intelligence information, the Intelligence Committee concluded that technology supplied by U.S. satellite companies enabled China "to improve its present and future space launch vehicles and intercontinental ballistic missiles." A senior Republican aide who took part in producing the report said it "confirms our worst fears about the Clinton administration policy of loosening satellite export controls and trying to deal with aggressive Chinese spying on high technology."

"China developed and implemented a covert action plan to influence policy and through illegal campaign contributions sought to loosen controls on critical technologies, and it worked," the aide said. The damage is substantial because "Chinese rockets are now or will become more reliable, more deadly, and more potent and could be used against the United States," he added.

The report reached the sensible conclusion that "any improvements in the PRC's space launch vehicles would be incorporated wherever practicable in the PRC's military ballistic missile program."

"The committee believes... the PRC will use the transferred information to improve its short-range ballistic missiles, intermediate-range ballistic missiles, and related technology. These missiles could threaten U.S. forces stationed in Japan and Korea, as well as allies in the region."

The satellite-missile connection is only one of the many dangers to America's national security caused by the Clinton-Gore administration. Another is China's entry into the Panama Canal.

CHAPTER FIVE
Panama Red

"I took the isthmus!"

—President Theodore Roosevelt

"I think the Chinese will, in fact, be bending over backwards to make sure that they run [the Panama Canal] in a competent and able and fair manner.... I would be very surprised if any adverse consequences flowed from the Chinese running the canal."

—President Bill Clinton, who later said he had misspoken

The date is July 2004. Chinese military forces based in southeastern China have spent the past two weeks firing short-range M-11 and M-9 missiles against military bases in Taiwan, devastating the island's military facilities and civilian infrastructure. The attacks were prompted by a statement from President Chen Shui-bian of Taiwan that his ruling Democratic Progressive Party would hold a conference to decide whether to change the name of the country from Republic of China to Republic of Taiwan. When the missile strikes finally end, Chen declares Taiwan a free and independent nation. The conflict continues.

In the watch center at the U.S. Pacific Command's Joint Intelligence Center in Hawaii, intelligence officers have been caught by surprise. The short-range M-9s and M-11s were launched with almost no visible preparation. The U.S. Space Command's Cheyenne Mountain complex in Colorado Springs first picked up on the missile launches when Defense

Support Program satellites detected the flashes of missile firings with its infrared sensors.

China had carefully studied U.S. military operations in the Persian Gulf, where American forces had six months to build up in Saudi Arabia before attacking, and the U.S.-led NATO air raids against Yugoslavia in 1999. In April 2004, just three months before the missile strike on Taiwan, the People's Liberation Army Second Artillery Corps, the unit in charge of strategic nuclear missiles, flight-tested the new Dong Feng-41 intercontinental ballistic missile. The new missile is China's most potent strategic missile. It is mobile, mounted on a truck that can be moved anywhere under cover of darkness and hidden underneath highway overpasses. The flight test was intentional. Much like China's August 1999 flight test of a new DF-31 missile, the DF-41 flight test was an ominous sign from Beijing to the United States that any intervention in a conflict with Taiwan would lead to nuclear war.

U.S. Pacific Command chief Admiral Dennis Blair's worst nightmare has come true. Despite his frequent visits to Beijing and meetings with top Chinese military leaders, China's attack on Taiwan means the United States could be at war with China. Blair orders a mobilization for sustained military operations in anticipation of a counterattack on Chinese missile bases in southern China. A phone call from the operations officer at the U.S. Southern Command in Miami compounds his fears. The officer reports that the Panama Canal has just been blocked and is impassible to ships. It was sabotaged by a Chinese merchant ship owned by the China Ocean Shipping Company (COSCO); the ship recently left the port facility owned by a subsidiary of Hutchison Whampoa Ltd., whose chairman, billionaire Li Kashing, has close ties to the communist government in Beijing. The loss of the canal as a strategic waterway for resupplying U.S. forces in the Pacific means that Admiral Blair will have to find new ways to bolster his forces. He knows that the loss of the canal means that more American soldiers will die.

Within days of the canal's closing, Admiral Blair receives an intelligence report classified "Top Secret—Gamma"—the highest secrecy level used to protect communications intercepts. The National Security Agency (NSA) in Fort Meade, Maryland, has sent an urgent report to

Pacific Command headquarters. NSA eavesdroppers working out of a secret listening post in Japan have picked up an alarming piece of intelligence from China's Second Artillery Corps command center. The command orders a forward deployed unit in Panama to remove the battery of DF-31 mobile ICBMs from the containers in the Pacific port of Balboa. The intercepted message says that the nuclear warheads for the missiles will arrive covertly within the next seventy-two hours. Checkmate.

*   *   *   *

The above scenario has never been played out in any of the Pentagon's war games. It would violate the cardinal political principle laid down by the Clinton-Gore administration: China is not a threat. But the prospect that China will use its facilities in Panama, as well as in other parts of the Western Hemisphere, is a real and growing national security threat.

How the Chinese gained a strategic toehold in Panama and other parts of the Western Hemisphere is a story of ignorance and failure to anticipate U.S. national security interests. It is a danger that could have been avoided, had it not been for the pro-China policies of the Clinton-Gore administration.

A STRATEGIC COUP

The history of the Panama Canal dates to 1889, when Congress chartered the Maritime Canal Company to build a shipping lane through Central America to open traffic for the first time between the Atlantic and Pacific oceans. Thirteen years later the Senate narrowly approved construction of what was called "the Big Ditch" in Panama. Today, the canal is vital for the growing East-West trade. Since 1990, container ship traffic has increased 8 percent, and the jump has caused lengthy delays for ships waiting to go through the canal.

When the canal was completed in 1914, it was a symbol of America's growing power. The United States helped create the country of

Panama—which before had been part of Colombia—in order to build the canal. The canal cost $387 million at the time, a figure equal to more than a billion dollars today, and some five hundred Americans died during the construction, many from tropical diseases.

In 1977 the United States and Panama signed the Panama Canal Treaty, which ceded control over the canal to Panama on December 31, 1999. The treaty did away with three other treaties, those of 1903, 1936, and 1955, that had guaranteed American ownership. The United States is still the number one user of the canal. About 13,000 ships pass through its locks every year.

China today has a major strategic presence in Panama. A Hong Kong corporation with ties to the Communist Party of China succeeded in leasing a port on either end of one of the world's most strategic waterways, Balboa on the Pacific and Cristobal on the Atlantic.

Article V of the implementing agreement for the Panama Canal Treaty makes specific provisions for the ports at Balboa and Cristobal, revealing just how important these facilities are. It states that all property belonging to the ports is "transferred without charge" to the Panamanian government. The article also states that the Panamanian government is responsible for "all rights over vessels within the lands and waters" of the two ports and that "movement of vessels to or from the piers and docks of the Ports of Balboa and Cristobal shall be subject to appropriate approval by the port authorities of the Republic of Panama." The implementing agreement grants the United States the power to control marine traffic within the waters of the canal operating areas, as well as at defense sites and within Balboa and Cristobal.

The strategic significance of Balboa and Cristobal is outlined in an annex to the implementing agreement. The annex gives the United States the right to use, "for the management, operation, maintenance, protection and defense of the Canal," a list of port facilities that the Panamanian government must keep in good order. The list includes six docks, one pier, a drydock, and related "facilities." The provisions contradict both political and intelligence assessments made by the Clinton-Gore administration that Chinese control of the two ports poses no danger.

China's presence in Panama, even through an ostensibly nongovernment firm, is part of a bigger strategy. Backed with nearly $600 billion in trade surplus, much of it gained from trade with the United States, China's communist rulers have quietly been expanding their economic power around the world. Despite statements by current and former U.S. officials that China's presence in Panama is not a threat, the facts show otherwise. The truth that has escaped the pro-China Clinton-Gore administration is that, unlike the administration, the Communist Chinese government has interests that extend beyond business and making money. China has strategic ambitions—one of which is to prevent the United States from interfering with China's power politics in the Pacific and with its attempts to dominate the region.

Beijing, through its ties to Hutchison Whampoa Ltd., scored a strategic coup in a shadowy 1997 deal that secured twenty-five-year leases— with options to extend them another quarter century—on the two port facilities of Balboa and Cristobal. The deal could have been stopped. Early in 1997 Panamanian government officials familiar with Chinese activities in the country told U.S. intelligence agencies that the Hong Kong conglomerate was spreading large sums of cash in Panama. Hutchison Whampoa's goal was to gain the winning bid on the port facility at Balboa, which had been operated by the Panama Canal Authority and was now being privatized. But the Clinton-Gore administration did nothing, and in February 1997 Hutchison Whampoa was awarded the leases on Balboa and Cristobal. Under Hutchison's agreement with the Panamanian government, the ports were to be run by a Hutchison subsidiary known as the Panama Ports Company.

The circumstances surrounding the Hutchison role in the contract were suspicious. William J. Hughes, the U.S. ambassador to Panama, outlined complaints by U.S. businesses against the Panamanian government in a letter to Panama's minister of commerce on March 1, 1997. Hughes stated that he had serious concerns about Panama's "unorthodox" bidding procedures that led to the Hutchison leases. "Over the past few months, representatives from numerous U.S. companies have come to see me to complain that the government of Panama is impeding their ability to invest and trade," Hughes wrote.

The embassy objected to the irregularities in the bidding process. Joe Johnson, a U.S. embassy spokesman in Panama City, said Hutchison's final agreement bore no resemblance to the bid request and raised questions about covert negotiations after others had submitted bids. Two American companies had lost out in the bidding. "There were a number of additional advantages granted to Hutchison after the solicitation process last summer," Johnson said. "The government of Panama... has not solved the commercial disputes. However, we're giving them time to work through this."

An internal U.S. Customs Service report also stated that Hutchison Whampoa won the port contracts through "an unfair and corrupt contractual bidding process."

Representative Dana Rohrabacher, California Republican, told the Senate Armed Services Committee in October 1999 that in investigating the port bidding process he found "corruption and a lack of transparency" that benefited Hutchison Whampoa and its chairman, Hong Kong billionaire Li Kashing, one of the wealthiest men in the world.

"Li Kashing and his Hong Kong–based company and subsidiaries are closely associated with the Beijing regime and have a history of acting as sources of funding or acting as intermediaries in deals for the People's Liberation Army," Rohrabacher said. "I learned from a number of sources in Panama that although Bechtel corporation was outbid, at least two other consortia involving American companies—such as Manzanillo Ports and Stevedoring Services of America—likely offered better bids for the ports but were outmaneuvered at the last minute by under-the-table payoffs. Hutchison also had the advantage in knowing that other facilities such as Albrook Air Field and the ports at the strategic Rodman Naval Station were included in the deal, while other companies reportedly did not have that information." Hutchison, in fact, had an option to lease the Rodman Naval Station but did not exercise it.

The 1977 Panama Canal Treaty was a culmination of liberal foreign policies that had a simple underlying theme: The United States is the primary cause of world problems. Diminish American power and you make the world safer, the argument went. But many conservative Americans decried President Jimmy Carter's "giveaway" of the Panama Canal. The canal treaty and the hollowing out of America's military forces helped elect President Ronald Reagan in 1980. Nevertheless, the Reagan administration never pressed its opposition to the treaty, and the protests against it eventually died down. Then in 1999 the Chinese threat to the canal, which had received little attention in the press, burst into public view with a letter written to the Pentagon by Senate Majority Leader Trent Lott.

GIVING AWAY THE FARM

Trent Lott was one of the few legislators to speak out against Hutchison's grab of Balboa and Cristobal, calling in May 1997 for an investigation of the shady bidding process. A document obtained by the *Washington Times* revealed that at least three U.S. companies had offered the Panamanian government better deals for the ports than Hutchison Whampoa had. According to a bid sheet produced by Panama's Ministry of Commerce and Industry, Hutchison's bid was lower than those of several companies, including Seattle-based Stevedoring Services of America (SSA), Bechtel International of San Francisco, and Cooper/T. Smith of Dallas. Hutchison offered Panama a fixed annual payment of $10 million, 7 percent of the gross revenues, and 10 percent of the ports' ownership. Bechtel's offer was higher on all counts: an $11 million annual payment, 7.5 percent of gross revenues, and 12 percent ownership. SSA topped Hutchison on at least two counts, with a fixed $11.6 million annual payment and 8 percent of gross revenues. Cooper/T. Smith outbid Hutchison on gross revenues, offering at least 7.5 percent. Panama instead withdrew its lease offer and awarded the port contracts to Hutchison, which agreed to pay $22.2 million a year to operate the ports. The government defended the transaction as a "straightforward business deal."

On August 1, 1999, Lott wrote a letter to Defense Secretary William Cohen stating that the Chinese shipping company had gained broad authority over the canal and could use the ports to deny passage to U.S. ships. "It appears that we have given away the farm without a shot being fired," the Mississippi Republican said in asking the Pentagon chief for his security assessment. "This administration is allowing a scenario to develop where U.S. national security interests could not be protected without confronting the Chinese communists in the Americas. U.S. naval ships will be at the mercy of Chinese-controlled pilots and could even be denied passage through the Panama Canal by Hutchison, an arm of the People's Liberation Army. In addition, the Chinese Communist Party will gain an intelligence information advantage by controlling this strategic choke point."

Cohen did not respond, a snub that left Lott angrier because the defense secretary was a Republican and a former Senate colleague from Maine. After several weeks of waiting, Lott directed the chairman of the Senate Armed Services Committee, Senator John Warner, to hold hearings on the threat to the Panama Canal.

"It is the perception of some of my colleagues and I [sic] that the Chinese involvement in Panama may not be straightforward and could, in fact, be a threat to our national security," Lott stated in seeking the hearing. "The transfer of control of the Panama Canal is one of the critical national security issues currently facing our nation and its impact will be felt for many generations to come." The committee, Lott said, urgently needs to investigate the contract by Hutchison Whampoa— a company reported to have ties to Chinese military and intelligence services.

The Clinton White House's first response to Lott's concerns was to dismiss them out of hand. The president's national security spokesman, David Leavy, said the treaty allows the United States to intervene militarily to defend the canal—even though there are no longer any American bases within a hundred miles. "Our team looked into this, analyzed it, and made a judgment... that we are satisfied that our interests will be protected, both in terms of national security and commercial," Leavy said. "We see no capability, on the part of China, which is a heavy user of the canal, to disrupt its operation. So I would caution people not to get too alarmist over this issue."

Lott, however, wanted answers to a series of questions:

- What power has Panama granted Hutchison Whampoa to operate the canal?
- What are the national security risks of Hutchison Whampoa's controlling container facilities in the Balboa and Cristobal ports?
- What are the national security risks involved in Hutchison Whampoa's eventually controlling former U.S. military bases in Panama?
- Does Hutchison Whampoa's chairman, billionaire Li Kashing, have ties to the Chinese Communist Party, China's People's Liberation Army, or Chinese intelligence activities?
- Does the 1977 treaty ensure that the United States can intervene in Panama to keep the canal open?
- Is China extending the range of its navy by commercially controlling the two Panama ports?

The hearing in October 1999 proved to be one of the best examples of Clinton-Gore "spin." The message: There is no threat to the canal or U.S. national security by Hutchison Whampoa's control over the ports.

A key witness was Marine Corps General Charles E. Wilhelm, commander in chief of the U.S. Southern Command, the military units in charge of protecting American interests in South and Central America. As part of the handover of the canal, the U.S. military pulled out of numerous bases in Panama, once the headquarters of the Southern Command. Wilhelm did not begin his testimony with the issue at hand, the Chinese threat to the canal. Instead he followed the State Department line about how well the military was implementing the 1977 treaty, a topic that no one on the committee had asked about. As for providing security for the canal, Wilhelm said the U.S. military was developing a "security strategy" that included help to the Panama Public Forces (PPF), the police forces. Panama has no standing army and is all but helpless. "We will help Panama develop a national level command, control, communication, and intelligence (C3I) system to enhance government responsiveness to national emergencies," the four-star general said. "We will assist the PPF to develop expertise in emergency and crisis action planning, to modernize their equipment, and to professionalize their security forces. The desired end-state is an effective Panamanian national C3I system and a modernized PPF capable of providing security for the Canal and playing an appropriate role in meeting common Panamanian and U.S. national security objectives." In essence, the United States would help the Panamanian police to communicate but would not give the police force the weapons and equipment to provide real defense. The general did not say when the Panamanians would be able to defend the canal or how they would do it with no U.S. military presence to support it.

But it was Wilhelm's assessment of the threat to the canal that was a real stretch. "We are not aware of any current internal or external threats to the Panama Canal, and we have no evidence that it has been targeted by terrorists or foreign governments," he stated. The answer was carefully worded by an officer trained to avoid political partisanship and to follow the orders of his commander in chief. "That said, we believe that the Canal must always be regarded as a potential target for both conventional and unconventional forces given its importance to global commerce and for military transits. The most likely threats to the Canal are internal and nonlethal." Only when pressed under questioning did Wilhelm acknowledge that Chinese companies like Hutchison Whampoa could be used by the Chinese government and that China does not hesitate to use its supposedly "commercial" state-run businesses to support its political and military objectives.

General Wilhelm was especially vague on the future threat and carefully avoided directly mentioning China and Cuba. He testified that future threats could include a "hostile foreign power" or transnational criminal organizations. "Cuba and China have strong economic interests in Panama but do not pose a threat to the security of the Canal *at this time*" (emphasis added). Wilhelm did not say when Cuba and China would emerge as future threats to the canal. But he noted that Cuba operates businesses in Panama to generate cash as a way of circumventing the U.S. embargo on the island. China has diplomatic relations with eighteen nations in the region and has links with more than two hundred commercial entities and joint venture enterprises in Latin America and the Caribbean. China quadrupled its investments in the region during the 1990s to $8.2 billion.

Hutchison's leasing of Balboa and Cristobal was dismissed as a purely economic and nonstrategic deal. "China's goals in Panama are to ensure unrestricted access to the markets and natural resources of Latin America and to promote China as a potential political and economic alternative to the U.S.," Wilhelm said. "In my view, the impact of Chinese commercial interests in Panama is less a local threat to the Canal and more a regional threat posed by expanding Chinese influence throughout Latin America."

Aside from China and Cuba, another threat to Panama is the illegal commerce in drugs, arms, and aliens, a problem Wilhelm said is undermining the stability of nations along the major trafficking routes, especially Mexico and Colombia. Wilhelm predicted that this kind of crime in Panama "will likely increase after the U.S. withdraws." But here again, he said, there is no "identified threat" to canal operations from the criminals. Is there an unidentified threat, a hidden danger? The general did not say. But he noted that the terrorist group Revolutionary Armed Forces of Colombia, known by its Spanish acronym as FARC, is using Panamanian territory as a safe haven and for rest and resupply between paramilitary actions. FARC terrorists are "scattered around Panama" but, according to Wilhelm, "pose no identifiable or verifiable threat to Canal operations or to the government of Panama." He did not elaborate on why the Colombian terrorists were harmless.

WHO WILL DEFEND THE CANAL?

So, if the canal is threatened, who will respond? The chairman of the Joint Chiefs of Staff, the top military officer, has assigned canal defense operations to Wilhelm's Southern Command. "We are prepared to act either unilaterally or jointly with the Panama Public Forces to fulfill these responsibilities," Wilhelm said. The command has carried out a "computer-assisted" military exercise—meaning no troops and equipment actually took part. The four-star general said the Pentagon has drawn up contingency plans for "the defense of the Canal" and is also looking at "alternative approaches" that will "ensure future safe passage of high value transits through the Canal."

The general's view is much softer than that of another witness, Caspar Weinberger, who served as President Reagan's secretary of defense. To Weinberger, any attempt to interfere with canal operations will be "catastrophic" because of the enormous economic and strategic importance of the waterway. Weinberger stressed that as long as the ports are controlled by a Chinese-owned company, the threat will always be there. "The company would not be able to survive if they don't do something the Chinese government tells them to," he said.

The hearing included other Clinton-Gore administration officials, all political appointees who were even more dismissive of the Chinese threat to Panama than was General Wilhelm. Brian E. Sheridan, assistant defense secretary for special operations and low-intensity conflict, appeared before the committee to minimize the importance of the canal. Other routes for some goods have "reduced the importance of the canal for U.S. commerce," he said. Still it remains "highly important"—a classification less than vital to U.S. national security.

How important is the Panama Canal? Four percent of all world trade and 13 percent of U.S. international shipping pass through the canal. Sheridan insisted that Hutchison Whampoa's control of the ports will not affect the current *privileges* of U.S. Navy ships to pass through the canal, nor will it *override* Panama's treaty obligations. So as long as everyone abides by the Panama Canal Treaty, there will be no problem. Sheridan pointed out that an amendment to the treaty gives the United States the "right to take such steps as each deems necessary... including the use of military force" to retake it. Of course, American troops— no longer based in Panama—could not be deployed from the United States quickly to prevent major disruptions of the canal by a determined foe.

Sheridan used even more spin to explain away Hutchison Whampoa, describing it as one of Hong Kong's oldest "British" trading companies. Li Kashing, however, purchased the company in 1979. Sheridan offered a careful assessment to explain away Li's ties to Communist China: "There is no public record of any mainland ownership of [Hutchison Whampoa and related corporations] either through direct investments or through membership on boards of directors."

And what did Hutchison Whampoa want with Balboa and Cristobal? "Our analysts believe that [Hutchison Whampoa's] primary interest in bidding on the Panamanian ports was to establish a Pacific Ocean hub for its shipping interests," Sheridan said. He suggested that the ports were insignificant and that ships passing through the canal do not have to use them. Besides, he said, a subsidiary of Stevedoring Services of America, Manzanillo International Terminal, and the Taiwan company Evergreen International still have port facilities on the Caribbean side of the canal entrance. Sheridan concluded his testimony by asserting that the leases for Hutchison Whampoa "do not limit or hinder military or commercial traffic or represent any greater threat to the Panama Canal than the 200 plus annual canal transits by Chinese flag vessels."

"The evidence we have does not suggest that China, through Hutchison Whampoa or any other firm, has the capability, the desire, or the wherewithal to seek to control the Panama Canal after its transfer to Panama on 31 December 1999," Sheridan said. "In the judgment of our analysts, Hutchison Whampoa's motivations are commercial."

It was the pattern of the Clinton-Gore administration to say one thing in public but keep the real story inside the cloistered realm of U.S. intelligence agencies. Three secret intelligence reports contradicted the official testimony of the Pentagon officials. They were obtained from the U.S. Southern Command and the U.S. Army under a Freedom of Information Act request by Judicial Watch, a conservative group whose political activism has brought numerous lawsuits against the government. A third internal report was from the U.S. Customs Service Intelligence Division.

The first report was labeled "SECRET NOFORN"—the designation that prohibits sharing the information with non-U.S. citizens. It was produced by the army's deputy chief of staff for intelligence on April 22, 1998. Its headline was unambiguous: "Panama: China Awaits U.S. Departure."

Below a photograph that was blacked out by army censors, the released portions of the report read as follows:

(U) According to a DIA Information Report, Li Kashing, the owner of Hutchison Whampoa Ltd. (HW) and Cheung Kong Holdings Ltd. (CK) is planning to take control of Panama Canal operations when the U.S. transfers it to Panama in Dec. 99.

(U) Li is directly connected to Beijing and is willing to use his business influence to further the aims of the Chinese government. He has been positioning his son, Victor Li, to replace him in certain CK and HW operations such as HW's Hong Kong International Terminals (HIT).

(U) Due to a decline in raw materials from within China, freight rates dropping due to excess tonnage in the market, and the current Asian financial crisis, corporate revenues should decline. Consequently, China is looking to expand into new markets (DIA, 221333Z APR 98).

(C) Analyst Comment: Li's interest in the canal is not only strategic, but also a means for outside financial opportunities for the Chinese Government. China, the canal's third largest user, consequently has a significant amount of influence. If China were to assume control of the canal operations, it would have to abide by the neutrality requirements of the Torrijos-Carter treaties.

The report directly contradicted Sheridan's assertion that Hutchison Whampoa had no strategic interest in taking over the canal. It also countered his attempt to downplay Li's ties to the Communist Chinese government. Sheridan's testimony was misleading or deceptive. It was also typical of the contempt for Congress shown by nearly every department and agency of the Clinton-Gore administration.

The second "Intelligence Assessment" was dated October 26, 1999— only four days after the Senate Armed Services Committee hearing on Panama. The report was labeled "SECRET//XI" and bore the headline "Panama: People's Republic of China Interests and Activities." The report was produced by the U.S. Southern Command Joint Intelligence Center, which includes representatives of several military and civilian intelligence agencies. The report said there was no "direct" ownership relationship between the People's Republic of China government and Hutchison Whampoa. According to the report, the subsidiary that will run the ports, Panama Ports Company, is responsible for tug boat operations, ship repair, and pilot services within Balboa and Cristobal. A key conclusion of the assessment was this: "Any potential threat posed by the presence of a pro-Chinese corporate entity in the Panama Canal zone is indirect." The report said it was "unlikely" that Panama Ports Company officials or employees would overtly sabotage or damage the canal "on orders from Beijing, as it would be contrary to their own financial interests and would undoubtedly elicit an immediate response from the U.S. and the international community."

So, the report stopped short of declaring that the Chinese were a direct threat. But the fact that it identified the Chinese as even a potential threat contradicts the Clinton-Gore administration's blanket dismissals of any threat whatsoever.

"Hutchison Whampoa's owner, Hong Kong tycoon Li Ka-Shin, has extensive business ties in Beijing and has compelling financial reasons to maintain a good relationship with the Chinese leadership," the report said. But having extensive business ties in Beijing is not the same as having business ties in New York or Detroit. Business ties to Beijing mean connections—*guanxi*, in Chinese. And connections in Beijing mean only one thing: extensive contacts and relationships with the Communist Party and People's Liberation Army officials who run China.

The report noted that "economic influence equals political leverage" and that archenemies China and Taiwan are vying for influence in many Latin American countries. "Currently 16 of the 30 countries worldwide which diplomatically recognize Taiwan are located in Latin America," the report said. In explaining how Hutchison Whampoa could use its economic power, the report said the company "could threaten to shift some business from Panama to its Free Trade Zone in the Bahamas, thus giving the company additional leverage over the Panamanian government."

How could China's presence in Panama pose a threat? The report's final declassified passage was short but succinct: "Hutchison's containerized shipping facilities in the Panama Canal, as well as the Bahamas, could provide a conduit for illegal shipments of technology or prohibited items from the West to the PRC, or facilitate the movement of arms and other prohibited items into the Americas."

China's illegal technology acquisition was never mentioned during the public Senate hearing, nor was China's proclivity to move arms and contraband into the Americas. This real China threat is allowed to be spoken of only in secret intelligence reports, lest China be offended.

The disclosure of the reports, in *Washington Times* articles by this author, drew little attention in most news accounts. But at least one member of Congress felt cheated: Senate Armed Services Committee Chairman John Warner demanded to know why he was not informed about the contents of the report by the officials who testified at the October 22, 1999, hearing. "I am concerned that this Pentagon report was not mentioned during our hearing or subsequently shared with the committee," an angry Warner stated in a letter to Defense Secretary Cohen.

The Customs Service intelligence report presented a dire picture of drug trafficking, money laundering, and growing Chinese involvement in Panama. The problems were getting worse as the result of the pull-out of U.S. forces and the failure of the Panamanian government to take steps to resolve them. "Panama's corrupt and ill-trained law enforcement units continue to be overwhelmed by trafficking efforts and are basically ineffective in their efforts," the May 2000 report said.

On Chinese involvement, the Customs Service noted that Li "reportedly has ties with the Red Chinese government." It stated that Shen Jueren, the Chinese Communist official who heads China Resources, and Li were partners in a Hong Kong bank. "This company has also established itself as a consolidator of ocean freight containers in Freeport, Bahamas," the report said.

China Resources owns 10 percent of Hongkong International Terminals, Hutchison Whampoa's flagship company, whose majority owner is Li Kashing, according to a 1997 memorandum from the American consulate in Hong Kong. Senate investigators identified China Resources in 1997 as "an agent of espionage—economic, military, and political." The firm has also been linked to the Lippo Group, which was implicated in illegal campaign donations to the 1996 Clinton-Gore reelection campaign.

The Customs report went on to say that "intelligence sources indicate that Chinese and Russian organized crime factions are active in narcotics, arms, and illegal alien smuggling utilizing Panama as a base of operations. The Chinese population in Panama has grown dramatically in the past five years, and the Chinese government maintains an embassy in Panama City."

As part of its pro-China agenda, the Clinton-Gore administration steadfastly rejected any suggestion that the Chinese company threatened the canal. "We do not see the Chinese-owned port facilities as a military or a national-security threat," said Kenneth Bacon, the Pentagon's spokesman, shortly after Senate Majority Leader Lott's letter to Cohen was made public. White House spokesman Joe Lockhart repeated the no-threat political line: "I can tell you with no uncertainty and no doubt that the United States does not believe that a Hong Kong company controlling, running the ports, loading and offloading ships at the Panama Canal poses any threat to the United States or to our national security, and that is an unequivocal statement."

When reports of Lott's and other senators' concerns about the canal were made public, Lockhart dismissed them with this snide comment: "That is the kind of silly stuff that gets out from time to time in this town. The security of the canal will be controlled by the commission controlled by Panama." He insisted the bidding for the port concessions was won fairly by the Hong Kong company. Lockhart was merely echoing the words of David Leavy, his fellow White House spinmeister, who had cautioned people "not to get too alarmist over this issue."

SOUND THE ALARM

Among the strategic facilities turned over to the Panamanian government was a deep underground intelligence facility. The facility is in Quarry Heights, where the U.S. Southern Command headquarters used to be located. In the middle of Ancon Hill, deep underground, was the Southern Command Intelligence Center. "From there we monitored and conducted intelligence operations for the Southern Hemisphere and Central America," a former intelligence official told me. "The place was top secret and built like a mini-Cheyenne Mountain"—the headquarters of the North American Aerospace Command in Colorado Springs that monitors worldwide missile launches and aircraft flights. "We just gave the whole facility to the Panamanians/Chinese," he said. Albrook Air Field, one of the facilities abandoned by the Pentagon, had been the base for regional surveillance operations for monitoring activities in Cuba and other parts of Central America. "There are many other military and intelligence facilities now gone," the former official lamented, including the Rodman Naval Air Station, which the Chinese had the option to lease, as well as military and intelligence facilities at Corozal, Corundu, Fort Clayton, Fort Sherman, and the Special Forces jungle training center. The former official said abandoning the military facilities was a strategic mistake for the United States. "We will pay dearly for this as surely as the sun rises," he commented.

Representative Duncan Hunter, California Republican and a former army ranger who saw combat in Vietnam, was one of the few members of Congress to sound the alarm. "The Panama Canal," Hunter said, "continues to be a critical choke point for the movement of American forces and supplies. Indeed, as the U.S. Navy has shrunk from 550 ships at the start of the decade to 350 ships today, the ability to shift units rapidly between oceans is vital. Strategists in Beijing certainly are aware of this as they consider American reactions to another crisis over Taiwan or anywhere else in Asia. The question is, why hasn't the Clinton administration considered this?"

President Clinton made clear he would not be concerned even if China did take over the canal. He was asked in November 1999 about the canal treaty and said he supported the turnover of the canal to Panama. "I think it's the right thing to do," he said. "I think the government of Panama is committed to maintaining the canal in an appropriate way and keeping it open and working with us to do so, and having good relations."

"You're not worried about China controlling the canal?" a reporter asked.

"I think the Chinese will, in fact, be bending over backwards to make sure that they run it in a competent and able and fair manner," the president said. "This is like them, like China coming into the WTO [World Trade Organization]. I think they'll want to demonstrate to a distant part of the world that they can be a responsible partner, and I would be very surprised if any adverse consequences flowed from the Chinese running the canal."

Privately, the remark drew groans from the president's aides. A spokesman had to put out a "clarification" carefully suggesting that the president may have misspoken. Several days later the president corrected himself. "It's important for the American people to understand that the canal, itself, will be operated and controlled entirely by the government of Panama, through the Panama Canal Authority," he said. "That is the locks, ingress and egress, access, openness—the canal is completely and totally within the control of the Panamanians." As for Hutchison Whampoa, Clinton stated, "They also do this in three or four ports in Great Britain. It's one of the biggest companies in the world that does this. The managing director is British. Most of the employees will be Panamanian. So I feel comfortable that our commercial and security interests can be protected under this arrangement."

But the activities of Hutchison Whampoa should have been disturbing. The alarm bells were sounded in two congressional aides' candid assessment of Chinese activities in Panama. Based on a fact-finding tour of Panama, Al Santoli, an aide to Representative Dana Rohrabacher, and Jim Doran, an aide to Senator Jesse Helms, the chairman of the Senate Foreign Relations Committee, concluded that U.S. national security is at risk in the canal.

The report revealed that China's presence is growing in the region. "U.S. and Panamanian security officials stated that Panama has become the central base of operations for Communist China in Latin America," the report said. "It is also a vital component to an emerging Chinese Communist strategy to dominate the Pacific and to undermine and isolate the United States. The No. 2 user of the canal, after the United States, is Japan, with China and Taiwan competing for the third position."

According to Santoli and Doran, the top Chinese government representative in Panama is a "senior intelligence officer" working out of a bank building in Panama City with fourteen assistants.

"Worldwide," the Santoli-Doran report stated, "China appears to be progressively positioning itself commercially and militarily along the key naval choke points between the Indian Ocean (its bases in Burma); the South China Sea (Hong Kong); the Straits of Malacca (the Spratly Islands and a growing role in Cambodia); the central Pacific (a major land satellite tracking station on Tarawa); the coast of Hawaii (a major ocean mining tract); the Caribbean (Cuba and the Bahamas); and now the Panama Canal. China's flagship commercial shipping fleet, China Ocean Shipping Company (COSCO), is directly connected to the People's Liberation Army and Chinese Communist government. COSCO ships have served as carriers for massive smuggling operations around the world—including the United States—of weapons, drugs and illegal aliens. In addition, COSCO has been used by the Chinese government to ship missiles and components of weapons of mass destruction to rogue nations such as Pakistan and Iran."

CHINA'S SOUTHERN STRATEGY

The Clinton-Gore administration has steadfastly refused to place China's Panama gambit into a larger strategic context. But one noted scholar has recognized China's strategic plan. Constantine Menges, a senior White House National Security Council specialist during the Reagan administration, is a professor at George Washington University in Washington, D.C., and head of the program on transitions to democracy at the Elliot School of International Affairs. Menges, who has a very good track record in projecting communist moves, reveals how the Chinese role in Panama is part of a new communist strategy dubbed "checkbook subversion"—the use of commercial activities and alliances to further geopolitical goals.

"I see China systematically trying to establish positions of influence in countries around the world where they can obtain benefits and where it might be useful at some future time to put pressure on the United States," Menges says. "The Panama Canal has long been considered one of the most strategically significant places on earth. It's of major importance to the United States for both military and commercial shipping and transit. I think the Chinese purpose in using bribery and corrupt methods to win the bidding for the contract on managing the ports at both ends of the Panama Canal has both a geopolitical and a commercial purpose. Geopolitically, China sees its location in Panama as a place where it can establish a base of influence in a small country, using political and commercial means, where it can work closely with its new ally Cuba to help those who oppose the United States in Latin America, and where it might also be able to position weapons such as medium-range missiles that potentially could be used to threaten the United States in times of crisis, or times of the choosing of the Chinese regime."

The large port facilities at Balboa and Cristobal include storage areas where shipping containers could easily be used to hide Chinese mobile, medium-range missiles. China has two new medium-range missiles that are transported and launched from truck launchers—a size easily concealed in shipping containers.

According to a classified assessment by the National Air Intelligence Center, China for the past several years has embarked on a program of upgrading older medium-range missiles to newer solid-fueled Dong Feng-21 missiles. The report, labeled "secret," also reveals that China's newest long-range mobile missile, the Dong Feng-31, is moved on trains in shipping containers. In fact the intelligence center showed a satellite photograph of the containers at the Wuzhai Missile and Space Test Center. The photograph showed what are believed to be the ICBMs in two containers, one holding the combined first and second stage and the other containing the upper stage with the warhead. The spy photographs make it clear that missiles could easily be shipped into Panama without being detected.

The larger Chinese strategy is to use China's huge trade surplus of $562 billion, obtained from its trade with the United States, Europe, and Japan, to buy influence through ostensible business arrangements in areas strategically important to China.

In Venezuela, China has developed close ties to President Hugo Chavez, a paratrooper who seized power in a coup in 1992 and was elected president in 1999. Chavez has said that Venezuela has "lifted itself up"—echoing Mao's 1949 declaration at the founding of the communist state that China had "stood up"—and copied China's official policy of creating a "multipolar world free of U.S. domination."

"We're trying to do what you did fifty years ago," Chavez said in Beijing. "We're beginning a revolutionary process, creating a new republic." Prime Minister Zhu Rongji of China, who is supposed to represent the new generation of less ideological communist leaders, offered praise for Chavez: "Although certain conservative forces at home and abroad are against your cause, the government and people of China are on your side."

Cuba, like Venezuela under Chavez, is another key element of China's developing strategy of subversion in the Western Hemisphere. In February 1999 China's defense minister, Chi Haotian, made a little-noticed visit to Cuba and, according to U.S. intelligence officials, concluded a new cooperation agreement with the regime of Fidel Castro. General Chi made clear that the growing ties between China and Cuba were not limited to economics. "Thanks to the development in the bilateral relations, the relations between the armies of the two countries have also seen fairly rapid development," Chi said during the Cuba visit.

Eleven months after Chi's visit, Cuba's communications minister, Silvano Colas, announced that Cuba has begun broadcasting official Chinese government radio broadcasts to the American continent for the first time. Colas denied that the cooperation involved intelligence gathering by China. Eight hours of daily Radio China International programming is being beamed into the United States. The programs are broadcast in Chinese, as well as Spanish, Portuguese, and English. Such broadcasts traditionally are used by spy services to communicate with clandestine intelligence officers, including China's large community of "illegals"—nationals trained to look and sound like Americans who remain hidden from view until activated by Beijing for intelligence or covert action purposes.

U.S. intelligence agencies also picked up information that China had begun cooperation with Cuba on electronic signals intelligence gathering, similar to the decades-old Soviet and now Russian electronic spying facility at Lourdes, Cuba. The intelligence site is believed to be located at a transmitting facility at Bejucal, Cuba. The Cubans said the cooperation with the Chinese involved modernizing the telephone system with China's Sinotech and Great Dragon Telecommunications companies working with the Cuban telephone company ETECSA and a second firm, Coprefil, that installed telephones on Cuba's Isle of Youth.

Menges sees a pattern—China moving into the hemisphere and lining up with anti-American forces and governments. The strategic goal would be to exploit the relationships to distract the United States from going to Taiwan's defense in the event of a conflict.

He cites the Hutchison Whampoa port facility in the Bahamas, in addition to its Panama Canal facilities. Moreover, China tried to obtain access to the old Long Beach Naval Yard in southern California through a lease arrangement with COSCO. COSCO failed to move into the facility but did manage to lease a major port facility in Vancouver, Canada.

"All of this is part of a pattern of establishing a presence in the Western Hemisphere that can be used against the United States if China believes it's useful to do so," Menges says. "A hypothetical example of that would be that in the event of a crisis about Taiwan, China might arrange that the Hong Kong port company Hutchison Whampoa, called Panama Port Holdings in the Panama context, do things that impede shipping through the Panama Canal. These might be made to look like accidents. They might organize strikes. Technical things stop working. There could also be demonstrations in Panama against U.S. ships, especially U.S. warships going through the Panama Canal, demands that they not be admitted to the Panama Canal."

The covert action side of the activities is only one end of the threat spectrum and could include secret backing for anti-U.S. terrorist groups in Latin America, who could be called upon to take action against American embassies and personnel in Latin America.

At the high end of the threat spectrum, China could secretly infiltrate missiles into its leased ports. "It is possible they could conceal medium-range ballistic missiles, of which China has some hundreds, in the port facilities in Panama which it alone will control access to," he says. "China could unveil them at some point and say they are nuclear warheads or high-explosive warheads, and these missiles could reach

Washington and other East Coast cities. It could be sort of a Chinese
Cuban missile surprise that might suddenly confront the United
States."

A U.S. national missile defense system—even if it were in place—
probably would not be effective at this close range because of the
depressed trajectory launches.

Menges is also concerned that Chinese support for anti-American
subversion in the region will affect Mexico, which is politically fragile
because of rampant illegal narcotics and the government corruption
that has come with it. President Hugo Chavez of Venezuela could begin
helping elements of the Mexican military that might seek to repeat the
kind of coup the colonel pulled off in his own country. "It's a situation
in which China has a large interest," Menges says. "China has expanding energy needs, and the combination of Chinese commercial relations with Mexico and the purchase of oil and Cuban covert action in
Mexico could be a very symbiotically effective combination for bringing a radical left regime in Mexico over time." The threat to the United
States in that scenario is obvious. Mexico's border with the United
States is two thousand miles long, and "this could pose a serious problem to U.S. national security," Menges notes. "All this could be done
through covert action and indirect means alone. There would be no visible activity, it would not involve the open use of military force by China
or Cuba but would involve an entirely covert campaign essentially to
change the character of the regime in a direction hostile to the United
States and friendly to China and Cuba."

China's connection with Cuba has received no attention from the
news media or from U.S. policymakers, who lack a clear understanding of Chinese strategic goals and ambitions. According to Menges,
China and Cuba have set up "silent partnerships" that will be used to
develop anti-U.S. policies in Latin America. "The goal is to set up
countries that are friendly to the dictatorships in China and Cuba, as
is the Chavez government in Venezuela and as a communist regime
in Colombia would be," Menges says. "There is a partnership, and the
commonality is that they are both communist regimes and they want
to hold power; they view the United States and its allies as dangerous

to them and to their future hold on power. Anything they can do to strengthen each other and strengthen groups within countries that are hostile to the United States is a way of impeding the ability of the United States to threaten their future control as communist regimes."

China's inroads into Panama and the Western Hemisphere are not the only method that Beijing is using to target its main enemy. China's proliferation of weapons of mass destruction is targeted at helping anti-U.S. governments around the world. The strategy is similar to this notion: "The enemy of my enemy is my friend."

CHAPTER SIX

Proliferation Subversion

"China must pay close attention to those countries that are opposed to American interests, or are potential strategic enemies. It must be borne in mind that the enemies of enemies are one's own allies. . . . Know this: the more the United States encounters trouble in other places in the world, the more difficult it is for it to concentrate its power on dealing with China and the greater the opportunities for China's existence and development."

—Chinese ultranationalist author He Xin

The American delegation was in Beijing to talk weapons proliferation. It was November 12, 1998, and the group was headed by John Holum, the director of the U.S. Arms Control and Disarmament Agency. The agency was later disbanded, leaving Holum an appointed but never confirmed undersecretary of state. Other officials included White House National Security Council staffer Gary Samore and Robert Einhorn, the State Department's point man on proliferation, as well as officials from the Pentagon's Joint Staff and the office of the secretary of defense. On the other side of the meeting table sat People's Liberation Army Lieutenant General Xiong Guangkai, the fast-track officer whose broad portfolio includes direction of Chinese military intelligence and PLA foreign diplomacy and liaison. Xiong is the hard-liner who once threatened to use nuclear weapons against Los Angeles if the United States defended Taiwan from a mainland attack. The topic of discussion was China's position vis-à-vis the twenty-nine–nation Missile Technology Control Regime (MTCR), whose countries agree not to sell missiles and related components to rogue states. China is a world leader in such sales. In fact, the Chinese Communist government and its action arm, the People's Liberation Army, use weapons proliferation as a way to wage indirect war against the United States.

"Studying the MTCR is not the same as joining the MTCR," General Xiong told the group with his characteristic grin. "But China is willing to work with the United States to expedite its study." China, Xiong asserted, did not want to see nuclear or missile proliferation in North Korea or in South Asia. This was just what the Clinton-Gore arms control team wanted to hear. Volumes of reports from U.S. intelligence agencies, however, show just the opposite: China is engaged in unrestricted weapons sales to North Korea, Pakistan, the Middle East, and North Africa. These sales of course increase the danger of war.

Xiong put the Americans on the defensive, saying that U.S. sales of missile defense weapons to Taiwan "constitute missile proliferation," criticizing in particular the recent sale of Patriot antiaircraft missiles. Clinton-Gore officials, on the other hand, never challenged him about Communist China's buildup of short-range missiles that made the Patriots necessary to Taiwan's defense.

Instead, State Department special adviser John Holum spoke in platitudes about how "[m]issile and nonproliferation cooperation are important to bilateral relations." He did, however, ask the Chinese about their recent shipment of telemetry equipment to Iran. The equipment is used to monitor missile test flights. Typically, Xiong didn't give him an answer.

CHINA'S ENEMY

Publicly and privately in meetings with U.S. government officials, China consistently denies that its arms sales are directed against the United States. The official line was put forth in February 1999 by Chinese Foreign Ministry spokeswoman Zhang Qiyue, who said, "Arms sales should be beneficial to the importing nation's defense capability, but should not be detrimental to regional security, peace, and stability." Zhang insisted, "China will not use arms sales to interfere in the internal affairs of the

importing nations," and asserted that Beijing maintains "a very responsible and cautious attitude" on selling arms and weapons know-how.

As with all communist governments, lying is standard practice. A
close look at Chinese weapons sales shows the spokeswoman's statement is false.

The CIA, even under the tight political constraints of the Clinton-Gore
administration that prohibit open criticism of China, has provided several reports to Congress on the issue, as required by law. The CIA
describes the Chinese arms sellers as "firms," though these "firms" are
owned by the communist government. From January to June of 1999, the
CIA reported, these firms "supplied missile-related items, raw materials
and/or assistance to several countries," including Iran, North Korea, and
Pakistan. The Clinton-Gore administration spin was that these companies were operating outside of official government control. But that is not
the case. The firms are owned and directed by the Communist Party's
Central Military Commission, headed by Chinese leader Jiang Zemin.

The intelligence reports received almost no attention in the press
for reasons that remain unclear. Are the news media not interested in
Communist China's arms sales? Or are there vested financial interests on the part of the major news organizations, especially the major
television networks, for avoiding any criticism of China? The communist government has a heavy-handed approach to news organizations
that report critically on China. Exposing China's dangerous weapons
sales would likely lead to expulsions of Beijing-based reporters or the
closing down of bureaus. That would leave the news organizations
unable to compete with other networks and newspapers for access to
Beijing.

The Clinton-Gore administration, for its part, has avoided acknowl-
edging Chinese military proliferation because it has legal implications,
namely, congressionally mandated sanctions. In April 2000 the State
Department announced that it was sanctioning North Korea and Iran
for missile proliferation activities. China, however, was not mentioned,
though it is an acknowledged—by the CIA and other intelligence
agencies—source of missile technology to North Korea. Curiously, one of
the laws mandating sanctions was sponsored by Al Gore when he was a

Tennessee Democrat in the U.S. Senate. Gore's key national security aide, Leon Fuerth, was aggressive as a Senate staffer in trying to put teeth into international agreements aimed at preventing the spread of weapons of mass destruction. But once he went to the White House as Gore's national security adviser, Fuerth signed on to the administration's policy of ignoring China's arms sales. A case in point: China's 1996 sale of Houdong fast patrol boats to Iran. The patrol boats were equipped with C-802 antiship cruise missiles. A navy admiral in the Persian Gulf, Vice Admiral Scott Redd, said the missiles were a threat to American ships and the 15,000 U.S. troops in the region. And the threat was not merely theoretical. In the late 1990s two of the Iranian Houdong missile patrol boats carried out a simulated, high-speed attack against the U.S. aircraft carrier *Kitty Hawk* and the cruiser *Cowpens*. The Iranian boats approached the warships and did not alter course until they were close enough to fire their C-802 cruise missiles. The simulated attack was then broken off.

Under legislation sponsored by Senator Gore and Senator John McCain, Arizona Republican, U.S. sanctions should be imposed on nations or companies that sell "destabilizing" weapons to Iran or Iraq. The measure was signed into law in 1992 as the Iran-Iraq Non-Proliferation Act. But as vice president, Al Gore has done nothing to enforce his own legislation. He was silent when Secretary of State Madeleine Albright dismissed the C-802 sale from China as insignificant. "The administration has concluded at present that the known transfers were not of a destabilizing number and type," Albright stated in a letter to Congress. According to national security specialist William C. Triplett II, the reason is related to the Clinton-Gore fund-raising scandals. Wang Jun, chairman of China's Poly Technologies, which made the sale of C-802s, visited the White House in February 1996 as a guest of President Clinton.

President Clinton and his national security adviser, Sandy Berger, decided that the only issue on which the administration would confront China—rather than "engage" it—was its abysmal human rights record. The reason: Polling data showed that it played well. So the Clinton-Gore administration has criticized China on its repression of Buddhists in

Tibet but has downplayed the significance of weapons that could be used against American servicemen and women overseas.

Worse, in a secret document reprinted in the appendix, the Clinton-Gore administration actually offered to reward China for its proliferation of missiles and other weapons technology by providing the communist regime access to U.S. high technology in exchange for joining the Missile Technology Control Regime. The deal even offered a "blanket" presidential waiver on all U.S. satellite launches. Instead of requiring a government review of which satellites can be fired into space on Chinese boosters—a sanction imposed in 1989 after the bloody massacre of protesters by Chinese troops—the White House wanted to give China easy access to cash from American companies looking for a cheap way to launch their satellites. But the Chinese rejected the deal because they refused to limit their weapons sales around the world.

Instead, since 1998 China has sharply increased its arms transfers. These sales are outlined in highly classified U.S. intelligence reports made available to this author by U.S. government officials. Only occasionally, when the reports could not be ignored, would senior Clinton-Gore officials announce that the U.S. government had "expressed its concerns" to Beijing. The diplomatic term for these notes is "demarches," but because of their softness, critics have dubbed them "demarshmallows."

The intelligence reports documenting the weapons transfers, more than anything, highlight the threat to the United States and international stability posed by Chinese arms proliferation. For that reason they deserve exposure. The government officials who provided them to me braved administrative punishment and even criminal prosecution to disclose them. The actions are a clear case of civil disobedience to protest the misguided and dangerous policies of the Clinton-Gore administration.

In early 1999 General Hugh Shelton, chairman of the Joint Chiefs of Staff, was concerned about numerous reports showing that China was covertly selling dangerous weapons and technology. Shelton ordered the Joint Staff intelligence chief, known as the J-2, to provide a report on Chinese proliferation, specifically arms-related transfers to the Middle East and South Asia. The study called for examining missile cooperation, technology transfers, production equipment sales, and training of personnel. The report, labeled "Top Secret," concluded, "The Chinese are proliferating on a consistent basis without technically breaking agreements with the United States."

The report included several examples. The National Imagery and Mapping Agency, an agency based in northern Virginia that provides intelligence reports based on high-resolution spy satellite photographs, reported in February 1999 that China had supplied Iran with "specialty steel components and materials" for missiles and had completed contracts for at least three deliveries of weapons-of-mass-destruction materials. Iran is building three long-range missiles designated Shahab-3, Shahab-4, and Shahab-5—the last a missile with enough range to strike targets in the continental United States.

On April 1, 1999, the National Security Agency, which conducts electronic eavesdropping of foreign communications, reported that Chinese government companies were supplying Iran with information on protective suits that would help the Iranians conduct combat with deadly chemical weapons.

According to the Joint Staff report, in February 1999 China helped Iran acquire "titanium stabilized duplex steel," which is used in building missiles. The destination for the material was a known Iranian rocket-development facility.

On March 25, 1999, China contracted with a Libyan government enterprise involved in developing a medium-range Al-Fatah missile. The Chinese company, identified as the China Precision Machinery Import-Export Company, agreed to train Libyan engineers in missile-related matters.

On April 1, 1999, Russia informed China that it was lifting all barriers to military-related technology transfers to the PRC. China, armed with its huge hard currency reserves, is in the market for weapons technology of all types, especially long-range missile know-how and ground-hugging cruise missile expertise. The Russians, in economic turmoil, are eager to sell.

Other intelligence reports based on sensitive space intelligence gathering have revealed that U.S. technology purchased by China has been forwarded to Pakistan, Beijing's key ally in South Asia. The material included missile production equipment. The Chinese company China Poly Ventures Corporation sent the equipment to the Pakistani national development center disguised in shipping documents as "Masada Cookware."

The National Security Agency reported in March 1999 that Iran's missile program had sent ten engineers to China for special training courses at Beijing University in inertial guidance and development techniques. The Chinese were careful to couch their missile cooperation with Iran under cover of working with Iran's short-range missiles. By claiming to cooperate on Iranian short-range missiles—those with ranges less than 186 miles and warheads lighter than 2,200 pounds—Beijing avoided U.S. criticism and sanctions. A senior White House official told me: "We have been concerned about Chinese assistance to Iran's missile program. One of the difficulties is that... the Chinese and the Iranians are working on tactical missile systems together, solid propellant systems, for example, and unfortunately that kind of technology, even though it is not prohibited by the MTCR [Missile Technology Control Regime], obviously has some carryover, and we're obviously working to try to persuade the Chinese that it is not in their interest to provide that kind of capability to the Iranians even though we can't claim that it's prohibited by any commitments that the Chinese have made." That statement was made in 1997. Yet China has continued its weapons sales without interruption.

China has failed to live up to its promises to abide by any arms control agreement. Beijing signed the Nuclear Non-Proliferation Treaty in 1992. It violated the agreement by helping Pakistan develop its nuclear weapons. Then, in 1998, President Clinton made a certification to Congress that China was not selling nuclear weapons technology to rogue states. The certification was required under a 1985 nuclear cooperation agreement with China. It said the United States could not provide China with civilian nuclear power technology and equipment unless the president certified that China was not helping other nations to build nuclear weapons. No other president had been able to make the certification because of the nuclear cooperation between China and Pakistan, Iran, and other developing nuclear powers.

The presidential approval was based on a 1996 Chinese government statement that Beijing would not sell nuclear goods to facilities hidden from international inspections. But in 2000 China said it would no longer accept any restrictions on its selling nuclear technology abroad. In announcing the deal with China, Clinton had called the 1998 nuclear accord a "win-win-win" that would boost U.S. national security, the environment, and American business. China had agreed to halt nuclear cooperation with Iran, and in exchange the United States would lift the ban on U.S. nuclear technology sales to China. Officially, Clinton-Gore administration officials insist there is "no evidence" that China has violated the agreement. But a classified U.S. intelligence report obtained by this author contradicts that claim. On April 2, 1999, a secret Defense Intelligence Agency (DIA) report exposed how the Atomic Energy Organization of Iran (AEOI) "intended to proceed with negotiations with the China Non-Metallic Minerals Industrial Import and Export Corp. (CNMIEC) for a large graphite production facility." A key Iranian nuclear weapons official, Ahmed Garib, was the contact point with the Chinese for the graphite project. The DIA concluded, "Based on other reports of AERC [Atomic Energy Research Commission, a part of AEOI] interest in graphite production, this facility could, if built, produce nuclear-grade graphite at a rate of some 200 tons per year." It was the first evidence of negotiations between the Iranians and the Chinese since 1997, when all cooperation was supposed to have stopped.

Aside from Iran, China is also trading with Saddam Hussein's Iraq, building a gas turbine electrical power generating plant worth $160 million. Any enemy of America is a possible customer for China.

THE NORTH KOREAN CONNECTION

For the United States, China's most dangerous proliferation activity is the help it provides to North Korea's long-range missile program. These missiles are targeted on U.S. forces in South Korea. They have increased in range and sophistication under the Clinton-Gore administration to the point where Pyongyang has a missile capable of reaching the United States equipped with a high-explosive warhead or a deadly biological or chemical weapons warhead. Soon North Korea could have missiles equipped with *nuclear* warheads capable of reaching U.S. soil. In its February 2000 report to Congress, the CIA acknowledged what had previously been discussed only in the extremely limited domain of classified intelligence reports: China was helping North Korea develop its long-range missiles. North Korea had already shocked the CIA with its August 1998 test of a Taepo Dong long-range missile that was capable of hitting the United States.

By identifying the missile assistance to North Korea, the CIA was admitting that it could no longer ignore what I had disclosed in the *Washington Times* six months before the February report. The intelligence reports were politically unwelcome by the Clinton-Gore administration, which saw them as undermining engagement with China. North Korea had been one area where Clinton's pro-China policy supposedly had produced benefits. Clinton-Gore officials never failed to point to China's diplomatic help behind the scenes in moderating North Korean behavior on missiles and nuclear weapons development. But now it was apparent that China was secretly boosting a missile program that directly threatens the United States.

In late December 1999, a Pentagon intelligence agency sent a top secret cable to senior government officials, including the secretaries of defense and state, the chairman of the Joint Chiefs of Staff, and the president's national security adviser. The report stated clearly that a Hong Kong company known as Pyramid Trading, or TNL Trading, was providing cover for missile technology to North Korea. "This is a deal for a direct shipment of Chinese missile technology," said an intelligence official who saw the report.

The reports were proof that Chinese President Jiang Zemin's assurances to President Clinton in the summer of 1998 were false. Jiang had said China would "actively study" joining the MTCR export control regime and would "tighten" export controls. But the facts uncovered by U.S. intelligence left no doubt that China had no intention of curbing

arms sales. For Beijing, it was a matter of national integrity. The hege-
monist United States would not be allowed to dictate to China what it
could and could not sell. And besides, the Clinton-Gore administration
had shown itself to be a paper tiger when it came to sanctions. As Lenin
put it decades ago, the capitalists will sell us the rope we will use to
hang them.

In 1998 Jiang joined Clinton for a rare unscripted press conference
in the large Western Hall of the Great Hall of the People, the communist government's palace and meeting place. Jiang announced that
both China and the United States had agreed "to prevent the proliferation of weapons of mass destruction," but he made no public mention of his promise to tighten Chinese export controls. The omission
was important. The fact that Jiang did not state publicly what he had
promised the president in private left doubts among skeptics in the
U.S. intelligence community. A White House fact sheet on the summit
stated that China "has begun to actively study joining the MTRC" and
that China has "announced that it has expanded the list of chemical
precursors which it controls" to prevent boosting third-world chemical weapons programs. The Chinese promises on biological weapons
also were vague. A statement on biological weapons called for establishing a protocol that would provide a "practical and effective compliance mechanism" and would improve "transparency"—diplomatic
code for Beijing's secrecy about its unconventional weapons and missile programs.

Although neither Jiang nor the White House fact sheet said that
China would curb missile transfers to South Asia, Clinton told reporters
there was "progress" on weapons proliferation, including "our joint
commitment not to provide assistance to ballistic missile programs in
South Asia and President Jiang's statement last week that China will
not sell missiles to Iran."

National Security Adviser Sandy Berger told reporters that, during
the meeting between Clinton and Jiang, the Chinese leader had said
both sides "had no plans to assist the Iranian nuclear program" and that
China would not "assist unsafeguarded nuclear facilities—read that

'Pakistan.'" As for missile transfers, Berger acknowledged that Chinese promises were "more ambiguous" and open to differing interpretations. "They said that they would adhere to the MTCR guidelines" but would not say when China would adopt "obligations of restraint" on missile sales as a member of the MTCR.

The North Korean missile technology transfers were part of a clear pattern of Chinese weapons sales. Other highly classified intelligence reports revealed that between 1998 and 1999 China had

- provided fiber-optic gyroscopes to North Korea;
- sold specialty steel for North Korean missiles;
- shared space technology with North Korea that U.S. intelligence agencies believe was a cover for missile technology sharing; and
- supplied accelerometers and special high-tech machinery to North Korean missile manufacturers.

The Cox Committee investigating Chinese weapons acquisition efforts also stated that there were indications of cooperation between China and North Korea on developing small nuclear warheads to fit on North Korea's long-range missiles.

The administration's response to the China–North Korea transfers was to cover them up. When I first disclosed the missile cooperation in July 1999 in the *Washington Times*, Secretary of State Madeleine Albright said, "We are concerned by reports that DPRK [North Korea] may be seeking from China materials such as specialty steel for its missile program." The administration, she noted, "takes the reports seriously" and would investigate them, and added that the State Department "raised our concerns with China and will continue to do so." But that was all the administration would do, express its concerns. The U.S. government applied no leverage and no threats to impose economic sanctions, as required by U.S. antiproliferation laws. Albright would not comment when asked about the missile transfers and the U.S. law that required the imposition of sanctions. But she insisted that the administration would "fully and faithfully implement the requirements of U.S. law." In reality, the State Department did nothing.

DOLLARS FOR CHINA

About a year and a half after Jiang made the empty promise to curb missile and weapons technology transfers, Bill Clinton announced an agreement with China that would result in Beijing's membership in the World Trade Organization (WTO). For Clinton it was another three-fer. "The China-WTO agreement is good for the United States, it's good for China, it's good for the world economy," he said. "Today, China embraces principles of economic openness, innovation, and competition that will bolster China's economic reforms and advance the rule of law. President Jiang Zemin and Premier Zhu Rongji have shown genuine leadership in committing China to open its markets and abide by global rules of fair trade."

Clinton went so far as to say that China's membership in the WTO would end the arms sales to rogue states. "The trade agreement is part of a broader agreement designed to bring China into global systems on issues from nonproliferation to regional security to environmental protection to human rights." The bilateral agreement, however, was classified by the Clinton-Gore administration as "Confidential" so that there could be no public scrutiny of the accord. After political pressure was applied from Republicans in Congress, the "U.S.-China Bilateral Market Agreement" was released on March 14, 2000. The document showed that the Clinton-Gore administration had given China a free pass on its continuing weapons sales, never even mentioning them in the agreement.

In fact, the agreement provides tremendous cover for continued covert sales of nuclear-, chemical-, and biological-weapons materials and technology, as well as missile transfers. A protocol of the agreement states that once it is a WTO member, "China's government would not influence, directly or indirectly, commercial decisions on the part of state-owned or state-invested enterprises. . . ." This means that when China's missile manufacturer sells missiles or components abroad, the government can claim complete ignorance.

In order for China to join the WTO, Congress has to pass legislation that would give China "permanent normal trade relations," what in years past has been called Most Favored Nation trading status, or MFN. The preferential trade status was denied under 1970s legislation that punished communist nations that had repressive emigration policies.

But in early 2000 the White House set up a "war room" to lobby for legislation lifting the restrictions. The group produced papers and responded to press reports that could weaken support for the bill. On proliferation, the White House released one report conceding that China still had problems with its sales of dangerous weapons. But rewarding Beijing with trade benefits would help the policy of "engagement" with China that was "key to advancing nonproliferation objectives," the statement said. "It is in our vital national interest that China embrace international nonproliferation norms, abide by them, and call upon others to do so as well. Our WTO agreement and provision of permanent normal trade relations (PNTR) status for China will advance these interests." But how? It didn't say.

The statement claimed that engagement had produced "steady programs in strengthening China's nonproliferation policy." It cited China's 1998 promise to prevent exports of "equipment and technology" that would in any way help India and Pakistan build nuclear weapons or ballistic missiles capable of carrying nuclear warheads. In 1997 and 1998, China, according to the White House, supposedly "put in place for the first time comprehensive controls on nuclear exports." Beijing also promised not to engage in "new nuclear cooperation with Iran," although its old cooperation was not defined, and China promised not to provide nuclear help to "unsafeguarded nuclear facilities" in Iran and Pakistan. But these statements were flatly contradicted by U.S. intelligence reports, including a DIA report of April 1999 and a top secret CIA report I published in my earlier book, *Betrayal*, which showed how Chinese and Pakistani officials collaborated on falsifying export documents to disguise assistance to Pakistan's nuclear arms program. (See the appendix of *Betrayal* for a copy of the document.)

According to the White House, "In 1994, China pledged to abide by Missile Technology Control Regime guidelines and not to export any

MTCR-class ground to ground missiles, and indicated during the president's 1998 trip that it is actively considering MTCR membership. China also stated publicly at that time that it has no plans to sell missiles to Iran and Pakistan." But there were no public statements by any Chinese official to support the last statement.

Still, the White House acknowledged, "We have continuing concerns. We are concerned about reports of the transfer of missile equipment and technology to Iran and Pakistan, and transfers of dual-use items that could be used by Iran in its chemical weapons program." An important caveat, but one that only those with access to classified intelligence reports fully understood. And typically, the White House fell back on its claim that it was working hard to curb any illicit Chinese weapons proliferation. "We are fully implementing U.S. law, including past imposition of sanctions related to China's export of missile technology and chemical weapons. We will continue to use the tools at our disposal to move China in the right direction."

The statement concluded that the failure to reward China with permanent favorable trade benefits "will not help us accelerate China's movement toward respect for and implementation of international standards for nonproliferation." The White House said it imposed sanctions in 1997 on seven Chinese entities for helping Iran's chemical weapons programs and threatened sanctions in 1996 after China assisted Pakistan's nuclear weapons program with ring magnets—technology used in making fuel for nuclear weapons. "We must continue to monitor China's activities closely," the statement said. But its method of continuing "to work with China toward a common understanding on effective export control policies and to strengthen existing national export control systems" has so far produced no results.

THE LIBYAN CONNECTION

The White House claimed that passing the China trade legislation and getting China membership in the WTO "will advance our national interest" by bringing Beijing into the mainstream and "encouraging respect" for international standards.

But the White House propaganda machine suffered a major setback on that very ground when fresh intelligence reports linked China to a new missile technology transfer, this time to Libya. The spinmeisters at the White House Trade Relations Working Group came up with a new way to explain away this latest violation of China's arms sales promises. China, you see, never promised not to sell missiles and technology to Libya, only to Pakistan and Iran. Technically, the working group could argue, Libya—not to mention North Korea—was not covered by the Chinese promises. So Beijing was not violating any agreement.

On March 2, 2000, a Pentagon intelligence agency again dispatched a highly classified cable to the most senior U.S. government national security and military officials. The report, based on sensitive information, stated that China was providing assistance to Libya's long-range missile program.

The intelligence agency identified the Libyan company involved in the Chinese missile technology transfer as Libtec International, which had been dealing with the state-run China Precision Machinery Import-Export Corporation (CPMIEC) since at least May 1999. The report stated that Libtec was probably "acting as a middleman between Libya's missile research and development program, the Al-Fatah project, and CPMIEC."

"In late February 2000," the report continued, "Libtec's Izz-al-din M. Abu Ghalya updated Su Bichun (aka Stephanie Su), director of CPMIEC's 5th Department, regarding: financial information [he] previously provided in mid-May 1999. Abu Ghalya amended his banking address concerning an unspecified transaction" related to his Credit Suisse bank account in Geneva.

"Libtec is a science and technology projects consultant and an import/export firm in Tripoli," the report noted. Abu Ghalya was a new figure on the CIA's weapons proliferation watch list and might be linked to Libya's nuclear program. "The scope of the Libtec-CPMIEC cooperation is unclear," the report said, adding that it may be related to "dual-use technology." The intelligence report suggested that the Libyan company was "a middleman between Al-Fatah and CPMIEC, whose cooperation has been by mutual consent, considered very sensitive and obscured by several banking entities, front companies and/or aliases."

The report was a smoking gun of Chinese duplicity in its dealings with the United States. China insists it is not helping rogue states build nuclear, chemical, and biological weapons and missile delivery systems. But the intelligence reports speak for themselves.

Libya is one of seven nations designated by the American government as a state-sponsor of international terrorism. Under the mercurial dictator Mu'ammar Gadhafi, the oil-rich nation has been responsible for notorious terrorist acts, most notably the 1988 bombing of Pan Am Flight 103 over Lockerbie, Scotland.

The Pentagon published its first and only report on international weapons proliferation in 1996. It stated that Libya is a major threat and that Gadhafi has shown he is willing and able to use chemical weapons and missiles against his enemies. And who are those enemies? "Libya sees the United States as its primary external threat," the report said. "Libya has a long history of subverting and destabilizing Arab and African nations by supporting coups, funding and training opposition forces and guerrilla groups, and plotting the assassinations of foreign leaders. Gadhafi has invaded, occupied, and/or claimed territory in all of Libya's neighbors except Egypt. He has at times supported foreign Islamic extremists, and he has frequently criticized Arab governments that have attempted to open dialogue with Israel."

The Libyan weapons program in 1996 was spending "several hundred million dollars" annually on its unconventional weapons and missiles, mostly in seeking foreign technology. Libya also is developing a "tactical" missile.

In early 2000 the Clinton-Gore defense secretary, William Cohen, reported, almost casually, that "Libya has chemical capabilities and is trying to buy long-range missiles." The information was a bombshell and highlighted the growing long-range missile threat. Why does Gadhafi want them? Cohen said Libya and other rogue states like Iraq and Iran do not want the long-range systems for use in regional conflict. "They want long-range missiles to coerce and threaten us—the

North American and European parts of NATO," Cohen warned. Other officials said later that the secretary was referring to secret intelligence reports indicating contacts between Libyan officials and North Korea—a major missile supplier that has been marketing the 620-mile No Dong missile and the near intercontinental-range Taepo Dong.

Perhaps goaded by Cohen's comments about Libya, on April 11, 2000, a Chinese Foreign Ministry spokesman said China had agreed to resume talks with the United States on arms proliferation matters. Beijing had canceled the discussions to express its anger over NATO's accidental bombing of the Chinese embassy in Belgrade, Yugoslavia. During a visit to Beijing in March 2000, National Security Adviser Sandy Berger had asked the Chinese to resume the talks, but there had been no hint during his visit that they would comply. When they did agree to talk, Gary Samore, the White House's proliferation specialist, was taken completely by surprise.

Interestingly, U.S. intelligence reports revealed that in March 1999 an agreement was reached between the Libyans and CPMIEC, which is a subsidiary of China Aerospace, the state company that had been linked to Chinese campaign contributions to the 1996 Clinton-Gore reelection campaign. Chinese technicians had been linked to Libya's indigenous Al-Fatah program as early as June 1998—the same month Clinton received assurances from Chinese President Jiang that China would not transfer missile know-how.

The China-Libya missile connection was a new proliferation danger. No mention of Libya was made in the CIA's semiannual report covering the first half of 1999. But the evidence of increased Libyan missile development began showing up late in 1999. On December 23 the intelligence community provided more bad news to policymakers. Intercepted conversations between Libya and China revealed that China was planning to sell a hypersonic wind tunnel to Tripoli's missile program. The wind tunnel is one of the most important components for designing missiles, since it shows how a missile in flight will withstand extreme pressures during launch. The intercepts also revealed that the Libyans were sending missile technicians to China. And the National

Imagery and Mapping Agency, which analyzes and reports on spy satellite photographs, reported that Libyans were enlarging a missile test facility as part of the development program.

In November 1999 British authorities intercepted a shipment of Scud missile components bound for Libya. The components were believed to have originated in North Korea and were labeled as having been sent from a Taiwan company—typical of a "false flag" operation designed to mask the real shippers. On April 12, 2000, Swiss authorities announced that they had arrested a Taiwanese businessman who was charged with attempting to smuggle Scud missile components to Libya.

Scuds can't hit the United States, but according to a congressional panel on missile threats headed by former Defense Secretary Donald Rumsfeld, Gadhafi warned his enemies in a 1990 speech: "If they know that you have a deterrent force capable of hitting the United States, they would not be able to hit you. If we had possessed a deterrent— missiles that could reach New York—we would have hit it at the same moment [as the 1986 U.S. air strike on Libya]. Consequently, we should build this force so that they and others will no longer think about an attack." Again, in 1995, he stated: "As things stand today I would attack every place from where aggression against Libya was being planned. I would even be prepared to hit Naples where there is a NATO base."

Gadhafi is not alone in the desire to launch missile attacks on the United States. In 1990 Abul Abbas, head of the Palestine Liberation Front, made similar remarks: "Revenge takes forty years; if not my son, then the son of my son will kill you. Some day, we will have missiles that can reach New York.... I would love to be able to reach the American shore, but this is very difficult.... Some day an Arab country will have ballistic missiles. Some day an Arab country will have a nuclear bomb. It is better for the United States and for Israel to reach peace with the Palestinians before that day."

On April 13, 2000, the day the China-Libya missile cooperation was identified, Secretary of State Madeleine Albright was testifying before

Congress and was asked about the front-page *Washington Times* article by this author.

"Libya possesses 300-kilometer-range Scud missiles and is actively pursuing acquisition and development of even longer-range systems," Albright told the Senate Appropriations Subcommittee on Foreign Operations. "The U.S. views Libya's efforts... as a serious threat to the region and our nonproliferation interests, and we have engaged in a number of ways in extensive efforts to impede the proliferation of missile equipment and technology to Libya." Of the newspaper report, Albright said, "We take all these reports seriously, and we have raised our concerns with the Chinese, and we are concerned about this." The concerns fell on deaf ears in Beijing. On June 9, 2000, the National Security Agency director reported that the head of Libya's Al-Fatah missile program was planning to visit Beijing's University of Aeronautics and Astronautics in the next few weeks. The university is the premier center for training missile engineers and technicians.

At the Chinese embassy, spokesman Zhang Yuanyuan quipped that he did not want to comment on an intelligence report "given what the CIA has just said about trying to locate a target in Yugoslavia." He was referring sarcastically to the CIA's public admission that it had fired an employee over the errant bombing of China's embassy in Belgrade. The CIA said its outdated maps had identified the building as a Yugoslav military procurement office. Zhang defended China's cooperation in building a railroad in Libya as one of several cooperative programs but said he was not aware of missile-related support from China.

Pentagon spokesman Kenneth Bacon said Libya's arsenal of short-range missiles was aging and as a result Tripoli has "made no secret of the fact that they would like to build longer-range missiles" capable of hitting targets 620 miles away from the North African country. "They do not have the indigenous technical capability, so they have been trying to work with other countries in the world in order to gain that capability," he admitted. But he would not say if China was helping the Libyans; he said only that the support was coming from nations in Asia. Asked if the

Chinese missile support violated China's stated promise to adhere to the guidelines of the MTCR, Bacon said China is not part of the export control regime but has promised not to transport entire missile systems. State Department spokesman James Rubin then said the U.S. government had notified the Chinese government about reports of its cooperation with the Libyan missile program. "We have engaged them about the issue of missile technology and equipment," he said, noting that U.S. worries about the Chinese missile program are "long-standing" and that Chinese leaders were informed about the role of state-run companies in the missile trade. Echoing the White House statement produced by the trade working group, Rubin added, "We will continue to work with China to bring its policies better in line with international norms."

Yet China's record when it comes to its promises is one of lies and deception. The secret listing of its proliferation activities is long. It includes transfers of weapons-of-mass-destruction technology and components, including ballistic and cruise missile know-how, to a host of rogue states—states the Clinton-Gore administration had relabeled as "states of concern" in an apparent effort to avoid offending them. The sales included transfers of weapons technology and components to Libya, Iran, North Korea, Syria, and Pakistan.

By July 2000, U.S. intelligence reports showed that the Chinese were continuing to secretly supply Pakistan with missile-related goods, namely, specialty steel, guidance systems, and technical expertise. When U.S. officials brought up the intelligence in meetings with representatives of Communist China, the Chinese would deny the reports.

The Select House Committee that investigated China's technology acquisition and spying warned that China's record of selling arms around the world has compounded the danger. "The PRC is one of the world's leading proliferators of weapons technologies," the report said. "Concerns about the impact of the PRC's thefts of U.S. thermonuclear warhead design information, therefore, include the possible proliferation of the world's most sophisticated nuclear weapons technology to nations hostile to the United States."

For the United States, there can be no greater danger than having its most sophisticated strategic nuclear weapons technology end up in the hands of nations like North Korea, Iran, and Libya.

CHAPTER SEVEN

Kindred Spirit

> *"Knowledge of the enemy's dispositions can only be obtained from other men."*
>
> —Sun Tzu

wo FBI agents sat in Notra Trulock's town house in Falls Church, Virginia, just outside of Washington, D.C. The tone of their questioning was hostile. "Do you have classified information in the house?" one of them asked. For the former Energy Department counterintelligence chief, it was the ultimate insult. Trulock was being accused of disclosing classified information improperly in a manuscript he had submitted to the CIA for publication in its journal, *Studies in Intelligence.* Instead of publishing it, the CIA had referred it to the FBI for investigation—which is why the agents were now in Trulock's home on this hot Friday evening, July 14, 2000. When Trulock asked to see a search warrant, the agents said they didn't need one, since they claimed to have the permission of the town house's owner, Trulock's friend Linda Conrad, who worked in the Energy Department's intelligence office. At one point during the raid, one of the agents went into a bedroom, started up a desktop computer used by Trulock, and downloaded the contents of its hard drive to a disk. The agents continued probing Trulock for over an hour, asking accusatory questions about classified information. He told them the truth: He had none.

"Screwed, blued, and tattooed," Trulock would later describe the interrogation, which came only days after his abrupt dismissal from the defense contractor TRW, Inc., a move Trulock is convinced was the work of political enemies. "This is what happens to whistle-blowers who speak truth to power in the Clinton administration," he told me.

In truth, Trulock had submitted the manuscript the FBI was now looking for to the Energy Department for security review, but the department had declined even to look at it.

The FBI raid on Trulock's house was harassment for his role in exposing one of the most damaging espionage cases in American history. He had uncovered Chinese espionage in the heart of the U.S. nuclear weapons complex. Chinese spies had scored a major coup; they had walked off with information on how to build Chinese versions of every warhead in the American nuclear arsenal. And the spying continues today.

The Trulock investigation was authorized by FBI Director Louis Freeh in consultation with Energy Secretary Bill Richardson, one of Bill Clinton's closest advisers. Trulock suspected that they singled him out because he had just published a shorter version of the manuscript as an article for *National Review* magazine. The article was highly critical of the Clinton-Gore administration's utter failure to aggressively pursue Chinese spying.

The administration wasn't interested in catching spies. Its highest priority was repressing its critics, especially those in American intelligence who had exposed the deception and politicization within the U.S. national security community under Bill Clinton. Trulock had been a major target ever since he quit the Energy Department after being pressured into a meaningless job and finally having his intelligence judgments questioned by an inspector general report that went to great lengths to cover up the entire Chinese espionage debacle.

The story began eighteen years earlier.

*   *   *   *

The telephone rang at the home of Gwo Bao Min, a former nuclear weapons engineer at Lawrence Livermore National Laboratory. It was December 2, 1982. The caller was Wen Ho Lee, another scientist who designed nuclear weapons at a second Department of Energy nuclear weapons laboratory in Los Alamos, New Mexico. Min was in trouble. He had been fired from his job at Livermore under suspicion of having passed nuclear weapons secrets to China. The conversation between Min and Lee was intercepted by the FBI, which was investigating Min. Lee guessed it must have been someone in China who revealed Min's identity to the FBI, and he promised Min he would uncover the informant. Although Min was never prosecuted and today lives in northern California, the exchange between Lee and Min would be at the heart of the most damaging espionage case in U.S. history, more damaging to American national security than the case involving Julius and Ethel Rosenberg, who passed nuclear secrets to Moscow in the early years of the Cold War. China had stolen the keys to unlocking the secrets of America's nuclear arsenal.

The first hints about the extent of the danger came on September 25, 1992, when the ground shook beneath the Chinese nuclear weapons test site about 120 miles north of Lop Nur, a town in the remote northwestern province of Xinjiang. The explosion was the first successful test of a small, compact warhead similar in design to the U.S. W-88. The fact that China had succeeded in building so small a warhead so quickly shocked many officials inside the U.S. intelligence community.

A spy working secretly in China for U.S. intelligence had revealed important details about the test. In short, China had made a quantum leap in the killing power of its nuclear forces. The spy revealed that during the 1992 test the Chinese had set off a relatively small 150-kiloton explosion using a special oval-shaped core. The shape of the core was the tip-off to analysts that China had discovered one of the most important secrets about American nuclear weapons.

And the Chinese had succeeded in doing so through espionage. The spying, which occurred under several earlier administrations, is continuing today. But the magnitude of the problem was kept secret and only became public in the late 1990s. The reaction to the espionage— or, really, the lack of a response—was the result of a pro-China policy that caused serious damage to U.S. national security interests. The inaction sent a signal to any would-be nuclear power: American nuclear secrets are up for grabs. Under the so-called "engagement" policy of President Bill Clinton, Chinese spying was ignored, minimized, and ultimately covered up. Nothing would be allowed to interfere with the deliberate policy of pretending China poses no threat to the United States. The story of how Chinese nuclear spies stole U.S. nuclear warhead secrets is about the failure of the United States government to protect its long-term national security interests.

China today is engaged in a major strategic nuclear weapons buildup. It is a buildup targeted at a single nation: the United States. Strategically, it includes two new road-mobile intercontinental ballistic missiles, the Dong Feng-31 and the Dong Feng-41; at least four new strategic nuclear missile submarines; and a host of exotic high-technology weapons including lasers capable of shooting down or blinding satellites. It also includes computer-based information warfare for launching crippling attacks on everything from electrical power to the computer networks used to keep commercial aircraft flying safely.

DECODING THE BOMB

Intelligence analysts working at the Department of Energy's Los Alamos National Laboratory wrote a classified analysis of the 1992 Chinese explosion that said the Chinese nuclear device tested near Lop Nur was shaped differently from any other known Chinese warhead. The device looked like an American warhead, and the scientists were concerned that the Chinese had obtained strategic secrets from the United States.

In April 1995 the Los Alamos analysts sent their classified memorandum to Notra Trulock, a political scientist by training who had worked at Los Alamos and who was director of intelligence for the Department of Energy. Four years later, Trulock would be hounded out of the department for his efforts to expose Chinese nuclear spying. No good deed goes unpunished, as they say. He had dared to challenge the pro-China policies of Bill Clinton. He had spoken bluntly about the Chinese strategic nuclear threat to the United States. He had revealed China's decades of nuclear-related espionage, and that the spying continues today.

Chinese espionage efforts against the weapons laboratories were not new to security officials. "But we were beginning to uncover the outlines of a broad and very successful Chinese intelligence assault against our nuclear weapons laboratories," Trulock told me. "These labs are the repositories of the secrets underlying the U.S. nuclear deterrent, accumulated through decades of U.S. nuclear weapons experience at the cost of billions of dollars." Trulock explained that he had tried to alert U.S. government officials ranging from his immediate superiors at the Department of Energy all the way to White House National Security Adviser Sandy Berger. Their responses were always "appropriate," but their actions never matched their expressions of concern. The Clinton-Gore administration viewed Chinese nuclear spying as a mere inconvenience, since the only strategy was to "engage" China's communist leaders—a policy that was ridiculed by China's communist leaders as the abject weakness of a decaying Western society.

"If our assessments of their perspective on their deterrent in the mid-'80s were correct, I think the Chinese now are moving much closer to having what they consider to be a credible deterrent," Trulock concluded. "And if they think the credibility of their deterrent is solid again, then that to me seems to open up a lot of other options for them, like Taiwan. The whole idea behind their deterrent is to keep us from intervening in the achievement of China's regional objectives."

Energy Department intelligence analysts learned that China had acquired U.S. secrets on at least seven of America's most modern thermonuclear warheads. The damage was known to key officials in the Clinton White House, the CIA, and the Pentagon, but the information was kept hidden from the American people to protect the Clinton-Gore policy of engagement.

It took a special congressional committee, one formed in 1998 to investigate Chinese acquisition of U.S. missile technology, to bring the story into public view. The Clinton-Gore administration fought the committee for five months, trying to prevent the release of classified intelligence information that exposed Chinese espionage, but in the spring of 1999 the committee's report was finally made public.

"The credentials of the scientists conducting the assessment, the nature of the evidence, and the quality of the technical judgments made for a compelling case," Trulock said. "Some of the nation's most experienced nuclear scientists participated in this work. Their contributions have never been recognized or acknowledged by their government."

The CIA, supposedly the nation's premier intelligence service, was "politicized" in the debate over Chinese spying. Its analysts tried hard to play down, minimize, and ignore the damage caused by the spying. The CIA even insisted that what the Chinese obtained by espionage could have been obtained in other ways, such as from leaks of classified information or from public documents.

But Notra Trulock gave me an inside account of the Chinese espionage case that revealed otherwise. The real issue was not whether a damaging spy scandal had occurred, but how the White House managed to contain the political fallout so that it touched anyone but the administration. The White House went into its "war room" media damage control mode. James Kennedy, the White House lawyer who handled the president's impeachment, was now put on the China spying story. The spin: Chinese spying was not our fault; it all happened in the 1980s. To influence news reporters and their coverage, he emphasized that the story was "old news," and if anyone were to blame, it would be the Republicans who were in power in the 1980s. When the Select Committee's bipartisan report was finally made public, the administration privately—and falsely—warned the major television networks that the report did not reflect the version based on classified information. If the media "went hard" with the story, the White House promised it had the means to discredit the report. So there was no story, or, at least, very little criticism of the Clinton-Gore administration.

"As the director of DOE [Department of Energy] intelligence, I was the talking head for the DOE group and bore most of the brunt of these attacks," Trulock recalled. "To his credit, Energy Secretary Bill Richardson did present me with a $10,000 (before taxes) bonus, but this didn't offset the fact that I had been demoted, relegated to a meaningless job, and eventually forced out of the department. Routine stuff for whistleblowers in this administration. But I also came under media fire of the type normally reserved for Ken Starr or someone involved in the president's public scandals. I read that I was a 'dangerous demagogue,' a 'great imposter,' 'obsessed,' that my 'style' was abrasive, and a host of other epithets. Reporters attributed a variety of motives to explain my involvement in this case, including imputations of racism and xeno- phobia. This was pretty heavy stuff for someone who has spent most of his career trying to stay out of the public eye. Of course, most of these allegations came from the very officials within DOE and the White House responsible for the cover-ups and stonewalling of the Congress and who had fought so hard to kill any meaningful security reform at the labs. Many of these were the perpetuators, if not the creators, of the very security lapses that made Chinese espionage possible in the first place."

TARGET: NUCLEAR ARMS

A classified U.S. intelligence report produced in late 1998 that I obtained revealed that the Department of Energy is under a major intelligence and espionage attack from a range of foreign intelligence services, not just the Chinese. The report, titled "Foreign Collection Against the Department of Energy: The Threat to U.S. Weapons and Technology," was stamped "Secret" and restricted from distribution to all foreign gov- ernments. According to the classified document, "The U.S. Department of Energy is under attack by foreign collectors—intelligence officers, as well as scientists, academics, engineers, and businessmen—who are aggressively targeting DOE nuclear, sensitive and proprietary, and unclassified information. The losses are extensive and include highly classified nuclear weapons design information to the Chinese."

The intelligence assessment was produced by the National Counter- intelligence Center, a relatively new agency based at CIA headquarters in Langley, Virginia. The center includes counterintelligence special- ists from various agencies charged with thwarting the activities of foreign spies. Officials from the CIA, DOE, FBI, the National Security Agency, and the Department of Defense are part of it. The secret report stated that China, Russia, and India "pose the most immediate threat and are dedicating extensive resources in the United States and abroad to gain knowledge of DOE information." The report made clear that the DOE facilities were seemingly oblivious to the threat. "DOE records show that over 250 known or suspected intelligence officers from 27 countries have visited or been assigned to DOE facilities in recent years." The report also noted that foreign intelligence agencies have engaged in "cyber" information collection—eliciting intelligence from e-mail communications and therefore allowing foreign spies to gain information "freely and repeatedly." The main target of the spying was the Department of Energy's primary product: nuclear weapons information. "Foreign collectors of nuclear information are interested in all facets of U.S. capabilities and past experience in the design of nuclear explosive devices," the report stated. "While the modern U.S. stockpile has tended to coalesce around a fairly narrow set of technical approaches to weapons design, the vast storehouse of information contained in the storage vaults and in the minds of personnel involved in all phases of the U.S. program represents a lucrative target for collectors."

The Energy Department is in charge of all aspects of developing and maintaining nuclear weapons. Its scientists and engineers lead the world in breakthrough research in high-energy physics, energy sciences, technology, superconducting material, accelerator technology, materials sciences, and environmental sciences. It has thirty-five sites around the United States, and the sensitivity of its work ranges from ultrasecret Special Access Programs to sensitive research and proprietary work with U.S. corporations. There are 10,500 DOE federal workers and another 120,000 contractors and support personnel. A total of 66,000 people hold "Q" level security clearances, giving them access to top secret data on the design, manufacture, or use of nuclear weapons.

Under the Clinton-Gore administration, foreign visitors were welcomed to this secret-rich environment with little concern for the security of U.S. nuclear weapons data. According to the classified intelligence report, foreign visitors from countries seeking nuclear arms data jumped more than 200 percent from the mid-1980s to the mid-1990s. In 1998 alone, some 25,000 foreign scientists visited or were assigned to Energy Department facilities. In one case in 1997, Russia's intelligence service ordered an agent working inside a U.S. weapons laboratory to find out about counterintelligence and security procedures, "including those used to screen and investigate foreign visitors and clear personnel for security clearances," the report stated.

The security at the Energy facilities was bad, and the department's ability to counter foreign spies was almost nonexistent. Trulock told me that when he took over Energy intelligence, counterintelligence was extremely poor. "Underfunded, understaffed, internecine warfare," he said. "The field counterintelligence people loathed and despised headquarters. Counterintelligence itself was starved. I thought it was a mess."

The intelligence report also highlighted the problem. The DOE counterspy program "has been undermined by a series of structural and systemic problems, including a lack of programmatic accountability and ineffectual centralized control over CI [counterintelligence] resources in the field," the report said. "These problems stymied efforts to assess, understand, and reduce the foreign intelligence threat."

The report outlined how China had scored major espionage coups. "During the period 1984 to 1988, China obtained through espionage the design information on a current U.S. warhead," the report said, referring to the W-88. "To obtain this information, the United States conducted tens of nuclear tests. Once obtained, the Chinese were able to accelerate their research and advance their nuclear weapons program well beyond indigenous capabilities."

China's methodology is unique. "Rather than send its intelligence officers out to recruit knowledgeable sources at facilities such as the national laboratories, China prefers to exploit over time the natural scientist-to-scientist relationships," the report said. "Chinese scientists nurture relationships with national laboratory counterparts, issuing invitations for them to travel to laboratories and conferences in China."

China's main intelligence service, the Ministry of State Security, or MSS, "encourages U.S. scientists to visit China," the report said, "expediting arrangements to enable Chinese experts to assess and develop these contacts. During the visit, the U.S. target is introduced to several senior officials and receives VIP treatment. The Chinese services' involvement is often not exposed and frequently will not lead to official recruitment of the individual, even though valuable information is obtained."

In addition, China is one of several nations that engage in electronic eavesdropping to obtain nuclear weapons information. China's electronic spies, along with those of Taiwan, France, India, Israel, Pakistan, and Russia, "are known to intercept U.S. satellite communications and in many cases have extensive capabilities to intercept other communications." The report noted that Russia has used its large eavesdropping facility in Lourdes, Cuba, to gain valuable nuclear weapons testing and research data from spying on the communications of Westinghouse and Varian corporations. From Varian's electronic communications, Moscow learned that technology transfers from the United States to China, including Varian equipment, were "being used by China for the development of nuclear power plants and nuclear weapons."

An appendix to the intelligence report, "Foreign Country Threats… Unique Approaches, Unique Requirements," summarizes the Chinese espionage threat:

China

China represents an acute intelligence threat to DOE. It conducts a "full court press" consisting of massive numbers of collectors of all kinds, in the United States, in China and elsewhere abroad. The Chinese have successfully employed a combination of open-source collection, all forms of cyberconnections, elicitation, and espionage to obtain information needed to advance their weapons program. China is highly reliant on many different types of technical specialists, scientists, and engineers. China is an advanced nuclear power, yet its nuclear stockpile is deteriorating. As such, China has specifically targeted DOE for the collection of technical intelligence related to the design of nuclear weapons and seeks information relating to the stockpile stewardship and reliability. This effort has been very successful, and Beijing's exploitation of U.S. national laboratories has substantially aided its nuclear weapons program (S/NF).

The Chinese intelligence-gathering assault on Los Alamos was relentless. In late 1998 and early 1999, a security analyst at the U.S. National Security Agency, which conducts electronic eavesdropping, discovered that Chinese computer hackers had stolen a large quantity of sensitive yet unclassified information. Using several American university computer gateways, the Chinese hackers downloaded the documents—whose paper equivalent would have been three-foot-high stack, and many of which contained the word "nuclear"—from a Los Alamos File Transfer Protocol (FTP) site on the Internet. The American analyst tracked the hackers to a Chinese government research institute in Beijing. It was a rare catch of government-sponsored computer intelligence activity.

Inside the Clinton-Gore administration, the whistle had been blown on damaging Chinese nuclear espionage. But not a single word about the activities was ever made public until many months later. The reason was simple. The president and his national security advisers covered up the damaging spy activities in an attempt to avoid complicating the engagement policy with Beijing. Under engagement, the administration was doing everything it could to help China modernize. The idea was that if we helped the Chinese, they would become friends of the United States. Instead, the Chinese gathered America's nuclear secrets and have become a more threatening regional and world power.

THE HANDBOOK FOR CHINESE SPIES

China's technology spying was also revealed in a Chinese government book obtained by this author. The 1991 publication was not a classified Chinese document, but its distribution was restricted. A copy of the book was obtained by the Defense Department and translated by the U.S. government. Its contents reveal the massive scope of the Chinese spying effort, which is focused primarily on the United States. The book is a guide for Chinese foreign technology spies who are tasked specifically with going after defense information and intelligence. It is called *Sources and Techniques of Obtaining National Defense Science and Technology Intelligence*, by Huo Zhongwen and Wang Zongxiao. The authors are teachers of intelligence at the China National Defense, Science, and Technology Information Center (DSTIC) in Beijing. This is the arm of the Chinese government that coordinates the sharing of technology information gathered abroad. The book is a one-stop shopping guide revealing China's vast storehouse of Western, and mainly

United States, defense technology and where to get it. The center is a key arm of the People's Liberation Army.

The authors explain that there is a difference between information and intelligence. "Intelligence is knowledge that is produced from activated information and targeted toward specific problems," they state.

As for the method of gathering information to be converted into intelligence, Huo and Wang encapsulate the Chinese way of spying: "Consider information piece by piece; place an excessive, one-sided emphasis on the absolute amount of the information collected; gauge the quality of collection work solely on the basis of the amount of information collected."

The book on defense technology spying is important because it reveals the lie propagated by Beijing that China's nuclear weapons development was based on indigenous development. It alarmed some Pentagon officials because of the massive scope of Chinese intelligence gathering. "Over 80 percent of all consumer requirements can be satisfied by overt information," the book states. The remaining 20 percent will be gathered through illicit means. "Generally speaking... classified information has the most intelligence."

"A common saying has it that there are no walls which completely block the wind, nor is absolute secrecy achievable," the book says, "and invariably there will be numerous open situations in which things are revealed, either in tangible or intangible form. By picking here and there among the vast amount of public materials and accumulating information a drop at a time, often it is possible to basically reveal the outlines of some secret intelligence, and this is particularly true in the case of Western countries. Through probability analysis, in foreign countries it is believed that 80 percent or more of intelligence can be gotten through public materials."

The book goes on to explain how "negligence" on the part of security review personnel often allows secrets to be made public inadvertently. A case in point: In the late 1970s a reporter published nuclear weapons secrets from Los Alamos that were thought to have been less sensitive nuclear rocket propulsion material. The Energy Department, according to the book, had mistakenly released the nuclear weapons material among an estimated 19,400 documents that should have remained secret, and the reporter published it in a 1979 article in *Progressive* magazine. "This incident tells us that, on one hand, absolute secrecy is not attainable, while on the other hand, there is a random element involved in the discovery of secret intelligence sources, and to turn this randomness into inevitability, it is necessary that there be those who monitor some sectors and areas with regularity and vigilance...."

The book lists an introduction to "national defense intelligence sources and materials" that includes:

- Publications of the U.S. Congress, such as committee reports and testimony, as well as the "big three" reports from the Pentagon to Congress: the Defense Department's annual report to Congress, its research, development, and acquisition report, and the annual military posture statement.
- Reports from the National Defense Technical Information Center and the National Technical Information Service. Science and technology information centers throughout China have been purchasing thousands of army, air force, and navy technology reports from these outlets since the 1960s.
- National Aeronautics and Space Administration (NASA) reports. China's DSTIC "keeps a full set of openly published NASA reports," numbering over one million documents.
- Reports from the American Institute of Aeronautics and Astronautics. The Chinese have gathered valuable intelligence from this nongovernmental academic group and its conferences and papers. Its products are "a major source" of missile and space flight data for China, and DSTIC boasts the only complete set of its documents.

The book also lists the Department of Energy as a key intelligence collection target for Chinese spies. "DOE reports come from several thousands of domestic sources, but the main ones are the department's eight main operations offices, its five main energy technology centers, its 18 large-scale laboratories, and their contractors," it states. "DOE reports are one of the four main categories of U.S. reports. They touch on every aspect of energy research and construction.... Actual experience proves that DOE reports are an important source of intelligence for our country's science and technology personnel engaged in energy research and construction. Besides this, DOE reports include a large number which are concerned with research into nuclear energy, and which involve dual military-civilian uses. Examples are reactors of various types (including those used on ships); nuclear power systems used in space; research, development, testing, and production of nuclear weapons; laser nuclear fusion technology; isotope separation technology; production and control of nuclear material; nuclear material safety issues; personnel security issues; secret information security issues; export control issues; nuclear weapons control issues; nuclear power stations, etc."

The authors conclude that Chinese intelligence officers pay "a great deal of attention" to these reports because "it is a source of intelligence with great value."

Just how great was not known until several years after the publication of the Chinese spying manual.

THE 20 PERCENT SOLUTION

The spying manual teaches Chinese intelligence operatives that not all of their efforts will involve searching Pentagon and U.S. government databases for technology secrets. Espionage is still necessary. "It is also necessary to stress that there is still 20 percent or less of our intelligence that must come through the collection of information using special means, such as reconnaissance satellites, electronic eavesdropping, and the activities of special agents purchasing or stealing, etc.," the authors state. One of the methods that would prove to be the most useful in building China's strategic nuclear arsenal is outlined in the book as "person-to-person exchange," where valuable information can be gained through personal contacts and meetings and discussions between individuals. "This is the procedure commonly used for collecting verbal information, but it is not limited to verbal communications. Participation in consultative activities is also a person-to-person exchange procedure for collecting information."

Such "person-to-person exchange" between American and Chinese scientists was pinpointed by Notra Trulock and his subordinates at DOE intelligence as a major source of the problem, one that the Clinton-Gore administration refused to recognize.

"This is a story of cover-ups, denials, disbelief, complacency, bungling, and gross ineptitude," Trulock told me in recounting the affair. "At several junctures along the way, administration and laboratory officials either refused to take steps to mitigate the potential damage from Chinese espionage or just never got around to dealing with the issue."

The spying has to be put into context. The Clinton White House was under fire over its policies that allowed China to improve the reliability of its strategic nuclear missiles through loosened export controls on satellites. And of course the administration was struggling to contain the political damage caused by disclosures about covert Chinese money that flowed into Democratic Party coffers during the 1996 reelection campaign. Trulock said he did not find "direct evidence" of a linkage between Chinagate scandals and the mishandling of the Chinese nuclear spying. "But it was always clear," he said, "that administration officials would not permit evidence of Chinese espionage to prevent them from using the national labs as bait to engage the Chinese in a number of administration policy initiatives. The FBI repeatedly warned DOE, lab, and National Security Council officials that the continued presence of large numbers of Chinese scientists at the national labs represented a significant risk to the protection of our nuclear secrets. But engagement was always more important than security or effective counterintelligence." Trulock believes nothing has changed despite the revelations about Chinese nuclear weapons espionage and China's extremely damaging acquisition of data on every deployed U.S. nuclear weapon, as well as some that were never deployed.

Trulock said the Clinton-Gore administration repeatedly ignored warnings that the end of the Cold War brought new dangers to nuclear secrets from foreign intelligence services. Some Energy officials understood the dangers of losing nuclear weapons data to foreign powers. "But these officials were pretty much driven out of the department by 1995 or left in 1996; their successors were clueless about the dictates of national security and even less comprehending of intelligence and counterintelligence," he said. "When I first became responsible for counterintelligence about this time [early 1995], the program was in a state of total disarray throughout the complex. Some modest efforts had been made to upgrade the program late in the Bush administration, but the newly arrived Clinton political appointees had brought these to a halt." FBI agents were pushed out, and counterintelligence funding was cut. "No money, a staff that lacked any direct counterintelligence experience and seemed indifferent to the hostile intelligence threat, and a reporting chain of command that cared more about hallway maintenance than foreign counterintelligence threats were hardly indicative of a serious approach to counterintelligence," Trulock said. "Up to this time, DOE political appointees were clearly signaling, by virtue of funding priorities and policies, that they viewed counterintelligence as a waste of time and resources. In short, the climate for espionage was ideal."

Trulock noted that the full-scale Chinese intelligence attack on U.S. nuclear weapons secrets became clear in the mid-1990s. But efforts to pursue spying were blocked by lab officials or Energy bureaucrats. Energy officials openly discouraged security, and later, when Chinese nuclear espionage became too blatant to ignore, senior Energy officials told Trulock that pursuing the spies "would destroy the reputations of the labs." When Trulock sought to provide a briefing to the congressional intelligence oversight committees, Deputy Energy Secretary Elizabeth Moler ordered him to keep Congress in the dark, Trulock claimed. "The only reason she offered was that she thought the Hill just wanted to hurt the president on his China policy," Trulock said.

Chinese nuclear forces lag behind American and Russian arsenals and are so much smaller in number—currently about twenty-four ICBMs—that many in the Clinton-Gore administration attempted with some success to label the nuclear threat insignificant. With the quality of their nuclear force at 1950s and 1960s levels, China's communist leaders realized in the 1980s that they needed to modernize or be left with a strategic nuclear force with little credibility.

China viewed America's deployment in the 1980s of the new Peace-keeper ICBM and the Trident D-5 submarine-launched ballistic missile as threats to its national security. "China's military writings and planning documents from the 1980s lay out strategic force modernization objectives clearly: In the future, China would develop a modern nuclear-missile force that would be survivable, accurate, lethal, and able to penetrate any potential enemy's ballistic missile defenses," Trulock said. China would field mobile missiles on land and at sea and would develop more accurate and more lethal warheads. As Trulock put it, "a new generation of nuclear warheads" would allow Chinese missileers to replace the single warheads with multiple-warheads on individual missiles.

China's solution was to develop smaller, lighter, and more efficient strategic warheads. "Smaller warheads have a number of other advantages, including lower requirements for nuclear material that would impose less of a burden on China's nuclear industry," Trulock said. "For these and other reasons, the Chinese concluded that the development of smaller, lighter, but more efficient nuclear warheads would become a key priority during the next stage of China's nuclear development. Better missile accuracy and greater warhead efficiencies could offset reduced nuclear yields."

Chinese technology spies focused on the state of the art in U.S. nuclear warhead design, the W-88, which was developed for the Trident D-5 missile. Los Alamos National Laboratory, in the highlands of northern New Mexico, began the final design in 1984. "China's selection of the W-88 was somewhat surprising," Trulock recalled, "since its technical sophistication seemed far beyond China's capabilities." U.S. nuclear designs use more exotic features requiring different geometries and small dimensions. They require more difficult production, maintenance, and support. The U.S. scientists, however, were the best in the world at understanding the challenges and overcoming them. It cost billions of dollars to do so. To make one warhead work, at least six underground explosions were carried out and a thousand non-nuclear tests performed. The W-88 was built over ten to fifteen years with at least a dozen underground test blasts at the Nevada Test Site.

The biggest obstacle to China's nuclear program was the Cultural Revolution. The anarchy unleashed by Mao and the communist government set back China's nuclear development by several decades, leaving the country with nuclear warheads that were large, heavy, inaccurate, and reliant on making a five-megaton blast—the explosive power of five million tons of TNT. "These warheads are inadequate for the type of missile force China intended to construct," Trulock said. The Chinese would need at least a threefold reduction in the weight of their warheads to meet future missile throw weight capabilities. To achieve that reduction would require a path of development that would progress slowly from one stage to the next through research, experimentation, and live testing. The cost would be enormous and would not fit with the national policy of Beijing to seek economic modernization first and military modernization last.

The Chinese found an easier way. They stole the warhead design from the United States. According to Trulock, China had acquired most of the warhead technology it needed by 1988. U.S. weapons laboratories began some limited exchanges with Chinese nuclear officials in the late 1970s. The visits continued throughout the 1980s. Some lab officials became concerned after the Chinese revealed they knew the top secret cover names for various classified U.S. weapons projects and asked probing questions about them. "Although this aspect of the U.S.-Chinese exchanges was fairly well known in intelligence circles from the mid-1980s on, apparently no one saw fit to impose restrictions on the exchanges or to question how the Chinese might have acquired such information," Trulock said.

TIGER TRAP

The first major espionage coup against U.S. nuclear secrets was China's acquisition of information about the "enhanced radiation" explosive, known as the neutron bomb. The scientist who provided the Chinese with the secret to this warhead, known as the W-70, worked at Lawrence Livermore National Laboratory in California. He was known by the code name "Tiger Trap." It was a trap that was never set. Tiger Trap

traveled to China in 1979 and met with Chinese officials involved in nuclear weapons development. He is believed to have provided extremely
sensitive information that was useful in China's effort to build small
warheads. Intelligence officials familiar with the case said that he had
also been caught with sensitive documents. Yet he was never arrested.
Counterintelligence officials sought to "turn" Tiger Trap into a double
agent who would work secretly for the United States. But Tiger Trap
refused to cooperate.

Tiger Trap was identified by intelligence officials as Gwo Bao Min, a
Livermore engineer who was fired from the laboratory in 1981 under
suspicion of passing secrets about the neutron bomb to China. The case
was mentioned for the first time in public in May 1999 in the final
report of the House Select Committee that investigated Chinese missile and nuclear weapons acquisition. The reference was cryptic:

> The Select Committee received information about the U.S. Government's
> investigation of the PRC's theft of classified U.S. design information for
> the W-70 thermonuclear warhead. The W-70, which is an enhanced radi-
> ation nuclear warhead (or "neutron bomb"), also has elements that can
> be used for a strategic thermonuclear warhead. In 1996 the U.S. Intelli-
> gence Community reported that the PRC had successfully stolen classi-
> fied U.S. technology from a U.S. Nuclear Weapons Laboratory about the
> neutron bomb. This was not the first time the PRC had stolen classified
> U.S. information about the neutron bomb. In the late 1970s, the PRC
> stole design information on the U.S. W-70 warhead from Lawrence
> Livermore Laboratory. The U.S. Government first learned of this theft
> several months after it took place. The PRC subsequently tested a neu-
> tron bomb in 1988. The FBI developed a suspect in the earlier theft. The
> suspect worked at Lawrence Livermore National Laboratory, and had
> access to classified information including designs for a number of U.S.
> thermonuclear weapons in the U.S. stockpile at that time. In addition to
> design information about the W-70, this suspect may have provided to
> the PRC additional classified information about other U.S. weapons that
> could have significantly accelerated the PRC's nuclear weapons pro-
> gram. The Clinton administration has determined that further informa-

tion about these thefts cannot be publicly disclosed without affecting
national security or ongoing criminal investigations.

China conducted five tests of its stolen neutron bomb technology
from 1988 on. The tests proved the weapon reliable, and Beijing hinted
at its use against Taiwan.

"In retrospect, it appears that design details for the primary and secondary components of this warhead were compromised to the Chinese,"
Trulock said. "In the United States, this warhead was intended for
delivery by the Lance tactical missile system and was developed in at
least three different variations including the enhanced radiation
model. Chinese interest in the warhead was most likely fueled by the
expanding presence of Soviet motorized rifle divisions on the Sino-
Soviet border and the likelihood that the Chinese might have to conduct attacks on their own territory in order to repel a Soviet invasion."

While the Clinton-Gore administration successfully deflected criticism of China's spying by blaming Republicans and insisting that the
espionage occurred during the 1980s, the evidence obtained by U.S.
intelligence showed that China's spying was ongoing. The FBI learned
through one of its agents that China was still working on the neutron
bomb well into the late 1990s. In addition, Beijing's nuclear weapons
scientists were having trouble getting the device to work properly and
tasked the Ministry of State Security, the primary civilian intelligence
service, to come to the United States and find the solution. The targets
again were the U.S. nuclear weapons laboratories that developed the
neutron bomb. They returned in 1996 for more secrets and were probably successful, although no one was ever caught.

THE SPY

Gwo Bao Min was born in 1939 and graduated from Taiwan National
University in 1962. He earned a master's degree in engineering from
West Virginia University and a doctorate in aerospace engineering from
the University of Michigan. He became a naturalized U.S. citizen and
joined Lawrence Livermore in November 1975. Min was employed

in Livermore's D Division, which studies the military uses of nuclear weapons. His assignment included research on ballistic missile defense, which was a key target of Chinese intelligence collection.

Dan Stober, a reporter at the *San Jose Mercury News*, was the first to disclose Tiger Trap's identity, about a year after the oblique reference to it appeared in the Cox Committee report. Min had been mentioned in a document released during court proceedings against Wen Ho Lee, who was charged in December 1999 with fifty-nine counts of mishandling extremely valuable nuclear weapons information. "It was clear from the beginning of the... investigation that Wen Ho Lee was the prime suspect because of a phone call that he had made to the subject [of the neutron bomb case]," said Robert Vrooman, a former counterintelligence director at Los Alamos. Other officials said the phone conversation was incriminating because it indicated that both men were sympathetic to helping China. A report to the Energy Department counterintelligence office by Wackhenhut, a DOE security contractor, stated that Lee had learned through the news media that Min "was having problems with some men in China" and knew that Min, like himself, was from Taiwan, so "out of curiosity" he called him on the telephone. The document identified Min as "Ko Pau Ming," but officials later said it was a different transliteration of Gwo Bao Min. The report said that Lee told the investigators that the FBI "learned of this call," presumably through electronic eavesdropping, and questioned him about whether he had any connection to the case. J. J. Lee, an engineering professor at the University of Southern California, told the San Jose newspaper that he had known Min since they were classmates in Taiwan forty years earlier. "He got a raw deal," Lee said. "He wanted to wipe out his memory of all that bad stuff. It [the neutron bomb investigation] certainly ruined his life."

Min was allowed to resign from Lawrence Livermore on February 10, 1981. The FBI came close to negotiating a confession, but at the last minute an agreement fell through. Without the confession, FBI officials felt they had a weak case, even though they continued to investigate Min after he left the laboratory. That's how the conversation between Lee and Min was intercepted. Min today lives a quiet life in Danville,

California, where he runs Grand Monde Trading. He declined requests to be interviewed.

SPECIAL DELIVERY

China's acquisition of neutron bomb secrets was a major loss for the United States, and not just because the W-70 design is the basis for the unique enhanced radiation weapon. If the secondary device is set up properly, the W-70 can be an advanced hydrogen bomb.

Even so, Trulock and his analysts were more concerned about the compromise of classified details of the W-88 because it had the best of everything. It was small in size and represented the culmination of decades of experience in building nuclear warheads. Trulock's group thought that perhaps it was Tiger Trap who gave up the W-88 secrets. The files on the Tiger Trap case were devastating. Min had access to a vast amount of secret weapons data, including material on command and control information. But Min had left Livermore before Los Alamos had supplied the laboratory with the secret design information on the W-88 warhead. "The results of looking at the Tiger Trap files were that, yeah, he had access to a lot of information, a lot of command and control information that really had not been recognized before," Trulock said. "But W-88, no. He left before the W-88 stuff showed up. So that really didn't help to resolve it."

Two Los Alamos analysts, Robert M. Henson and Lawrence A. Booth, concluded after analyzing intelligence reports that there was enough information to suggest that the new Chinese warhead was a copy of the W-88.

The working group was already examining whether spies had stolen W-88 design secrets when the CIA presented more evidence. In July 1995, a packet of secret Chinese-language documents showed up at CIA headquarters by international courier, a present from a Chinese government official. The DHL delivery package contained an intelligence bombshell: hundreds of classified Chinese documents that could only have come from deep within the Chinese Communist government. One document contained classified data on the W-88, namely, three key dimensions and a diagram showing how various components of the four-foot-tall warhead were located inside its metal cowling.

A CIA officer from the agency's Directorate of Intelligence, the branch in charge of analysis, took details of the document to Department of Energy headquarters, saying the information was relevant to the DOE's investigation. Nevertheless, the CIA at first refused to allow Trulock and the Energy intelligence officials to see and analyze the document. The chief of the CIA directorate of operations himself insisted on maintaining tight control over all the material.

Then, in a classic case of intelligence agency bureaucratic turf battling, the CIA, which lacks expertise in nuclear weapons matters, secretly contacted a scientist at Los Alamos and asked him to provide the agency with the dimensions of the W-88 in order to compare them with the dimensions in the Chinese document. The scientist recognized the end run around Energy's intelligence shop and contacted Trulock in Washington.

Energy officials now demanded to see the complete translations of the Chinese documents. CIA Director John Deutch, a former deputy defense secretary, tried to block them, but eventually Trulock succeeded in gaining access to the key W-88 document. The document, written by a Chinese government institute involved in nuclear weapons, confirmed the lab officials' fears. "Everybody looks at it and says, 'They got the W-88,'" Trulock recalled.

The document, dated 1988, provided details of China's plans for developing nuclear warheads. It explained why the Chinese believed their nuclear deterrent was losing "credibility" and surveyed the nuclear arms programs of the "Big Five" nuclear powers—the United States, the Soviet Union, France, Britain, and China itself. Most of the nuclear weapons information, however, was about the U.S. arsenal.

In the document, the Chinese recognized that their strategic nuclear deterrent was vulnerable and was going to remain vulnerable unless steps were taken to modernize it. The way to reduce that vulnerability was to develop mobile missiles that could be hidden easily, moved rapidly on roads, and set up and fired with little or no warning time. It would require a major step forward from the 1950s-era, liquid-fueled missiles currently deployed. Chinese nuclear weapons designers recognized that the current warheads were too heavy and too big and would not fit on the mobile strategic missiles. The answer was to produce a small warhead, the best example of which was, according to the document, the W-88. "The W-88 was the benchmark for them," Trulock said.

The document then proceeded to give the dimensions of the W-88 warhead. It did not outline the composition of the materials, the fuel, or other data. The key detail in the twenty-page document was the shape of the atomic trigger used to set off the massive secondary explosion. It showed that the shape of the trigger was not spherical and that it was located inside the long nose cone's forward component. The Chinese also knew that the secondary device was spherical in shape and were able to identify the width of the casing that surrounded the trigger device to within a millimeter of the actual W-88 casing.

The document was bad news for the Clinton-Gore administration. It was the smoking gun of Chinese spying from a source intelligence officials call a "defector-in-place"—a Chinese government official with access to secret nuclear weapons documents who is cooperating with the CIA. To confuse things, however, the agency would later determine that the agent was actually "under control" of the Chinese government. A CIA official said agency analysts were unable to explain the agent's behavior. They could determine only that he had provided Chinese classified documents and that the documents contained classified U.S. nuclear weapons design information. One theory, the CIA official said, was that the agent was a legitimate defector but was discovered by Chinese counterintelligence officials and later "turned" into a Beijing-controlled double agent. Jack Downing, the CIA deputy director of operations, the top spy who had served as station chief in both Beijing and Moscow and retired from the agency in 1999, was convinced the defector had come under control of the Chinese government at some point after he provided the documents to the CIA.

A former FBI counterintelligence official involved in the case said the big question about the walk-in was why the information was passed to the CIA. Did the intelligence community ever answer the question? "No," the former official told me. "There's some opinion that they [the

Chinese] made a mistake in allowing him to pass that. Maybe. There's also some speculation that they wanted it passed so that the Taiwanese might know that they have this capability, to scare them a little bit more. And you know, I don't know which way to come down on that. I do know that the Chinese are masters at deception, and it goes back to Sun Tzu." In counterspy terms, the Chinese are experts at manipulating and creating illusions. "What you see with the Chinese is not really what's there." The information could have been passed by mistake, although "I find that difficult to believe," the official said.

Trulock believes that questioning the motives of the Chinese agent was part of a campaign by pro-China officials within the U.S. intelligence community to downplay the revelations about Chinese nuclear espionage. "Much of the information about the walk-in document in the public domain is misleading, in some cases false," Trulock said. "Much of this was spread around by DOE officials after the publication of the Cox Report and was clearly intended to discredit this important clue to Chinese espionage successes," Trulock said.

And the Chinese were certainly successful. The information in the Chinese document included classified data on seven U.S. thermonuclear warheads—the W-88 Trident submarine D-5 missile warhead, the W-56 Minuteman II, the W-62 Minuteman III, the W-70 Lance, the W-76 Trident C-4 missile warhead, the W-78 Minuteman III Mark 12A, and the W-87 Peacekeeper. It also included the enhanced radiation version of the W-70 that is the neutron bomb.

"Much of the information was indeed classified, certainly during the mid-1980s, but related to more general warhead characteristics," Trulock said. "The W-88 data, on the other hand, was quite detailed with regard to size, geometry, and configuration. For example, dimensions were provided which were accurate to three significant figures for both the nuclear primary and secondary of the warhead."

Was the information obtained from warhead blueprints or related documents? "The simple answer is we really don't know," Trulock said. He noted that critics who doubt that China conducted nuclear espionage seized upon this fact to undermine the harsher conclusions of the Cox Committee.

"The walk-in document was prepared for a Chinese institute respon-sible for developing missile reentry vehicles, or the shell encasing a nuclear warhead," Trulock stated. "The purpose of the document appeared to be to demonstrate to this institute the future directions of Chinese warhead development. As such, there was no need to reveal additional information on the W-88; in particular, there was clearly no requirement to discuss the composition or materials used in the W-88. Did the Chinese have these and other details and simply conclude that the intended recipients of the document had no 'need to know' the rest of the information?" Trulock believed that was possible. Among DOE scientists, who knew the most about it, some believed that only U.S. knowledge could have allowed the Chinese to test a small warhead suc-cessfully in 1992. Others thought it possible that the Chinese could have developed the warhead without lengthy testing.

The bottom line is that the first Chinese test was a success. "To many of our scientists with their detailed knowledge of Chinese nuclear developments, this Chinese success came as a shock," Trulock said. "In the end, the study group concluded that the Chinese had used this information to accomplish this feat."

Trulock also believed that the Chinese goal in targeting U.S. nuclear weapons was the know-how that would provide shortcuts and road-maps to the right solution to the problem of small warheads. "Knowing the correct solution to a tough scientific or technical problem can result in immeasurable savings for a foreign lab or research institute," he said. "Blueprints would be best, but technical solutions, dimensions, geometries, and other details are locked in the minds of scientists who have spent years working on these warheads. They 'know' this infor-mation as well as they know their own social security numbers or the dates of their children's births."

Since the source of the information, as the Chinese spying manual pointed out, is in the Department of Energy nuclear weapons labora-tories, it is logical that the espionage targeted the weapons scientists.

"So there is no disputing the fact that the Chinese acquired impor-tant classified nuclear weapons secrets through espionage, at least within official circles," Trulock said. "The massive declassification of

DOE documents in 1993–1994 could also offer a rich mine of materials to assist the Chinese or other foreign nuclear pretenders. But as with the Soviet case, we will probably never know whether the Chinese acquired actual blueprints unless China's intelligence archives are opened to Western researchers."

The W-70 thermonuclear warhead in particular is believed to be Beijing's choice for arming the new DF-31 ICBM that China flight-tested in August 1999. The missile was put on display in October 1999 in the fiftieth anniversary celebration of the Communist Party's founding of the People's Republic.

"A new nuclear warhead—lighter and smaller—had to be developed for this missile, and we believed the Chinese completed testing of such a warhead for the DF-31 in the mid-1990s," Trulock said. "Testing of a nuclear device resembling the W-88 was also completed by 1996; we forecast that this warhead would be deployed on either a longer-range ICBM or a new Chinese submarine-launched ballistic missile (SLBM) to be deployed sometime in the mid-2010s, according to the latest intelligence community forecasts. Many of the other Chinese acquisitions were also intended to support or sustain these and other nuclear warhead programs."

Chinese spying allowed Beijing to save time, money, and human resources on developing new nuclear warheads. By some scientists' estimates, China saved a decade or more of development time. As Trulock put it: "Most importantly, the Chinese learned the correct technical path to follow. They were able to avoid the blind alleys and cul-de-sacs experienced by the United States in decades of nuclear weapons research and development. The United States blazed the trail, but the Chinese acquired a road map and a clear set of markers to follow the U.S. path of development."

"Espionage revealed what worked and what did not," Trulock added.

With two new warheads based on the W-88 and the W-70, "the information had been used to accelerate the development of modern thermonuclear warheads for new generations of mobile intercontinental range ballistic missiles, both land- and sea-based," Trulock concluded.

The damage is not theoretical. The new Chinese force of mobile strategic missiles will be more than a retaliatory force. "Such systems might be effective against U.S. forces operating in or staging forward to intervene in a future Taiwan Straits crisis and still retain a second-strike capability against the U.S. homeland," Trulock said. "Such a force would never match the arsenals built up during the Cold War by the United States and Soviets, but this did not seem to be the Chinese objective. China would be only the second nation to deploy a road-mobile ICBM, and, if successful, such an arsenal might approach that of the U.S. or Soviets in terms of qualitative characteristics. Confronted with such a reality, would a U.S. president be willing to trade Los Angeles for Taiwan?"

ROYAL TOURIST

U.S. intelligence also learned from sensitive information that Chinese intelligence wanted new information related to nuclear testing. The target this time was the U.S. Stockpile Stewardship Program—an ambitious, expensive, and risky program to maintain U.S. nuclear weapons without big underground tests. The Chinese wanted information on the tools, techniques, and knowledge base for this program. Over the next decade the U.S. government will spend about $45 billion on the program. Despite the Chinese nuclear spying, the Clinton-Gore administration continued to push its openness programs and thus opened new avenues for Chinese intelligence collection at U.S. weapons laboratories.

The Chinese were seeking the data the United States had gained from over a thousand U.S. nuclear tests. Specifically, they wanted special codes that are used to conduct simulations of various warhead explosions when run on supercomputers that perform millions of calculations per second. A key target was a special technology developed at the Lawrence Livermore Laboratory called "inertial confinement fusion." Some of that was obtained from Peter Lee, an American who spied for China. He cooperated with Chinese nuclear weapons scientists starting in the mid-1980s and continuing until his arrest in 1997.

"Lee was a world-class diagnostician who had worked at both Lawrence Livermore and Los Alamos throughout the 1980s," Trulock said. "In 1997, he admitted providing information to Chinese nuclear weapons scientists on diagnostic techniques employed by the labs at the Nevada Test Site. His knowledge of such technologies would be of great benefit to a program intent on developing smaller, lighter nuclear warheads."

DOE security and counterintelligence officials repeatedly warned Energy and lab officials about the new Chinese intelligence targeting. "Not once were we taken seriously," Trulock said. "Not once did any lab official undertake an investigation of computer security, nor did any DOE or administration official order the labs to undertake such an inquiry. We were repeatedly told that lab computer security was good and that thefts of nuclear weapons data from the labs' computer networks were inconceivable." They were wrong.

The intelligence report on foreign targeting of Energy facilities cited earlier exposed the vulnerability of the labs' computer systems. It noted that there were 324 attacks on unclassified computer systems at the labs between October 1997 and June 1998. "Prudence alone would seem to dictate that we ought to consider our nuclear weapons simulations codes and testing data compromised," Trulock said. "While not a substitute for real nuclear testing, this information coupled with advanced computing capabilities would augment and complement the data collected by the Chinese from their 1990s testing series."

The Clinton-Gore administration's handling of the Peter Lee spy case was typical of its pro-Beijing policies. The FBI had planned to arrest Lee on November 6, 1997. But the White House put off the arrest. The reason: President Jiang Zemin of China was to visit Washington. Jiang joined Clinton for a press conference on October 29, 1997, where Clinton announced, with no touch of irony, that he was lifting a ban imposed and maintained by several presidents that prohibited U.S. nuclear power companies from selling technology to China because of Beijing's notorious track record for helping states like Pakistan develop nuclear arms. Clinton ignored the numerous intelligence reports showing that China secretly continued to work with Pakistan's nuclear weapons program. But before U.S. companies could sell their technology, a presidential certification would be required. Clinton thus told reporters that the certification "will allow our companies to apply for licenses to sell equipment to Chinese nuclear power plants, subject to U.S. monitoring."

This was the agreement that Clinton called a "win-win-win"—but that proved to be a bust, bust, bust, because China failed to promise that it would not take U.S. technology and sell it to other nations.

The White House, as stated, ordered the FBI to delay the Peter Lee arrest to avoid offending the Chinese, especially because of the nuclear cooperation agreement. White House aides were acutely aware of how it would look if the president agreed to sell China nuclear power technology while its spies were stealing U.S. nuclear weapons secrets.

According to U.S. government officials close to the Peter Lee case, China also issued a blunt warning that the outcome of the Peter Lee case could upset China-U.S. relations. The threat worked.

Senator Arlen Specter, Pennsylvania Republican and chairman of the Senate Judiciary Subcommittee on the Courts, questioned top Justice Department officials on the case. The Justice Department had restricted the prosecutor in the Peter Lee case from seeking tougher charges, charges that could have brought Lee a life term in prison or even the death penalty. Instead, Lee was allowed to plea bargain. His sentence was minimal. Federal District Judge Terry Hatter sentenced Lee to a five-year suspended sentence, twelve months in a halfway house, a $20,000 fine, and three thousand hours of community service. The fix clearly had been in from the same White House that had delayed his arrest.

The damage from this case, code-named "Royal Tourist," was extremely serious. Lee admitted under questioning from FBI agents that he had provided Chinese nuclear weapons scientists with details of classified U.S. nuclear testing simulation technology. He also gave the Chinese secrets of antisubmarine warfare, lecturing in Beijing on the subject on May 11, 1997. "At one point in his presentation, Lee displayed an image of a surface ship wake, which he had brought with him from the United States," the Cox Committee report states. "He also drew a graph and explained the underlying physics of his work and its applications. He told the PRC scientists where to filter data within the graph to enhance the ability to locate the ocean wake of a vessel."

The charges against him included one count of transmitting defense information improperly and one count of making false statements to the U.S. government. On December 8, a full month after Jiang's visit, Lee pleaded guilty to passing classified U.S. defense information to Chinese scientists during a 1985 visit and falsifying reports of contacts with Chinese nationals in 1997. The Cox Committee concluded that between 1985 and 1997, Peter Lee "may have provided the PRC with more classified thermonuclear weapons-related information than he has admitted."

Specter was convinced the investigation was botched by the Clinton-Gore administration but was never able to find out the reasons why. Suspiciously, the Justice Department concluded the plea agreement with Peter Lee without conducting an assessment of the damage to U.S. national security. "That plea bargain was entered into without any damage assessment by the Department of Defense," Specter said. "The Department of Justice entered into a plea bargain... in the face of offenses that could have carried the death penalty or life imprisonment." Jonathan Shapiro, the assistant U.S. attorney who prosecuted the case, testified before Specter's committee that he had wanted to prosecute Lee on spy charges but was forced to make a deal on lesser charges because of decisions by senior Justice Department lawyers. The navy also hampered the prosecution by giving conflicting statements about the submarine secrets compromised by Lee, Shapiro said. A Justice Department memorandum stated that Shapiro should be told "vigorously and repeatedly that the FBI is much more interested in the intel yet to be garnered from Lee than in punishing felons." But Specter pointed out that Lee did not cooperate as required by the plea agreement, and yet no action was taken against him.

The U.S. intelligence community's conclusion: Lee had provided China with "significant material assistance to the Chinese nuclear weapons programs," in the words of an official assessment provided to Specter's Senate subcommittee.

WEN HO LEE: KINDRED SPIRIT

In September 1995 Notra Trulock began wrapping up the analysis conducted by DOE scientists and intelligence analysts about the W-88 warhead. The assessment was clear: China had been provided with classified
information on the design of America's most modern nuclear warhead.
Trulock had been working closely with the FBI when he finally made an
official referral to the bureau in September 1995. The response was
unusual. "We finished up and we tried initially to refer it to the FBI, and
the FBI kicked it back to us and said, 'Too old, too cold. How about if
you guys do an administrative inquiry?'" Trulock was disappointed. An
administrative inquiry is nothing more than a records check. Only travel
records and security files could be checked. The investigators had no
power to check bank and financial records that might reveal payments
from the Chinese. And it would be less thorough because the inquiry
limited investigators to checking within Department of Energy facilities. Trulock had no authority to investigate Pentagon officials who
had access to W-88 secrets. But it was a way to help the FBI narrow
the field of potential candidates and suspects. The inquiry lasted from
November 1995 to May 1996. The FBI seemed to be in no hurry to catch
a Chinese spy.

"Our results were formally transmitted to the FBI in June 1996; the
FBI then opened a full field investigation in July 1996," Trulock said.
"FBI officials told us that they would be seeking technical surveillance
and [would] undertake a host of other investigative measures in pursuit of this investigation. I was later surprised to learn that no attempt
to obtain technical coverage was made until a year later—in July 1997."

The DOE, working with a veteran FBI counterintelligence agent who
specialized in Chinese spying, T. Van Magers, had come up with a list
of seventy "leads"—people with access to warhead data within DOE
who could be spies. The people on the list included former student rad-
icals and Maoists who had continued their adherence to Marxism-
Leninism-Maoism even after being employed in classified nuclear
weapons work. The list was then narrowed down to twelve people and
sent to the FBI for further investigation.

Trulock briefed his boss at Energy, Undersecretary Charles Curtis, on the case. "It's clear that the Chinese have gained access to U.S. restricted data," he said. "And also the access to this data has enabled the Chinese to make material progress in the development of their road-mobile missile system." The Chinese had saved hundreds of "man-years" of research and "billions" of dollars. The initial assessment was that China got secrets that "might have come from espionage," Trulock stated. The Energy analysts also had a specialist conduct an assessment of whether the Chinese could have gained the W-88 secrets from open sources. The answer was definitively no.

Regarding the Chinese document, Trulock said Energy officials were not in a position to make judgments about the veracity of the agent who provided it. "But a careful review of the technical details by lab scientists showed the warhead data contained in the document to be correct and highly classified," he said. "Other information in the document was also accurate and did in fact exist within the time frame under question. There were no historical inaccuracies within the document. Regardless of the credibility of the source, the document seemed genuine, and we needed to learn the origins of the compromise of this information. My job at DOE was to try to protect secrets from foreign intelligence services. We had been presented with a Chinese-originated document that contained some of our most sensitive nuclear weapons information. We needed to know how and where the Chinese had acquired this information. We had a hard time understanding the FBI's actions in this regard."

Trulock said the DOE administrative inquiry did not single out Wen Ho Lee as the chief suspect. While his name was on the list sent to the FBI in June 1996, "his name was not the first on the list, nor was he the only individual under suspicion." Trulock believed the FBI would recognize the case as a high priority national security investigation. But the FBI's actions showed otherwise.

"For me, allegations against Mr. Lee regarding his security violations and mishandling of hundreds of computer files containing classified nuclear weapons data reinforce the basis for including him on our original list," Trulock said. "Obviously, given their prior history with him, the FBI didn't need DOE to highlight Wen Ho Lee for them. At DOE, we fully expected the FBI to pursue each of the leads that we had provided them. The FBI had the resources, manpower, and authority to conduct a real spy hunt; DOE had just done some of the preliminary legwork."

Trulock said the FBI singled out Lee and his wife, Sylvia, who also had worked at Los Alamos, early on in the investigation. Sylvia is a naturalized citizen who was born in China's Hunan province. She worked as a computer technician at Los Alamos from 1980 to 1995 and held a top secret security clearance. As Trulock recalls, the FBI immediately focused on Lee, and it was apparent that the bureau had its own sources of information. By March 1996, one FBI agent said privately, "It's Wen Ho Lee, and we're going to get him." The FBI said its investigation of Lee and his wife began on May 30, 1996, based on information supplied by the Energy Department.

Travel records showed Lee and his wife had traveled to China twice, once in 1986 and again in 1988. Investigators placed Mrs. Lee on the list because she held a clerical job at Los Alamos and had met with the visiting delegations of Chinese scientists. Wen Ho Lee had access to W-88 design information and numerous other secrets about U.S. warhead design and manufacture. He was born in Taiwan and was a hydrodynamicist and engineer who worked in Los Alamos's X Division, the most secret part of the laboratory because of its information on nuclear arms. He worked in the division from 1980 to 1998, when he was dismissed from Los Alamos.

THE HUG

One of the most significant pieces of information about Wen Ho Lee was his appearance in the early 1990s at a meeting of visiting Chinese officials in New Mexico. The top official at the meeting was Hu Side, vice president of the China Academy of Engineering Physics, the Chinese state organization in charge of developing nuclear weapons. Hu visited the three U.S. nuclear weapons laboratories, including Los Alamos, in February 1994, a month after he had become the head of the Chinese nuclear weapons program. His host was Sig Hecker, then director of Los Alamos. On a visitor information form, Hu stated that the purpose of his trip was to see the laboratory and "discuss laser technology and its applications." "My specialty is applied physics," he wrote. "I have been working in this field for about 35 years." That was an understatement; Hu is considered the father of China's nuclear weapons.

According to intelligence officials, Wen Ho Lee showed up uninvited but was nevertheless welcomed. At some point, Hu came up to Lee and embraced him. An informant overheard Hu tell the gathered Chinese scientists that Wen Ho Lee had made important contributions to China's nuclear weapons program. The information was passed to the FBI many months later by the source, who witnessed what intelligence officials are calling "The Hug."

The FBI, according to court papers, believes Wen Ho Lee passed classified nuclear secrets to Chinese officials during 1986 and 1988 meetings in his hotel room in Beijing. The day before he was fired, Lee told investigators: "Did I pass W-88 information to unauthorized person[s]? I know from my mind, I didn't do it. I have nothing. I have never passed any information to any unqualified person...."

FBI Agent Michael W. Lowe stated in an affidavit that Wen Ho Lee had at first denied trying to contact Min in 1982. But after the FBI told him the conversation had been intercepted, "Lee admitted he had called the Lawrence Livermore employee and had previously misled the FBI about the contact."

Even though Trulock referred the results of the administrative inquiry to the FBI on July 1, 1997, months went by and nothing seemed to be going on in the way of a serious investigation. Trulock faced a dilemma. If a spy was stealing nuclear weapons secrets, the first step should be to stop the loss of classified and sensitive information. The investigation required utmost secrecy to avoid tipping off the suspects. But allowing someone who is suspected of passing secrets to China to continue to have access to those secrets posed even greater dangers.

Energy Secretary Hazel O'Leary told Trulock that, before he could provide briefings about the case to the House and Senate intelligence oversight panels, White House National Security Adviser Sandy Berger must be notified. Trulock complied, and Berger told Trulock and Energy officials to go ahead and brief Congress.

A former FBI official involved in the case told me the investigation faced problems from the start. Justice Department officials in the Office of Intelligence Policy Review refused a request to seek the approval of a special federal court to put a wiretap on Wen Ho Lee. Justice refused despite the fact that the FBI had compelling reasons for wanting to put Lee under surveillance, including his travel to China, the hug from Hu Side, and the bureau's determination that Lee was about to begin work with a Chinese national research assistant, which raised concerns that the assistant might have a connection to Chinese intelligence. "There was a reasonable suspicion, we believed, to go forward," the former FBI official told me. Nothing doing. The decision was made by Richard Scruggs, a friend of Attorney General Janet Reno from her days as a prosecutor in Florida. A secret internal Justice Department report later criticized Scruggs for turning down the wiretap request.

Reno escaped responsibility for the botched surveillance request because, under Justice Department procedures, she was not informed about rejected requests.

On March 6, 1999, the *New York Times* broke the sensational story of how Wen Ho Lee was the prime suspect in the investigation of Chinese nuclear spying. The story would earn reporter Jeff Gerth a Pulitzer Prize, newspaper reporting's highest award. Trulock believes that the newspaper's stories were crucial in highlighting the problem. He is convinced the entire problem would have been covered up without Gerth's reporting.

Two days later, Energy Secretary Bill Richardson ordered the University of California—which was in charge of running Los Alamos on behalf of the Energy Department—to dismiss Lee, whom he had no direct authority to fire.

As the former FBI official put it, "With Wen Ho Lee we were in the reasonable suspicion, borderline probable cause [phase], and then everything went public, and there's not much you can do about it after that." With the chief suspect unmasked, the FBI's chances of uncovering hard evidence of activity had evaporated.

Wen Ho Lee denied he was a spy. Lee was born in Taiwan in 1939 and became an American citizen in 1974. He first came to the United States in 1964 to attend Texas A&M University, where he eventually received a doctorate in mechanical engineering. He worked at Los Alamos for twenty-one years, mostly in the nuclear weapons division. Lee said in an interview broadcast on CBS's *60 Minutes* in August 1999, "I devote the best time of my life to this country, to make the country stronger, particularly in the nuclear weapon area, and I try to make the country stronger so we can protect the American people. But, suddenly, they told me I'm a traitor."

He was never charged with treason, however, or even espionage. Instead, the case was in tatters due to Justice Department mishandling and the eventual public disclosure, which some officials believed was a deliberate leak by Energy Secretary Bill Richardson to mitigate the political fallout. Consequently the FBI was left with pursuing lesser charges of mishandling classified nuclear secrets.

Shortly after the case became public, Clinton was asked about it at a press conference on March 19, 1999. His remarks showed that he was still committed to helping China become a modern world power, whatever the cost to the United States.

A reporter asked: "Mr. President, how long have you known that the Chinese were stealing our nuclear secrets? Is there any trust left between the two nations? And some Republicans are saying that you deliberately suppressed the information from the American people because of the election and your trade goals."

The president deftly handled the question, showing his skills as a master of political spin:

> Well, let me try to respond to all those things. First of all, the latter charge
> is simply untrue. We were notified—Mr. Berger was notified sometime
> in 1996 of the possibility that security had been breached at the labs,
> the Energy Department labs where a lot of our nuclear work is done, in
> the mid-'80s—not in the 1990s, but in the mid-'80s—and that there was
> an investigation being undertaken by the FBI.

Then, sometime in the middle of 1997, he was notified and I was notified that the extent of the security breach might have been quite extensive. So we had the CIA looking into that, the Energy Department
looking into that, and the FBI investigation continued with the cooperation, the full cooperation of the Energy Department. In early 1998, I pro-
pounded a presidential directive designed to improve security at the
labs. And as you know, Secretary Richardson's been talking quite a bit in
recent days about what has been done since that directive was signed
and what continues to be done today.

The security directive was simply a presidential order giving the FBI
greater authority over Energy Department counterintelligence and
requiring polygraph tests for laboratory scientists with access to the
most sensitive nuclear weapons secrets. The laboratories, however,
have resisted the implementation of the order. When a polygraph, or
lie-detector, test was ordered for all who had access to nuclear weapons
secrets, the lab scientists revolted. They signed petitions against the
practice and even circulated instructions on how to cheat the tests,
which measure heart rate, skin response, and breathing in response to
questions.

The president said there were two questions which had to be kept
separate. First, was there a security breach in the mid-1980s, and if so
did it result in espionage? "That has not been fully resolved, at least as
of my latest briefing," he said. The second question was whether action
was taken soon enough. "I am confident that we in the White House
have done what we could to be aggressive about this."

Aggressive in what way? It was clear the White House was aggressive, but not in seeking to find out whether Chinese spies had stolen
American nuclear warhead secrets.

The president made it clear that there would be no penalty for Chinese spying. "I don't believe that we can afford to be under any illusions
about our relationship with China, or any other country, for that matter, with whom we have both common interests and deep disagreements," Clinton said. "I believe the course I have followed with China is
the one that's best for America—disagreeing where we have serious

disagreements, pursuing our common interests when I thought it was in the interests of the United States."

The president insisted "categorically" that "it never crossed my mind that I should not disclose some inquiry being undertaken by the United States government for reasons of commercial or other gain. That is not true. I just think we should always pursue what is in the interest of the United States.... I think that if anybody did, in fact, commit espionage, it is a bad thing and we should take appropriate action. But in our dealings with China, we should do quite simply what is in the interest of the American people, and that's what I intend to do." The president said he understood that the spying investigation "has not yet determined for sure that espionage occurred." The tone was set for all the investigations to follow, and the imprimatur of the president went a long way in influencing the outcome of the probe.

Clinton said that if espionage had occurred, "I will be very upset about it." He then announced that retired Senator Warren Rudman, a New Hampshire Republican and head of the President's Foreign Intelligence Advisory Board (PFIAB), would conduct an inquiry into the matter.

THE RUDMAN PANEL

Warren Rudman provided the perfect cover for White House political damage control. One of his first tasks was to request all the raw intelligence and investigative files from the FBI. It was something both the Justice Department's Internal Security Section and the FBI were loath to do. They knew the White House could use the information to discredit the sources or leak details to friendly reporters to make sure the investigation never succeeded. Rudman bristled at the suggestion that he was in any way a stalking horse for the president. But the PFIAB is a White House operation, despite the window dressing of being headed by a former Republican senator. The final report of PFIAB criticized the abysmal security at the weapons laboratories, calling it science at its best, security at its worst. However, the report sought to minimize the prospect of Chinese espionage. It referred to "leaks and thefts" as if they were in the same category, thus reducing the implication of espionage by Beijing.

The report said that "intelligence gathering" by China is a challenge to the weapons labs. "More sophisticated than some of the blatant methods employed by the former Soviet bloc espionage services, PRC intelligence operatives know their strong suits and play them extremely well," the report said. "Increasingly more nimble, discreet and transparent in their spying methods, the Chinese services have become very proficient in the art of seemingly innocuous elicitations of information. This modus operandi has proved very effective against unwitting and ill-prepared DOE personnel."

But on the real issue of how China obtained warhead secrets, the panel, echoing the official White House political line, balked. Disputing the claim about "wholesale losses of nuclear weapons technology," the report concluded that "the factual record in the majority of cases regarding the DOE weapons laboratories supports plausible inferences—but not irrefutable proof—about the source and scope of espionage and the channels through which recipient nations received information." The report was a whitewash of Chinese spying. It would be used conveniently by supporters of the president to refute the much more dire claims of the Cox Committee. It was another example of the lawyerly approach to manipulating public opinion. In this case, the White House intelligence board, supposedly an independent panel headed by a Republican, had presented a contradictory view, and that view was adopted by many sympathetic news reporters. "The classified and unclassified evidence available to the panel, while pointing out systemic security vulnerabilities, falls short of being conclusive," the report said. "The actual damage done to U.S. security interests is, at the least, currently unknown; at worst, it may be unknowable."

The PFIAB was once the preserve of intelligence professionals, scholars, and "wise men" who provided the president with independent advice on often complicated intelligence matters. Under Bill Clinton, the board became politicized. Stanley Shuman, a New York investment banker, and Richard L. Bloch, chairman of a Texas real estate investment firm, were appointed to the intelligence panel on July 24, 1995, according to White House records. Federal Election Commission records indicate that both men contributed a total of $220,000 to the Democratic National Committee between June 1995 and May 1996, suggesting that the going price for a seat on a White House panel is about $100,000. Shuman was one of the 938 friends of Clinton who was allowed to spend a night in the White House. The sixteen-member board is granted access to a wide variety of secret intelligence. For its investigation of Los Alamos, the board requested a mass of raw intelligence files that law enforcement and intelligence officials told me they didn't want to surrender because they feared that the White House would use the information to discredit the probe, as it had done in past investigations.

Rudman attacked reports by this author that exposed the transfer of raw files. He claimed the reports were "a clear and deliberate challenge to my own integrity." Rudman continued: "The documentary materials from the Justice Department and the FBI... were requested so that I could fully understand each of the alleged violations of security at our weapons labs. Such an understanding is essential if our special investigative panel is to fulfill properly the substantial responsibility with which it has been charged." The fact remains that it would have been very easy for any one of the people in the PFIAB office to provide what they saw to the president and his advisers.

FBI officials said the PFIAB requests were part of the Clinton-Gore administration's pattern of seeking the most sensitive information, including the nature and identity of sources. Once passed to the White House or political appointees linked to it, the information would inevitably be compromised in public, making investigations and intelligence gathering against Chinese targets more difficult.

As part of its investigation of Lee, the FBI searched his computers and found numerous unauthorized transfers of nuclear weapons data. Agents also set up a "sting" operation aimed at enticing Lee into revealing his activities. But the operation did not work. John Lewis, the FBI's National Security Division chief, who oversaw the case, said the FBI had its suspicions. "There was some smoke, but we had no conclusive evidence," Lewis told *Newsweek* magazine.

THE INDICTMENT

On December 10, 1999, Lee was indicted on fifty-nine counts of mis-handling classified nuclear weapons design and testing information. The classified information was related to "the design, construction, and testing of nuclear weapons," the U.S. Attorney's office in New Mexico stated. The specific files included:

- Data files that contained information relating to the physical and radioactive properties of materials used to construct nuclear weapons.
- Input deck/input file information that included descriptions of the exact dimensions and geometry of nuclear weapons that were used in connection with the design and simulated testing of nuclear weapons and the computer instructions to set up a simulated nuclear weapons detonation.
- Source codes used for determining by simulation the validity of nuclear weapons designs and for comparing bomb test results with predicted result.
- Nuclear bomb testing protocol libraries reflecting the data collected from actual tests of nuclear weapons.
- Data concerning nuclear bomb test problems, yield calculations, and other nuclear weapons design and detonation information.
- Computer programs necessary to run the design and testing files.

The charges also included violations of the Atomic Energy Act and carried a maximum penalty of life in prison. The downloaded files were "legacy codes"—vital secret data that could be extremely valuable to China in conducting computer simulations of nuclear weapons. The downloading occurred in 1992, 1993, and 1997. To highlight its effort in bringing the indictment, the U.S. Attorney's office stated that over sixty FBI agents and dozens of computer specialists, along with technical specialists such as scientists, engineers, and technicians, from both the FBI and the DOE, took part in the probe. The office proclaimed that it had conducted more than a thousand interviews and searched more than a million computer files. The number of data bits examined by investigators was estimated to be "over four trillion." The press release noted that "several searches" were also carried out.

The U.S. Attorney's office made no mention of the delay in putting Lee under electronic surveillance or the fact that his Chinese national researcher was allowed to return to China. The investigation was botched. One former federal prosecutor put it this way: "As we used to say, thick indictment, thin case." In other words, the indictment against Lee was lengthy, but the prospects for conviction were not bright.

John Lewis of the FBI's National Security Division said Chinese intelligence presented unique problems. "We did not have a lot of hardcore Chinese espionage cases," he told me. "Remember the old East German target. The East Germans used to do something that was very difficult for us. They would only make their meetings inside of East Germany. They get their people in there. Safe houses, etc. The Chinese do the same thing. They are very reluctant to make hard-core meets [FBI-ese for meetings] anywhere but inside China. That's why we were so concerned about people traveling there. They are on their turf, in their environment, under their control."

Friends of Wen Ho Lee came to his defense. An Internet site was created to include details of the ongoing case. "Dr. Wen Ho Lee has suffered incalculable damage to his reputation, career and family," the site said. The site accused the government of singling out Lee as a victim of politics, blame avoidance, budgetary ambitions, and stereotypes about Lee's loyalties. Also, the Wen Ho Lee Defense Fund was set up to help with legal expenses.

Some of the government's case was revealed in pretrial maneuvering. FBI Agent Robert Messemer, a veteran counterspy, told a closed hearing in December 1999 that Wen Ho Lee had a "continuing association" with Chinese intelligence.

With so little to go on, the government's strategy was to keep Lee in jail for months on end in the hope that he would seek a plea agreement of a lighter sentence in exchange for cooperating in a damage assessment and debriefings with intelligence officials.

The strategy paid off. Kindred Spirit came to a close in September 2000. In a plea bargain, Lee was convicted of one felony count of mishandling nuclear data. All other fifty-eight counts in the federal indictment were dropped. The prison term was reduced to the nine months he had already served in jail, and he was freed. As part of the agreement, Lee promised to cooperate with investigators for six months in explaining what happened to the seven missing computer tapes. Lee also promised to explain his visits to China and his relationship with Chinese intelligence and nuclear officials. "On a date certain in 1994, I used an unsecure computer in T-Division to download a document or writing relating to the national defense," Lee said in a brief statement that was part of the plea bargain.

Intelligence officials do not know what motivated Lee to gather the secrets in classified Los Alamos computers and transfer them to unsecure systems and portable tapes. The leading theory is that he wanted to have something to fall back on if he should lose his job during employee cutbacks. There were also suspicions that Lee was providing secrets to Taiwan.

U.S. Attorney Norman Bay said that Lee was prosecuted for "what he did," not because of his race. If Lee fails to reveal all during debriefings, he will be prosecuted for perjury or obstruction of justice, Bay promised.

According to investigators, Lee downloaded nuclear weapons information months before he traveled to Taiwan in March 1998 and gave a seminar at the Chung Shan Institute of Science and Technology. The institute is a secret military facility where Taiwanese scientists work on nuclear and missile research. It was where Taiwan had been building a nuclear bomb until work was halted under pressure from the United States in the 1980s. While at the Taiwan institute, Lee used a long-distance telephone to dial in to the Los Alamos computer and transfer two unclassified documents from a file that also contained secrets. Investigators believe the trail left by Lee could have allowed Taiwan's intelligence service to obtain his password and user identification to gain access to the computer system at Los Alamos.

THE PROBLEMS CONTINUE

The public exposure of the loss of U.S. nuclear secrets prompted Energy Secretary Bill Richardson to declare that he had fixed all the problems. He assured the American people that nuclear secrets were safe. But in June 2000, Los Alamos officials discovered that two computer disks containing highly classified information on nuclear weapons were missing. The disks were used by an emergency response team, and the data on them included information about U.S., Chinese, Russian, and French nuclear weapons. The disks were later discovered hidden behind a copy machine in the X Division, the unit in charge of designing nuclear weapons. A federal grand jury was convened after several officials at the lab gave conflicting answers to investigators about the circumstances surrounding the missing disks. Richardson and other officials claimed there was no evidence of espionage. But the sad fact is there is no way to know whether someone removed the disks, copied their contents, and then returned them.

"Regrettably, this is just one more potentially catastrophic security failure which has become an all-too-familiar pattern of security failures at the Department of Energy," said Senator John Warner, Virginia Republican and chairman of the Senate Armed Services Committee. The Cox Committee report on the Wen Ho Lee case is considered the worst-case scenario. But it is also the most credible because it is relatively untainted by the spin from the White House. It said that China "has stolen classified information on all of the United States' most advanced thermonuclear warheads."

The House Intelligence Committee formed a special panel to investigate security problems at the Energy Department. Its conclusions, released in the summer of 2000, were harshly critical of the Clinton-Gore administration's approach to spy catching and protecting secrets. The group was headed by Paul Redmond, a former CIA counterspy chief who earlier had compared Chinese nuclear spying at U.S. weapons laboratories as similar in magnitude to the Rosenbergs' spying.

The Redmond report singled out the Clinton administration's first Energy secretary, Hazel O'Leary, for what it said were "many of the CI [counterintelligence] and security problems at the laboratories." For instance, O'Leary did away with color-coded security badges that helped identify whether persons were in unauthorized locations—such as those with large amounts of secret information. Why? She believed the colored badges were unfair, a form of discrimination.

The Redmond panel stated that the security scandal at the Energy Department was part of a pervasive, administration-wide problem of deemphasizing security after the Cold War. "The State Department, for example, embarked on its now infamous 'no escort' policy, the Defense Intelligence Agency issued 'no escort' badges to Russian military intelligence officers, and even the Central Intelligence Agency precipitously abandoned its policy of aggressively recruiting Russian intelligence officers," the report stated. The government "must ensure that such laxity will never again be encouraged or tolerated."

The report also ridiculed the Clinton-Gore administration's widely-reported claims to have repaired the problems: "Statements to the effect that all is now well in the CI [counterintelligence] area are nonsense." Security and counterintelligence shortcomings "cannot be fixed overnight," the report said. "Such statements serve only to strengthen the position of those at the laboratories who would wait out the effort to improve CI and thus make the job all that much harder. Our yardstick for assessing the CI program will be their future success in catching spies."

It was all too clear to any observer that in the upper levels of the Clinton-Gore administration there was no interest in catching spies, especially those working on behalf of China. As the persecution of Notra Trulock demonstrated, the administration was more interested in silencing critics than in protecting the nation's secrets.

I. C. Smith, a retired FBI agent who spent years countering Chinese intelligence and espionage activities, considers American leaders ignorant about the nature and scope of the Chinese intelligence threat. "In essence, the inference by many of the 'China is no threat' group was that an agrarian country could not pose an intelligence threat to such a technological marvel as the U.S."

Smith told me that top officials viewed intelligence threats from the standpoint of the military threat, and thus the KGB was given greater credence as a spying threat than more sophisticated intelligence agencies like the East German Stasi and the Chinese Ministry of State Security. "This is true today," he said. "There are those that will argue that we could give the Chinese the plans for our most sophisticated weaponry and they could not catch up with us."

Smith noted that the Chinese may be less effective at utilizing secrets gathered by their spies, but "this does not mean that we should put our guard down." Instead, the United States should "make them pay for every scrap of information that they obtain.... To steal it shortcuts the process and allows them to continue to divert money from research and development to other areas to keep the government afloat."

"The United States must not be so shortsighted that we will forego our security just because a generation from now the Chinese will still be behind the U.S. technologically," Smith said. "We must adopt the attitude of the Chinese and look to generations a hundred years from now. We cannot afford to mortgage future generations' security just to satisfy a current trend of appeasement."

Smith observed that American leaders today show "little intellectual capacity for counterintelligence," the often arcane understanding of how foreign intelligence services work against the United States. "The shortsighted view of the PRC... is that China doesn't pose a threat," he said. "After all, they aren't out there making dead drops, communicating via shortwave radio, paying cash concealed in hollow rocks, etc., as is the expected norm for the spy business. This view became dominant in the FBI and even, to a large extent, the intelligence community, and this resulted in the FBI essentially de-emphasizing counterintelligence in general, and in the China counterintelligence program in particular."

"This led directly to the debacle of the Wen Ho Lee investigation," Smith added. "The FBI's counterintelligence program was relegated to a poor third place in the National Security Division amidst talk of completely shutting down the program. The lessons of Tiger Trap and Larry Wu-Tai Chin had been conveniently lost. For many in the FBI, if the counterintelligence program didn't produce an espionage case per month with its attendant arrests, media exposés, etc., then it wasn't worth pursuing."

According to Smith, the FBI's failure to aggressively pursue Chinese spies played into the Clinton-Gore administration's pro-China policies. "No one in the administration protested the reduction of resources in the China counterintelligence program," he said. "In essence, the FBI, wittingly or not, played directly into the hands of the administration."

During the twenty years since the normalization of relations with China, threatening Chinese intelligence and espionage operations have never been fully recognized. Smith said that warnings about the danger were largely ignored by policymakers "predisposed to take an opposite view" of the threat.

Smith, who understands the Chinese intelligence threat as well as any current or former U.S. national security official, believes the key to the problem lies in Beijing's communist government. "The PRC's communist government needs an adversary," he said. "And having an adversary is key to communism remaining in power. That is the justification for violations of their own constitution exalting freedom and other concepts and the pervasive police apparatus that keeps them in power."

There is a penalty for going against the grain of the misguided conventional wisdom on China, Smith said. "To state such views was to be viewed by the pro-PRC intellectuals in this country as a 'warmonger,' of 'limited intellect,' a 'gumshoe,' and viewed with contempt," he said. "This was not the view that resulted in enhanced career opportunities and certainly did not result in being embraced by China and [receiving] invitations to Chinese embassy functions or trips to the Great Wall. In effect, a hard-liner toward China was simply ostracized and banished to the fringes of policymaking in government and certainly within some individual agencies."

The FBI's Chinese counterintelligence program today is probably as weak as it has ever been. Agents assigned to it are said to be demoralized and inexperienced and to lack support from FBI senior officials.

China's nuclear espionage—spanning decades—is meant to provide the nuclear power to achieve a single goal: to deter the United States from defending Taiwan.

CHAPTER EIGHT
Flashpoint Taiwan

"Use reality, make a noise in the east, but strike to the west.
Cut time and strike in multiple waves."

—Senior PLA Colonel Wang Benzhi, on plans for missile strikes against Taiwan

"DSP reports five events from known ICBM bases in western China." The airman's voice was tense but carried an air of nonchalance, a sign of rigorous training. He was inside a dimly-lit command bunker nearly a mile beneath Colorado's Cheyenne Mountain, along with twenty other airmen, soldiers, and sailors from various branches of the U.S. and Canadian militaries. He was in the headquarters of the U.S. North American Aerospace Defense Command, known as NORAD. At NORAD, they think about the unthinkable, twenty-four hours a day, seven days a week. Closed to the outside world by huge steel doors designed to withstand a nuclear attack, the NORAD bunker is where military personnel scan the globe from computer terminals looking for signs of any missile launch on earth. The launches are watched by infrared sensors around the world, primarily the constellation of satellites with the nondescript name of Defense Support Program (DSP).

The five hot pops picked up by the DSP satellite over China were the first sign of trouble. Less than a minute later came more bad news: "Sir... we have multiple missile launches. Stand by for target report." A few seconds later, the intelligence officer on duty broadcast further details: "Intel indicates probable launch of five ICBMs from China. Intel assesses this to be combat against North America."

It was September 3, 1999, and the Chinese missile attack was only an exercise. But it was a sobering reminder of how the strategic nuclear threat against the United States has not gone away with the demise of the Soviet Union. And this time the button could have been pushed in Beijing, not Moscow. A nuclear war with China over its dispute with Taiwan is a real danger. And even though the Clinton-Gore administration went to great lengths to ignore it, the danger is growing.

A short time after the airmen announced the beginning of the simulated Chinese nuclear combat, five red lines emanating from western China streaked across the computer map in the command center. Each line represented the flight path of a Chinese CSS-4 intercontinental ballistic missile, or ICBM, headed directly for the United States. China's twenty-four silo-based missiles are old by American standards, but they can hit targets more than eight thousand miles away and are the backbone of China's strategic nuclear force. The missiles are based on the design of America's first generation of missiles, which China obtained from a defecting U.S. missile engineer. Each of the CSS-4s carried a huge five-megaton warhead with the equivalent of five million tons of TNT—enough to blow up an entire city. The NORAD computerized attack warning network had already plotted the targets of the incoming ICBMs. They appeared as dots on the giant computer map: Seattle, Colorado Springs (where the Cheyenne Mountain complex is located), Chicago, New York, and Washington, D.C.

Air Force Colonel Allen Baker, NORAD's director of operations, explained how nuclear war with China would proceed. Once the Chinese missile launches are confirmed from multiple electronic sensors such as satellites and radar stations on the ground or at sea, the next step would be to pick up the special telephone to the White House. "At this point, I'd be telling the president how many minutes until Washington, D.C., is gone," he said. Flight time from China to the capital: about thirty-five minutes. Asked if the U.S. military had the means to shoot down the incoming missiles, Baker said, "Absolutely nothing." A National Missile Defense system to handle a limited attack such as the Chinese strike or one from a single North Korean missile is being developed but may not be deployed for several years, he said. So why track the missiles? "We're tracking them so we can tell our commanders exactly what is happening so they can figure out what their response is going to be," he said. "If they take out Washington, D.C., do we want to take out Beijing? I don't know. That's their decision."

NORAD's 1999 missile exercise also showed that the U.S. military could not afford to give up its strategic nuclear deterrent, despite efforts by the Clinton-Gore administration to pretend it is no longer needed. Only months earlier the president had announced that U.S. strategic nuclear missiles would no longer be targeted on China after China promised to "detarget" its missiles and not aim them at American cities. On June 27, 1998, Chinese President Jiang Zemin appeared at a press conference after meetings with Clinton in Beijing. He announced: "President Clinton and I have decided that China and the United States will not target the strategic nuclear weapons under their respective control at each other. This demonstrates to the entire world that China and the United States are partners, not adversaries."

As with so many other statements by the Chinese Communist leader, Jiang lied. The proof arrived in a form common during the highly politicized Clinton-Gore administration. It was kept hidden from public view as part of a classified intelligence assessment. On December 2, 1998, the Pentagon's Defense Intelligence Agency (DIA) reported that the People's Liberation Army conducted exercises that included simulated nuclear missile attacks on Taiwan and U.S. military forces in the region. The exercises began in late November and ended in early December. Involved in the maneuvers were road-mobile CSS-5 medium-range missiles that were spotted by U.S. spy satellites as they moved up and down roads along China's coast. The DIA report, based on sensitive intelligence gathered by U.S. spying systems, also spotted activities linked to the exercises by silo-based CSS-2s. The DIA's analysts determined that the missile units were conducting mock nuclear attacks on Taiwan and against U.S. Army troops based in South Korea. Marine Corps troops on the Japanese island of Okinawa and mainland Japan also were targeted with strikes. As one official who saw the report put it, "They were doing mock missile attacks on our troops."

A White House official confirmed the intelligence report and said that both weapons had "never been pointed our way before." But the official sought to downplay the threat by insisting that the missiles were older weapons systems, noting that the CSS-2 was first deployed in 1971 and the CSS-5 in the 1980s. "The important point is these are not new missiles," he said.

The important point missed by the White House—intentionally—was that the missile exercise directly threatened the 37,000 troops based in South Korea and the 47,000 troops in Japan, including about 25,000 Marines on Okinawa. Moreover, the exercise was evidence that Jiang's promise about detargeting was hollow. Or was it? Jiang had referred to "strategic" nuclear weapons. Apologists for Beijing argued that the CSS-2s and CSS-5s that were moved around during the exercise technically may not be in the same category as longer-range ICBMs. The U.S. Air Force National Air Intelligence Center dispels that notion. In its annual report on "Ballistic and Cruise Missile Threats," the center stated that medium-range missiles "are strategic systems" armed with nonconventional warheads. Pentagon officials concluded that the simulated attacks were a sign that China is prepared to go to war with the United States over the issue of Taiwan.

One element of the missile exercise that surprised DIA analysts was the PLA's use of "obscurants"—smoke and particle-filled clouds that were dispersed around the mobile missiles to protect them from attacking forces, namely, U.S. precision strike weapons. The masking involves spraying clouds of small particles around the missiles that can cause laser tracking devices to bounce off their intended targets and can fool airborne U.S. weapons operators into guiding bombs on the wrong target or on an improper aim point on a target. The Chinese missiles were seen ready for launch on their mobile truck launchers, although none was fired. The use of the obscurants was an indication to DIA officials that the Chinese were conducting the exercise in anticipation of future attack by U.S. warplanes equipped with laser-guided bombs and precision weaponry. In August 2000 the air force moved several dozen air-launched cruise missiles to the island of Guam, perhaps in anticipation of a conflict over Taiwan.

The PLA's forty liquid-fueled CSS-2s, with ranges of about 1,922 miles, are being replaced in most regions of China with the more advanced, solid-propellant CSS-5s, with a maximum range of 1,333 miles.

Richard Fisher, a specialist on the Chinese military, believes the Chinese may interpret the June 1998 detargeting pledge to exclude shorter-range nuclear missiles and include only long-range ICBMs. The targeting of U.S. forces in the recent exercise highlights the most important aspect of any future Chinese military threat to the region. "Chinese doctrine puts special emphasis on missile forces, concealing mobile forces for obtaining surprise, and using a wide variety of current and future nuclear and non-nuclear warheads," Fisher said.

MISSILE BUILDUP

Taiwan is a mountainous island about the size of West Virginia located off the southern coast of China. It has a population of about twenty-two million people, and, unlike its archenemy, it is a thriving multiparty democracy. It is also a major international trading power with more than $218 billion in global trading.

Taiwan's military has about 430,000 soldiers and is equipped with weapons obtained primarily from the United States. But U.S. arms sales to Taiwan have been cut back sharply by the Clinton-Gore administration.

Meanwhile, Communist China has dramatically built up its military forces over the past decade. The most alarming Chinese military development was identified by the DIA in October 1998. A report labeled "Secret" outlined a major buildup of short-range ballistic missiles opposite Taiwan. The report was based on sensitive intelligence indicating intricate knowledge of PLA missile planning. Up until 1998, the missile deployment had been modest and was limited to a garrison of CSS-6 missiles at Leping. What the DIA had uncovered was a Chinese plan to have a total of 650 missiles by 2005. According to the DIA, in 1998 China had 150 missiles near Taiwan and would add about fifty new missiles a year until it had achieved its objective.

The missile escalation was a clear sign to the Pentagon that China was engaging in a major buildup of its forces near Taiwan. The buildup could mean only one thing: China was planning military attacks against the island. The new missiles include the two versions of the

CSS-7 short-range ballistic missiles, designated Mod 1 and Mod 2. The DIA report said the Mod 1 had a range of 350 kilometers and the Mod 2 was capable of hitting a target as far away as 530 kilometers.

On December 5, 1999, the DIA again issued a secret report updating the short-range missile buildup. The conclusion was not good news for American military planners. "The DIA believes there are at least 40 CSS-7 missiles in Chinese military bases near Taiwan," said one intelligence official familiar with the report's conclusions. "This gives China the ability to target Taiwan with little or no warning." The report stated that China's goal was to have five hundred short-range missiles within range of Taiwan by 2005, allowing the PLA to target all of Taiwan's major military bases. "They will be able to take Taiwan with little or no warning," the official said. The report identified a third missile base under construction along China's coast. At the time of the report, the brigade-sized base being built near the town of Xianyou was nearly complete, and U.S. satellite spy photographs showed that the layout of the buildings and storage sheds was similar to that of the missile brigade headquarters located at Leping, where CSS-6 missiles are based. In addition, the report identified a second CSS-7 base at Yongang. The new base also was colocated with tunnel storage areas for the missiles, a sign that the Chinese were protecting the systems not against Taiwanese military forces but against U.S. bombers equipped with precision-guided bombs and missiles.

Pentagon analysts viewed the missile buildup as ominous since it showed that Beijing's intention was not to conduct aircraft or seaborne assaults against the island but to launch barrages of missiles. A Pentagon report to Congress made public in June 2000 stated that Beijing views ballistic missiles, as well as ground- or sea-hugging cruise missiles, as "potent military and political" weapons that can be used against Taiwan. "In an armed conflict with Taiwan, China's short-range ballistic missiles likely would target air defense installations, airfields, naval bases, C4I nodes and logistics facilities," the report said. C4I stands for command, control, communications, computers, and intelligence.

As was typical during the Clinton-Gore administration, public reports were politicized to downplay the China threat. An internal Pentagon report obtained by this author warned that the danger from the

short-range missile force was growing. "A large arsenal of highly accurate and lethal theater missiles serves as a 'trump card,' a revolutionary
departure from the PLA of the past," this internal report said. "The
PLA's theater missiles and a supporting space-based surveillance network are emerging not only as a tool of psychological warfare but as a
potentially devastating weapon of military utility."

Even after this reporter published the intelligence on the missile
buildup, President Clinton did not demand that China stop the destabilizing deployments. Clinton was asked about the deployments at a
press conference on December 8, 1999, and he said he had "grave concerns" about the growing threat. "China is modernizing its military
in a lot of ways, but our policy on China is crystal clear. We believe there
is one China," Clinton said. The phrase "one China" means that whatever happens, Clinton stands with Beijing. He said that the dispute
between the mainland and Taiwan should be resolved through dialogue and that "we oppose and would view with grave concern any kind
of violent action."

"There's been a lot of buildup of tension on both sides that I think is
unnecessary and counterproductive," Clinton said.

But Taiwan has never threatened the United States. Communist
China has, and its threats went nearly unchallenged by the Clinton-
Gore administration. One of the most alarming statements appeared
in the official PLA newspaper, *Liberation Army Daily*, on February 28,
2000. The newspaper is the official organ of the PLA and reflects the
views of its most senior leaders, notably Central Military Commission
Chairman Jiang Zemin. American intervention in a conflict between
Taiwan and China would lead to "serious damage" to U.S. national
security, the newspaper said. The article warned in only slightly veiled
language that China would resort to long-range missile attacks against
the United States during a conflict with Taiwan. "China is neither Iraq
nor Yugoslavia but a very special country," the newspaper stated.
"[O]n the other hand, it is a country that has certain abilities of
launching strategic counterattack and the capacity of launching a long
distance strike. It is not a wise move to be at war with a country such
as China, a point which the U.S. policymakers know fairly well also." A

war with China would force the United States to "make a complete withdrawal" from East Asia similar to the loss in Vietnam, the article said. Pentagon officials were surprised by the harsh anti-American tone of what amounted to an official threat by China against the United States.

But instead of criticizing China for its threat, the Pentagon's official spokesman sought to explain it away. Kenneth Bacon told reporters during a regular briefing that "Chinese doctrine" does not include "first-strike" nuclear attacks. "And there is nothing new in that article that changes that," he said. The answer was misleading because the PLA commentary made no reference to a "first-strike" missile attack. The article was referring to the use of nuclear weapons as a deterrent or as retaliation for U.S. conventional forces' intervention in a war between Taiwan and China.

The PLA's threatening article was written by PLA Colonel Zhu Chenghu, deputy director of the Institute of National Security Studies at the National Defense University in Beijing. He is an influential military hard-liner who wrote in 1998, "Although the Asia-Pacific region has been relatively stable since the end of the Cold War, there are also many uncertainties there. If certain hot-spot problems are not handled properly, they may cause conflicts, confrontations, and even war in this region, thus wrecking the peace, stability, and prosperity of the region."

DOCUMENT 65

The missile threat against the United States reflected official policy, as revealed in an internal Chinese military document obtained by dissidents in China. I received a copy of the report, known as "Document 65." It was dated August 1, 1999, and signed "General Political Department of the People's Liberation Army." The CIA has a copy and has analyzed its contents but is uncertain whether it is a genuine leak or a deliberate disclosure. The DIA also has a copy, and Defense officials who have seen classified Chinese government documents said Document 65 is written in a format similar to known secret materials that defecting Chinese officials have delivered.

The document declared that "a most important task" of the Communist Party of China is the reunification of Taiwan and that all military units, both combat and noncombat, must "be well-prepared for the war based on the rapidly-changing relationships with Taiwan." It stated that the "Taiwan issue has long since become a trump card by the anti-China forces and deteriorated into a malicious tumor that hinders the development of our motherland. Playing the Taiwan card and using it to contain China is a manifestation of the old Cold War thinking in the new international arena and an important means of opposing China by a handful [of] politicians in the U.S. Congress who cling desperately to the Cold War thinking. In terms of social system, it is expressed as anti-Communist thinking; in terms of outlook, it is revealed as naked racial discrimination. In view of this situation, to resolve [the] Taiwan issue and achieve the reunification as soon as possible not only involves our sovereignty and national dignity, but also directly relates to our country's development and important strategy in opposing world hegemonism." The reference to world hegemonism is code for Beijing's view of the threat from the United States.

China, according to the document, seeks a peaceful reunification with Taiwan but will not give up its option to use military force, as Taiwan announced in 1991. That was the year Taipei declared it was no longer the government of all of China and thus no longer sought to take back forcibly what was lost during the 1940s civil war. In the context of military force, the document disclosed for the first time the idea that the Taiwan issue would not be allowed to "drag on indefinitely." And because of Taiwan President Lee Teng-hui's remarks of July 9, 1999—when he declared that Taiwan "has been a sovereign state since it was founded in 1912" and called for relations with China on a "special state-to-state" basis, thereby challenging Beijing's "One China" policy—the Chinese military has been given "solid grounds for achieving reunification using military power." Still, China remains committed to peaceful reunification for the long-term interests of Beijing, Document 65 declared.

As for world affairs and Taiwan, Document 65 stated that the timing of reunification, peaceful or forceful, had been hampered by the

United States. Europe would not join the United States in fighting a war with China, it stated. "When deciding on the timing, we must... use diplomatic leverage to minimize international resistance."

What followed next was the internal PLA and Communist Party view on how to prevent the United States from defending Taiwan from a Chinese military attack. "Based on strategic considerations, the CMC [Central Military Commission] has decided to disclose, when appropriate, some information on strategic weaponry so that the U.S. will exercise some caution in decision making and be aware that it would have to pay a price if it decided to intervene in a military conflict. The purpose is to prevent the U.S. from being deeply involved even if a war becomes unavoidable so that the losses on both sides of the Taiwan Straits will be minimized throughout the war. The main point is deterrence, which is the test for a peaceful solution. The test is within the strategic scope of taking initiative and promoting good timing." The document noted that relations between Washington and Beijing were at "a low ebb" due to the May 7, 1999, NATO bombing strike on China's embassy in Belgrade, Yugoslavia. The bombing was accidental and based on faulty CIA maps, but China remains convinced the attack was deliberate and intended to draw China into a world war.

The document also had an alarming passage discussing war with the United States:

> Taking into account [the] possible intervention by the U.S. and based on the development strategy of our country, it is better to fight now than in the future—the earlier, the better. The reason being that, if worst [sic] comes to worst, we will gain control of Taiwan before full deployment of the U.S. troops. In this case, the only thing the U.S. can do is fight a war with the purpose of retaliation, which will be similar to the Gulf War against Iraq or the recent bombing of Yugoslavia as far as its operational objective is considered, namely, to first attack from the sky and the sea our coastal military targets, and then attack our vital civil facilities so as to force us to accept its terms like Iraq and Yugoslavia. This is of course

wishful thinking. However, before completely destroying the attacking enemy forces from the sea and their auxiliary bases which together constitute a threat to us, even if we successfully carry out interception and control the sky, our military and civil facilities will still incur some damages. The damages will be more extensive if the war cannot be ended within a short period of time and the U.S. cannot launch the second and third strategic strikes, which will take a toll on the economic development of our country. If the above scenario cannot be avoided, an early war will delay the success of our reform whereas a later war will jeopardize the full achievement of the reform.

The Chinese document asserted that the United States military has not been tested in a major conflict with a large nation like China. China's forces will be able to defeat the United States because the U.S. military will become "exhausted" from long-distance warfare. "It can be safely expected that once the U.S. launches an attack, the front line of the U.S. forces and their supporting bases will be exposed within the range of our effective strikes. After the first strategic strike, the U.S. forces will be faced with weaponry and logistic problems, providing us with opportunities for major offensives and [to] win large battles." The document reveals what Pentagon specialist Michael Pillsbury has called "dangerous misperceptions" by China about the United States. It is just these kinds of misperceptions that could lead to a war.

As for nuclear war, the Chinese military "does not foresee" a strategic nuclear exchange because the United States has shown no willingness to fight a massive conflict over Taiwan. Also, China is willing to suffer "major losses" of its forces, but the United States, as demonstrated in Vietnam, is not. The document stated that the United States backed off its deployment of two aircraft carrier battle groups near Taiwan in 1996 after spy satellites detected the departure from Lushun harbor of China's four nuclear submarines. "So far we have built up the capability for the second and the third nuclear strikes and are fairly confident in fighting a nuclear war," the document said, noting that the Central Committee of the ruling Politburo "has decided to pass through formal channels this message to the top leaders of the U.S. This is one of the concrete measures that we will take to prevent the escalation of war in the spirit of being responsible."

THE DF-31

The PLA did not wait long to follow through on its promise to demonstrate a new strategic weapon. On August 2, 1999, one day after Document 65 was produced, the same warning center that conducted the simulated Chinese nuclear attack on the United States monitored a real missile launch. A Defense Support Program satellite picked up the flash and relayed it to the air force watchers in Cheyenne Mountain around 10:00 PM Mountain Daylight Time.

The test firing of the Dong Feng-31, or East Wind, came less than a month after Taiwanese President Lee Teng-hui called for "state-to-state" talks between Taiwan and China, which angered Chinese Communist officials, who refuse to acknowledge Taiwan's current and historical independence. The strategic nuclear missile test was intended as a signal to the United States about the consequences of intervening in the dispute. China's strategic nuclear missile program is cloaked in utmost secrecy. Within the U.S. intelligence community, it is on the list of "hard targets" for U.S. spying. Thus, it was striking to CIA and DIA analysts that for the first time Beijing announced through its official Xinhua news agency that a new missile had been tested. "China successfully conducted a launching test of a new type of long-range ground-to-ground missile within its territory," the news agency announced. In addition to the U.S. defense satellites, the missile test was closely followed by a special U.S. intelligence-gathering ship with the code name *Cobra Judy*. The ship, the USS *Observation Island*, was positioned in waters off China. The missile was launched from a test facility at Wuzhai Missile and Space Center in central China and tracked to impact in a remote area of central China.

As it had done with all of China's threatening military and intelligence activities, the State Department attempted to play down this new strategic nuclear missile development. "We do not have any basis to conclude that the timing of this launch is linked to the issues with Taiwan," claimed State Department spokesman James Rubin. "This test-firing has been expected for some time and why they specifically chose today is something for them to explain, but it's not an unexpected development in the course of their modernization program." For the Clinton-Gore administration, China's strategic nuclear modernization program, rather than threatening the United States, was something to be welcomed. In the liberal "multipolarity" worldview espoused by the president and his top advisers, anything that diminished America's role as sole superpower was a good thing.

China had used missile tests for political messages before—including firing M-9 short-range missiles dangerously close to Taiwan shortly before its 1996 presidential election. And a ground test of a DF-31 was conducted during President Clinton's ten-day state visit to China in June and July of 1998.

For the CIA, the DF-31 was the culmination of China's continuing effort to acquire both missile and warhead technology from the United States. It is this mobile intercontinental-range missile, with a maximum range of about five thousand miles, that will be the first to use stolen U.S. warhead know-how. If it is a single warhead, it will be the W-70 copy. Should China seek to expand the lethality of its small missile arsenal, as it promises to do in response to U.S. national missile defenses, the W-88 look-alike warhead will be applied, probably in threes. The missile is expected to contain special space launcher technology obtained from U.S. companies during cooperation on satellite transfers in the early 1990s.

The DF-31 is the world's second truck-launched missile, after Russia's SS-25 and follow-on SS-27, also called Topol M. Intelligence analysts believe the DF-31 is the first of two new mobile missiles to replace the old CSS-4 arsenal that is liquid-fueled and takes much longer to fire. The lengthy preparation time makes the older missile vulnerable to preemptive attacks. The DF-31 is believed to be for use against Russia and India—China's two regional strategic nuclear rivals. For the United States, the longer-range version, the DF-41, will be developed several years after the DF-31 is deployed. It will have a range of about 8,600 miles and will be able to hit all parts of the United States. The DF-31, by contrast, can reach only the western United States.

The new mobile missile also was judged by the DIA to be capable of launching multiple warheads, a quantitative and qualitative step forward over China's current arsenal of single-warhead missiles. A classified report stated several months after the test that the August 2 flight included a single dummy warhead combined with several decoy warheads. The decoys were a clear sign that the Chinese are anticipating future U.S. missile defenses. Adding more warheads on their missiles aims to defeat the antimissile shield.

The Pentagon and the CIA watched the DF-31's development closely. A secret report from the National Air Intelligence Center, located at Wright-Patterson Air Force Base in Ohio, stated that the DF-31 is a major strategic threat. "The DF-31 ICBM will give China a major-strike capability that will be difficult to counterattack at any stage of its operation," the report said. "It will be a significant threat not only to U.S. forces deployed in the Pacific theater, but to portions of the continental United States and to many of our allies." The DF-31 will "narrow the gap" between the current Chinese missile arsenal and those of U.S. and Russian strategic forces.

Congressman Christopher Cox, chairman of the Select Committee on U.S. National Security and Military/Commercial Concerns with the People's Republic of China, believes the DF-31 test confirmed the forecast of his panel's final report. It highlighted new dangers to the United States. "It is a significant modernization that will make the PRC one of only two countries in the world with a road-mobile nuclear force," Cox said. "In effect, this will give the PRC a first-strike capability against every country in the region except Russia, while limiting U.S. options were we to intervene against aggression."

TAIWAN ARMS

With China building up its missile forces, the danger of conflict in the Taiwan Strait is growing. Taiwan's last major weapons purchase was 150 U.S. F-16 fighters in the early 1990s. The jets were sold, however, without advanced avionics systems that give them greater capabilities for flying and fighting in bad weather. The omission was intentional and aimed at preventing Taiwan from having an edge in an air conflict with China in the military hardware balance. The special aircraft pods were approved for sale in June 2000, but their final transfer may take years. Taipei also purchased a version of the Patriot antiaircraft missile that was used against Iraqi Scud missiles during the 1991 Gulf War. But serious flaws in those missiles were discovered after the missile batteries were kept turned on for long periods of time. The Pentagon secretly replaced a number of Patriot batteries in Kuwait, Saudi Arabia, and South Korea after learning of the glitch in early 2000. A Pentagon report to Congress in 1999 stated that Taiwan's strategic objectives against China included maintaining "air superiority," maintaining the ability to defeat a PRC blockade of the island, and countering an aerial or amphibious assault on Taiwan.

Admiral Dennis Blair, the commander in chief of the U.S. Pacific Command based in Hawaii, said in an interview in November 1999 that the missile buildup was destabilizing the region and showed the need for the United States to provide more defensive arms and weapons systems to Taiwan to maintain a balance of power. The four-star admiral said the United States would be justified in providing missile defenses to the island under the 1979 Taiwan Relations Act. "We're talking about a balance here," Blair said, "and a count of 500 or 600 [missiles] to very few defenses doesn't seem like a very good balance."

Curiously, Blair had a different tone in a private meeting with a group of Senate staff aides four months earlier. The admiral had taken over from Admiral Joseph Prueher, whose softness toward Beijing was rewarded with an ambassadorship there. Blair had informed Defense officials privately that he would be tougher on China than his predecessor had been. But at a meeting on Capitol Hill in late 1999, Blair criticized President Lee Teng-hui of Taiwan for calling for relations on a "state-to-state" basis between the mainland and the island. The communist rulers in Beijing regarded the statement as a step toward independence and were furious, of course. Blair told the staffers that Taiwan had become "the turd in the punch bowl" of U.S.-Chinese relations.

What was worse was Blair's subsequent remark that if Taiwan were to declare itself an independent nation, "I don't think we should support them at all." The remark was the clearest sign that the Clinton-Gore administration had aligned itself with the communist regime in China against democratic Taiwan.

"It was a dangerous remark," said a Senate aide who attended the meeting with Blair. "The problem is China, not Taiwan."

THE IMPORTANCE OF TAIWAN

When Lee Teng-hui announced his desire for state-to-state relations between Taiwan and the People's Republic of China, he also remarked, "We would like to take a more active role in the Chinese mainland's modernization process; therefore, we hope that the authorities there can proceed with democratic reform to create favorable conditions for democratic unification. This is the direction of our efforts. We want to maintain the status quo and maintain peace with Beijing on this foundation." Lee noted that Taiwan plays a crucial role in Asia. "Taiwan is important for two reasons: its safeguarding of democracy and human rights and its important strategic position in the Western Pacific region."

Indeed, Taiwan is located in one of the most important strategic waterways in the world. Ships bringing oil from the Middle East to the region must pass through the South China Sea. Goods bound from Asia to Europe and the Middle East travel in the opposite direction. It is not just fervent nationalism mixed with communism that is driving China's demands for reunification. The strategic motivation is China's desire to expand its influence far beyond Chinese shores. U.S. intelligence analysts refer to it as Beijing's "two island-chain strategy." China is seeking hegemony over strategic waters extending several hundred miles, including Taiwan, which sits at the north end of the vital sea lane. Eventually, China wants to expand the first island chain to cover up to a thousand miles from its coast.

The evidence of China's covert strategic expansion into the Pacific has been ignored by most major news media. But as in the past, the expansion has been highlighted in great detail in classified U.S. intelligence reports. On January 29, 1999, the National Military Joint Intelligence Center, the Pentagon's central clearinghouse for intelligence related to joint military operations, reported that spy satellite photographs of the South China Sea revealed that Chinese military forces were expanding a military air base on Woody Island. The construction involved building petrochemical storage facilities. Intelligence analysts said the construction of fuel storage tanks will support China's new Russian-made Su-27 fighter bombers. The air base is located on part of the Paracel Islands chain that is administered by China but claimed by Vietnam. The Woody Island base where the new fuel storage tanks are being built is about 260 miles east of Da Nang, Vietnam, in the South China Sea, and about four hundred miles south of Hong Kong.

The construction on Woody Island was troubling for pro-China supporters in the United States because it contradicted the notion that Communist China has no territorial ambitions outside its own borders. "This is part of ongoing Chinese efforts at power projection throughout the region," said one official familiar with the intelligence report. In a report in the *Washington Times*, this author first disclosed the new military construction on the Paracels, which China calls the Xinsha Islands. This disclosure followed other troubling reports of China's expansion of military facilities on another disputed island chain, the Spratly Islands, further south near the Philippines. The Spratlys are a series of islets claimed by several countries; they are believed to have large reserves of oil and natural gas. The islets have been the scene of several clashes between Philippine and Chinese military forces.

Pentagon officials believe the construction on Woody Island is for a fuel depot for Su-27s or Chinese FB-7 fighter bombers to increase the range of the jets and allow them to be able to reach the Spratlys, in case of future conflicts with the Philippines. Philippine military aircraft bombed a Chinese installation on Mischief Reef in the Spratlys in 1995, and Chinese warships were spotted there in 1999, as were new Chinese military facilities on the islands.

China specialist Richard Fisher said the military base on Woody Island can be used for a variety of military aircraft. "As we look into the next decade, [airborne warning and control jets] could operate out of Woody Island, directing both offensive and defensive operations aimed at controlling access to the South China Sea." In fact, China's new Phalcon Airborne Warning and Control System (AWACS) plane, which was purchased from Israel amid protests from the United States, could use the island as a strategic refueling base. The Phalcon, similar to the U.S. AWACS command and control plane, is built on a Russian-made IL-76 aircraft, and when deployed by the PLA it will provide much greater capabilities for conducting long-range warfare, including support for the Su-27s. China has at least eighty-seven Su-27s and is expected to buy about three hundred of the advanced jets from Russia. It is also developing several other fighter bombers. In July 2000, Israel's government bowed to U.S. pressure and canceled the planned sale of the Phalcon aircraft. The action angered Chinese President Jiang Zemin, who chastised the American defense secretary, William S. Cohen, during a Beijing meeting. Intelligence officials said they expect the Chinese to continue shopping for airborne warning and control jets, probably from Russia.

The official government news agency, Xinhua, has tried to dismiss Western intelligence reports by saying that Beijing plans to turn Woody Island, which it calls Yongxing, into a tourist resort. However, the facility currently holds a small contingent of PLA troops and a satellite tracking station. The military development of Woody Island ties in with the expanding reach of Chinese military power, as underlined in a classified 1996 Pentagon report on aerial refueling. It said that by 1997 "Chinese tanker and receiver aircraft probably will be able to perform some long-range escort, air-to-air and ground attack missions over the South China Sea or elsewhere in the region." China has converted at least twenty B-6 bombers into long-range refueling tankers and recently equipped up to twenty-four F-8 fighters with aerial refueling pods for extended-range missions. The refueling capability has extended the F-8's combat radius from 431 miles to 632 miles, enabling China "to conduct combat missions over the South China Sea, near Taiwan, along the Sino-Indian border and over the East China Sea."

"Steady progress in air refueling will give China a power-projection capability over the South China Sea by the turn of the century," the Pentagon report said.

BAD INTENTIONS

The buildup of China's missile forces opposite Taiwan did not make headlines in the *New York Times* or *Washington Post*. Nor did the major television networks show interest in the story. But inside the Pentagon the missile deployments were viewed with alarm. Even the DIA in its classified reporting cables did not capture the context of what was going on. One Pentagon officer did, however. Air Force Major Mark A. Stokes, who was an air attaché at the U.S. embassy in Beijing from 1992 to 1995, outlined the full extent of the missile operations in an internal paper produced in 1999. Stokes exploded the orthodox pro-China view—a view espoused by many of America's China hands—that the People's Liberation Army is a "junkyard" army incapable of matching American military power for the next twenty or thirty years. Stokes has it right: China's strategy of missile power threatens not only Taiwan but also American forces in Japan and Hawaii.

"The People's Republic of China is developing one of the most daunting conventional theater missile challenges in the world," his report said. "A large arsenal of highly accurate and lethal theater missiles serves as a 'trump card,' a revolutionary departure from the PLA of the past. The PLA's theater missiles and a supporting space-based surveillance network are emerging not only as a tool of psychological warfare, but as a potentially devastating weapon of military utility." Theater missiles include not only ballistic missiles that travel through space and reenter the atmosphere at high speed, but also aircraft-launched ground attack missiles and cruise missiles guided by onboard computers. The report reveals that the Chinese are developing systems of surveillance that can monitor large areas and can provide targeting data almost instantaneously. Beijing is working on an overwhelming theater missile advantage over Taiwan and is adjusting its doctrine to focus on launching massive, no-warning attacks.

From the early 1990s to mid-decade, Chinese military forces showed no serious interest in attacking Taiwan. The only forces deployed close to the island were a "symbolic" force of ground troops, warships, and military aircraft within three hundred miles of Taiwan. "Now, however, PLA modernization—and theater missile development in particular—is motivated in large part by a desire to use decisive military force as a means to deter Taiwan independence sentiment and strengthen the PRC's hand in a reestablished cross-Strait dialogue," the report said. The sober message in the buildup is that Chinese military leaders have adopted the view that "force may eventually have to be used" against the island. Chinese military leaders learned Iraq's lesson from the 1991 Persian Gulf War: Do not allow U.S. military forces months to build up prior to attack. "Successful use of overwhelming force through preemptive strikes to quickly resolve the Taiwan Strait issue could preclude U.S. intervention by presenting Washington and the international community with a fait accompli," the report said.

The report provided the details of a military buildup opposite Taiwan that was clearly meant to be used in the future, not merely as a diplomatic tool of political coercion. The report outlined the following weapons and support developments:

- **Satellite surveillance:** By 2005 to 2010, China will deploy a space-based surveillance system made up of radar-imaging satellites for all-weather monitoring; signals intelligence-gathering satellites to pick up all electronic communications and signals; high-resolution photographic satellites for early warning, missile targeting, and mission planning; and high-resolution imagery satellites for intelligence and damage assessment in conflict. The radar imaging satellites, similar to the U.S. synthetic aperture radar satellites known by the code name "Lacrosse," would be used for tracking U.S. aircraft carriers and submarines far from China's shores.
- **Theater ballistic missiles:** The backbone of the PLA's military operations is deployment of conventionally armed ballistic missiles as part of Beijing's "deep attack strategy." In addition to the deploy-

ments of 310-mile-range CSS-6s (M-9s) and 186-mile-range CSS-7s (M-11s), China will use medium-range CSS-5 missiles. The CSS-5 has a range of up to 1,333 miles; it is a nuclear-armed missile but is being converted to precision strike conventional warheads. The missile cannot be stopped with Taiwan's Patriot air defense missiles.

- **Missile technology advances:** China is adding "terminal guidance" to its missiles. The system allows onboard computers to match stored images of the ground with flight data. High-explosive warheads are being augmented with advanced warheads, including cluster bomblet warheads, exotic electromagnetic pulse warheads that knock out electronics, penetrating warheads for attacking hardened targets, and fuel air explosives that create huge blasts for much greater accuracy.

- **Missile defense countermeasures:** Anticipating the deployment of regional antimissile defenses, Chinese military developers are planning to defeat missile interceptor systems by large-scale "saturation" missile strikes, maneuvering warhead reentry vehicles, stealth warhead and missile design, decoy warheads, and onboard electronic jammers. Also under development are special missile coatings designed to thwart laser guns, like the air force's new Airborne Laser weapon. Moreover, the PLA is working on low-trajectory ballistic missiles that can defeat missile defenses.

- **Land attack cruise missiles:** China, with Russian assistance, is building at least three new cruise missiles modeled after the ground-hugging U.S. Tomahawk. The PLA could field its first Tomahawk-like cruise missile, the XY-41, in the early 2000s. The new missiles include a modified Silkworm antiship cruise missile with a range of up to 248 miles. A second missile, the YJ-8, will be modified from China's version of the French Exocet antiship cruise missile and will have a range of between seventy-five miles and 186 miles and will rely on U.S. Global Positioning System satellites for its guidance system. The PLA also is working on an antiradar missile similar to the U.S. HARM—High-speed Anti-Radiation Missile. The YJ-9 missile appears to be similar to Russia's KH-31P, which China has said was developed to shoot down U.S. AWACS jets and to attack Patriot anti-missile radar as well as the Aegis battle management radar deployed on U.S. and Japanese advanced destroyers.

The PLA is not just building hardware for large-scale theater war. It is making extensive improvements in its organizational and battlefield planning. For example, the report stated that "the key to success of a theater missile campaign is concealing the forward deployment of brigade elements. Surprise can only be achieved through denial of foreign human and technical intelligence access." The PLA is hardening its communications lines and working on plans to knock out U.S. satellites in space, as well as increasing its ability to track U.S. satellites in space.

The Stokes report was most revealing in laying out the scenario for a lightning missile strike on Taiwan. The plan calls for "no-warning" attacks on the island with missiles, backed by aircraft sorties and special operations attacks to prevent a buildup of U.S. forces. The goal of the attacks would be to knock out all communications and information systems, defeat Taiwan's air forces, and control the waters around the island by knocking out ships. "PLA conventional ballistic and land attack cruise missiles would attempt to paralyze Taiwan's command and control system by... cutting off fielded military forces from the civilian and military leadership in Taipei," the report said. The weapon of choice will be antiradar missiles. To gain air superiority, China would attack airfields, runways, weapons storage facilities, command posts, and fuel depots. Sea superiority would include missile attacks on ports. The missiles can be launched within forty minutes of the order to do so. The report quoted PLA writings as stating that Taiwan could be paralyzed by missiles "in as little as 45 minutes."

TARGET: U.S.A.

The Stokes report stated that the PLA would use four hundred missiles in its opening attacks, or about half of its regional missile forces. The attacks would come from all angles to frustrate missile defenses. Key targets would include Taiwanese military leaders. The report noted that the PLA could attack "the heart of Taiwan's political and military leadership" such as the presidential palace and the defense ministry, which could be blown up with as few as five missiles.

In anticipation of U.S. involvement, the PLA "has indicated a willingness to use highly accurate [short-range ballistic missiles], [medium-range ballistic missiles], and [land attack cruise missiles] against U.S. assets, to include key bases in Japan and aircraft carriers operating in the Western Pacific," the report said. China has practiced using its missiles against the carriers and would also fire missiles against regional U.S. air bases, naval facilities, and key command and control and support facilities. The unclassified report made no direct mention of the December 2, 1998, DIA report on the missile exercises against U.S. bases, but this was an oblique reference to it.

Stokes warned in his report that the combination of advanced surveillance, large numbers of ballistic and cruise missiles, and a shift toward surprise attack is a serious threat to the stability of the region. The force would provide Beijing with a "decisive edge" over Taiwan in a conflict and "could also hold U.S. forces in the Western Pacific at risk should a decision be made to intervene."

To protect its missile power strategy, Beijing has launched a "propaganda campaign" against U.S. regional antimissile defenses, presenting what the report called a bogus claim that missile defenses will spark an arms race. Stokes also noted there is a "mutually supporting dynamic" between Communist Chinese officials and U.S. critics who oppose missile defenses.

"Confidence in a quick military victory could lower the perceived cost of conflict and thus increase Beijing's incentives to use force," the report stated. Unchallenged by a Taiwanese missile defense, Beijing's first strike force "raises the danger of preemptive war."

This raises the danger that Taiwan will decide to renew its efforts to develop nuclear weapons. "Taiwan is considered by some to have the capacity to develop nuclear weapons quickly if the need should arise," the report said. It also could encourage Taiwan to launch a defensive war against China. The report quoted U.S. military doctrine on the preferred method of countering enemy missiles: "Attack and destroy or disrupt theater missiles prior to their launch."

Stokes believes that Beijing will not moderate its missile deployments near Taiwan. "Theater missiles are an integral part of the PLA's overall modernization objections," he said. "As long as the PLA seeks to develop the kind of force that could give the PRC a decisive military advantage over Taiwan, then the ability to freeze or roll back theater missile deployments will be limited." Still more should be done to try to convince the communist leaders in Beijing that the missiles are destabilizing and that dealing with Taiwan through military force "is not a viable option."

In sharp contrast to Stokes's analysis, the official Pentagon report sent to Congress on Chinese military activities in relation to Taiwan was a highly politicized unclassified report made public in June 2000. The twenty-six-page report was replete with excuses for why Beijing either would not or could not attack Taiwan. But as for explaining the strategy of the Chinese, it made clear that the military buildup by Beijing was preparation for a possible future confrontation with the United States. Chinese military doctrine anticipated fighting a technologically superior foe like the United States. "Moreover, a cross-Strait conflict between China and Taiwan involving the United States has emerged as the dominant scenario guiding PLA force planning, military training, and war preparation," the report said. The big question in the dispute over Taiwan, of course, is whether the United States will defend it in the event of a mainland attack.

Clinton's first comments on the Taiwan Strait crisis of 1999 followed a telephone conversation between the president and Chinese leader Jiang Zemin on July 20 of that year. Clinton was asked by reporters during a Rose Garden ceremony at the White House whether Jiang had threatened to use force against Taiwan and whether he would use force to defend Taiwan. The president replied, "We had a conversation in which I restated our strong support of the 'One China' policy and our strong support for the cross-strait dialogue, and I made it clear our policy had not changed, including our view under the Taiwan Relations Act that it would be—we would take very seriously any abridgement of the peaceful dialogue." China, Clinton said, knows U.S. policy well, and repeating the so-called "One China" view for Beijing's benefit and "encouraging Taiwan to support that" would be "helpful in easing some of the tensions." He called the telephone exchange with the Chinese leader "a very positive conversation, far more positive than negative."

The next day, at a formal press conference, the president was asked again whether the United States would intervene militarily if China attacked Taiwan. He again declined to answer directly, stating only that U.S. policy is governed by the Taiwan Relations Act. "We made it clear.... And a few years ago we had a physical expression of that, that we don't believe there should be any violent attempts to resolve this, and we would view it very seriously." He was referring to the two air-craft carrier battle groups sent to waters near Taiwan in March 1996 after China conducted menacing war games that included several short-range missile firings. But the United States also tilted away from Taiwan by canceling a trip by a Pentagon delegation to express U.S. anger over Lee Teng-hui's statement of the obvious—that there are two Chinas, one communist and one democratic. Clinton defended the trip cancellation at his press conference. "I didn't think this was the best time to do something which might excite either one side or the other and imply that a military solution is an acceptable alternative," Clinton said. "If you really think about what's at stake here, it would be unthinkable."

The White House made only a passing reference to "fully imple-menting" the Taiwan Relations Act and keeping "robust unofficial" ties with Taiwan in its December 1999 "National Security Strategy for a New Century" report outlining U.S. foreign and defense policies.

The Taiwan Relations Act states that the decision to recognize Beijing diplomatically "rests upon the expectation that the future of Taiwan will be determined by peaceful means." It also states that "any effort to determine the future of Taiwan by other than peaceful means, including by boycotts or embargoes," would be viewed as "a threat to the peace and security of the Western Pacific area and of grave concern to the United States." The act allows the United States to "provide Tai-wan with arms of a defensive character," although that is not defined

further. And last it states that it is U.S. policy "to maintain the capacity of the United States to resist any resort to force or other forms of
coercion that would jeopardize the security, or the social or economic
system, of the people on Taiwan."

The position of National Security Adviser Sandy Berger and his top
China aide, Kenneth Lieberthal, was that because they viewed Taiwan
as a part of China, the United States could not plan to defend the country from itself. It would be tantamount to intervening in the internal
affairs of China—the exact position of the communist leaders in Beijing.
Lieberthal was regarded as among the most pro-Beijing officials in the
Clinton-Gore administration. Berger's relations with the Chinese go
back to his days as a trade lawyer for Hogan & Hartson, when he was in
charge of joint U.S.-China ventures with American companies. During
a visit to China in March 2000, China's foreign minister, Tang Jiaxuan,
referred to Berger as "our old friend" who had been the key player in
keeping relations with Beijing on track.

In Auckland, New Zealand, in September 1999, Clinton again stated
the need for peaceful resolution of the latest crisis following a meeting
with Jiang Zemin. When the Chinese leader was asked if he continued
to advocate attacking Taiwan over the question of independence, Jiang
stated: "Our policy on Taiwan is a consistent one. That is, one, peaceful unification, one country–two systems. However, if there were to be
any foreign intervention, or if there were to be Taiwan independence,
then we would not undertake to renounce the use of force."

The Chinese were posturing in advance of Taiwan's March 2000 election, which ended more than five decades of Kuomintang rule and
brought the pro-independence Democratic Progressive Party to power
under the leadership of Chen Shui-bian.

China's rulers did not repeat the attempts at intimidation that they
had used in 1996. No large-scale exercises were held, and no missiles
were fired. But Beijing engaged in a war of words. The first salvo came
with the release on February 21, 2000, of an official government "white
paper," with the title "The One-China Principle and the Taiwan Issue."
The 7,400-word document provided the communist perspective on the
civil war that ended in 1949 but led to the anticommunist Nationalists'

controlling Taiwan. Citing a "serious crisis," the document added a new condition for using force to reunite Taiwan under communist rule. In the past, Beijing had laid out the conditions for the use of force as occupation by a foreign power, development of nuclear weapons, and a declaration of independence by the Taipei government. The key phrase was: "If the Taiwan authorities refuse, sine die, the peaceful settlement of cross-Straits reunification through negotiations, then the Chinese government will only be forced to adopt all drastic measures possible, including the use of force."

Premier Zhu Rongji of China then delivered a finger-pointing threat to the people of Taiwan on March 15, 2000. The statement was clearly aimed at influencing the voting in Taiwan set for three days later. The official Beijing line was that the election was a "local election," but Zhu told Taiwanese voters not to elect Chen Shui-bian president. The islanders "are in a very critical and historical juncture, and I advise all people in Taiwan not to act on their impulse since this juncture will decide the future of both sides across the Straits. I am afraid you won't have another opportunity to regret." The threatening statement apparently backfired, since the Taiwanese elected Chen.

The Taiwanese people stood up for their democratic rights, but the Clinton-Gore administration did not side with them.

The clearest example was the failure of the president and his advisers to live up to the obligations under the Taiwan Relations Act to provide for Taiwan's defensive needs. For seven years Taiwanese military officials went to Washington, met with U.S. officials, and requested new weapons. Without fail, the requests were turned down, the latest rejection coming in April 2000 when the Clinton-Gore administration denied Taiwan's request to buy advanced air defense weapons and Aegis ships costing up to $1 billion each. When it comes to supporting American business, the Clinton-Gore administration is happy to arrange deals between big campaign donors and the communist government in Beijing. But for democratic Taiwan... nothing doing. The administration approved the sale of advanced medium-range air-to-air missiles, known as AMRAAM, but refused to allow the missiles to be stationed on the island. The decision drew criticism from Senator Jesse Helms, chairman of the Senate Foreign Relations Committee. "What is Taiwan to do? Call FedEx for its AMRAAMs after China attacks?" Helms asked.

The Clinton-Gore reelection campaign benefited from thousands of dollars in covert contributions from China, much of it linked to Chinese government sources. The Clinton-Gore policy on export controls allowed China to improve its long-range strategic nuclear missiles, which are targeted on American cities. The administration ignored Chinese inroads into the Panama Canal. It ignored China's sales of nuclear, chemical, and other weapons and missile goods to rogue states. It made sure that China paid no price for stealing secrets of U.S. nuclear warheads. Fundamentally, the Clinton-Gore administration treated China the way Chamberlain treated Hitler—except worse. Chamberlain's interest was to prevent war. The Clinton-Gore administration merely wanted to enrich its campaign coffers and friendly corporations. It would be a tragedy for the twenty-two million people of Taiwan—and for the United States—if they are sacrificed to Communist China, all in the hope of a windfall of corporate profits for Democratic Party donors. But that was the direction of Clinton-Gore policy.

An American China Strategy

The People's Republic of China is the most serious national security threat the United States faces at present and will remain so into the foreseeable future. This grave strategic threat includes the disruption of vital U.S. interests in the Pacific region and even the possibility of a nuclear war that could cost millions of American lives.

Yet under the "engagement" policy of President Clinton and his advisers, the China threat has been wished away with meaningless platitudes and unrealistic expectations that China will somehow evolve peacefully into a benign democracy. It is a policy of weakness and passivity that ill serves America's national interests.

In stark contrast, China's hard-eyed communist rulers have set out on a coolly pragmatic course of strategic deception that masks their true goals: undermining the United States around the world and raising China to a position of dominant international political and military power. They seek to push the United States out of the vital Pacific region and achieve virtual Chinese hegemony in Asia. In a world growing more interdependent by the hour, China's ambitions cannot be shrugged off.

The reason Americans should take the threat from China so seriously is that it puts at risk the very national existence of the United States. And the reason the world should take the China threat so seriously is that our country, by virtue of its wealth and power, is the leading force for freedom and democracy everywhere. Without this leadership, there is little hope of a better life for all mankind.

The China threat demands a strategic response from the United States, not ad hoc policies that have failed to promote real change within the dictatorial government in Beijing. Under the Clinton-Gore administration, China was dismissed as a threat or even a potential threat. The apparent reason for what amounted to a policy of appeasement was trade and business interests, combined with the compromising of Bill Clinton by Chinese interests that contributed heavily to his campaign funds. But there is also a more sinister reason: an ideological affinity for China's supposedly "progressive" brand of communism among top White House advisers and even the president himself. Going beyond the Left's long-standing and relatively harmless "anti-anticommunist" infatuation, this blinkered view sees China as the last best hope for the triumph of Marxist ideas.

These wishful thinkers desperately want China and its communist rulers to prosper, in hopes that the misguided idealism of their college days will thereby survive the universal discrediting of communism in the past decade.

U.S. intelligence officials have made it clear that the failure of the Clinton-Gore administration to understand the China threat and do something about it started at the top. A White House list of intelligence priorities of interest to the president and his national security advisers did not even include China as a principal target. The list was sent to the Central Intelligence Agency and heavily influenced how senior intelligence officials gathered, analyzed, and reported secret intelligence to the policymakers. The absence of China from the target list demonstrated that Bill Clinton did not want to know what China was really doing.

To address the China threat adequately, U.S. leaders must first understand the threat, then develop and implement a strategic plan to eliminate the threat. Such a plan must include at least the following elements:

- **Launch a major intelligence "blitz" against China:** U.S. intelligence agencies today have very limited capabilities for gathering strategic intelligence information from China. The small number of China specialists within the U.S. intelligence community must be augmented with as many as 2,500 to 3,000 China specialists. The CIA and the Defense Intelligence Agency must devote most of their resources to developing networks of agents inside China's Communist Party, the government, the People's Liberation Army, and related organizations. China's more open economic situation has created tremendous espionage opportunities. Electronically, the National Security Agency must be tasked to build up its eavesdropping capabilities and other signals intelligence and code-breaking capabilities targeted at China. The National Reconnaissance Office, in charge of spy-photographic satellites, should be tasked to develop greater surveillance, reconnaissance, and intelligence-gathering capabilities directed at the difficult target of Chinese government and military activities. Analytically, the orthodox notion of a nonthreatening China should be replaced with a hardheaded realism based on American national interest. Without knowing and understanding both the threats and the opportunities presented by China's communist regime, American leaders will be unable to formulate strategic policies. A massive intelligence collection effort is needed.

- **Develop a strategic plan:** The United States needs to carry out a comprehensive effort to analyze and formulate strategic policies for dealing with the China threat, both short-term and long-term. The starting point is to recognize that, despite the Clinton administration's policies—and partly because of them—the communist regime in Beijing is not evolving in a democratic, nonthreatening direction. Instead, it is becoming more threatening. China's communist government has realized that the economic precepts of Marxism-Leninism do not bring prosperity. But it obviously has not considered the real problem: its brutal communist dictatorship. It has modified its economics without recognizing that its guiding ideology is fundamentally flawed and would have to be discarded to truly bring about reform. An American strategic plan must begin with a solution that includes a democratic alternative. The Communist government must be replaced and a process of "de-communization," similar to de-Nazification following World War II, must be adopted.

- **Strengthen alliances in Asia:** The United States should seek to develop a strategic alliance as part of a larger policy of pressuring China into adopting noncommunist democratic reform. The United States must play the leading role in Asia, acting as a force for freedom and democracy. The alliance must be aboveboard in frankly identifying China as the major threat to peace, stability, and freedom in Asia. The alliance should include Japan and South Korea in Northeast Asia, the Philippines and other friends in Southeast Asia, and India in Southwest Asia. India's turn toward reliance on nuclear weapons is a direct result of the pro-China policies adopted by the Clinton administration. The result has been greater instability in Southwest Asia, with India and Pakistan engaging in a nuclear standoff. To the north, the United States must do everything possible to end the emerging anti-U.S. alliance between Russia and China. More must be done to help Russia democratize, and U.S. benefits should be used as leverage to prevent its alliance with Beijing. The policy can be likened to "containment" of China in the same way the West contained the Soviet Union during the Cold War. The United States needs to appeal directly to the Chinese people, just as it appealed to the people in the Soviet bloc, to reject communism. The Chinese people need symbols and hope, not a U.S. government that kowtows to unelected dictators. They need to know that the United States will be a beacon of hope for them, helping them to be not only prosperous but also free and governed democratically. The People's Republic of China should be admitted to the fraternity of free nations only when it becomes free.
- **Bolster American military forces:** The foundation for a strategic policy toward China is a strong United States military and an effective national security posture in the Pacific. The Clinton administration has systematically weakened the nation's capabilities across the board. Under Clinton, the military became a social experimentation laboratory for liberal attacks on a fundamentally conservative institution. Budget cuts combined with expanded nonmilitary missions have devastated military preparedness and morale. The unprecedented disarmament since the collapse of the Soviet Union in 1991 must be halted. Military alliances in Asia must be reestab-

lished along with diplomatic alliances. Because China is sharply building up its missile forces, a U.S. national missile defense directed at countering China must be deployed as soon as possible. China has shown no willingness to curb its buildup of short-, medium-, and long-range missiles, and the development and deployment of a U.S. missile defense to counter them must be speeded up. The missile defenses will neutralize the key element of China's program of power: nuclear missiles, both intercontinental and regional.

- **Create a pro-democracy Pacific community:** A key strength of America is its diversity, and Asian-Americans have played one of the most important roles in our society. The Beijing government regards all Chinese living abroad as its citizens, based on common ethnicity. The Americans among the so-called overseas Chinese must take the lead in forming a new Pacific community that will promote American values of democracy and freedom. The ultimate goal would be to work together with all people in the Pacific community of nations—including those in North and South America—to bring about the peaceful replacement of the communist government in China with a democratic alternative. A fundamental element of this community would be the clear announcement that the United States will never abandon the people of Taiwan and that Taiwan will never be traded away into the slavery of communist rule.

The United States today is a Pacific and therefore Asian power, as much as it is an Atlantic and European power. As such, we have a great stake in the freedom and prosperity of the region. Failure to promote democracy and freedom will leave Asia in the hands of a Chinese dictatorship that within three decades could become the region's—if not the world's—dominant power.

APPENDIX

The Documents

Te following pages offer a sampling of government documents that reveals how China has become the most serious problem for U.S. national security during the
Clinton-Gore administration. These documents, some of which are
classified "secret" and "top secret," represent important evidence that
has been kept from the American people or played down in an effort
to minimize the scope and nature of the China threat. They present a
stark record of how the Clinton-Gore administration has threatened
U.S. national security as well as the safety of our allies and our servicemen and women abroad.

Portions of a secret report produced in late 1998 by the U.S. counterintelligence community that highlight the foreign intelligence assault on U.S. nuclear weapons laboratories. (18 pages)

**Foreign Collection Against the Department
of Energy: The Threat to US Weapons and
Technology** (C NF)

Summary (U)

*Information available
as of 6 November 1998
was used in this report.*

The US Department of Energy (DOE) is under attack by foreign collectors—intelligence officers, as well as scientists, academics, engineers, and
businessmen—who are aggressively targeting DOE nuclear, sensitive and
proprietary, and unclassified information. The losses are extensive and
include highly classified nuclear weapon design information to the Chinese.
Many foreign collectors find DOE's unclassified and declassified information as valuable as the classified information. They have repeatedly demonstrated the intent and capability, given the opportunity, to collect against
DOE's vast holdings of technical knowledge and experience, thus circumventing expensive and time-consuming research and development efforts.
Regardless of the collector, the ultimate recipients of the information are the
foreign research institutes and defense establishments, which in turn apply
this knowledge to advance their own scientific and technological efforts.
(S NF)

Foreign collectors rightly view DOE as an inviting, diverse, and soft target
that is easy to access and that employs many who are willing to share information. DOE believes that extensive interaction with foreign scientists is
essential to maintaining its international scientific leadership. There are significant counterintelligence implications attached to this culture, however,
as it offers foreign collectors abundant opportunities to gain access to DOE
facilities and personnel. Following are examples of such opportunities:

• Approximately 25,000 foreign scientists visited or were assigned to DOE
  facilities in the past year; more contacts go unreported because they are
  not considered extensive.

• DOE's frequent participation in international scientific and academic
  exchanges and the frequent travel overseas of DOE employees lead to or
  expand access for foreign collectors. DOE employees are especially vulnerable to foreign collectors trained in elicitation. (S NF)

Foreign collectors are targeting both classified and unclassified DOE information. Whether stolen, elicited, or simply downloaded from the Internet,
DOE information is enormously valuable. While we did not conduct a damage assessment of the information lost, individual cases clearly demonstrate
that such information has saved other countries substantial time and money
and has undercut US policy, security, and competitiveness. (S NF)

...ent surveys the activities of 12 countries that pose significant ...threats to DOE. There are others targeting the unique and valu- ...entific and technological information held by DOE that still need to ...ved:

...na, Russia, and India pose the most immediate threat and are dedicat- ng extensive resources in the United States and abroad to gain knowledge of DOE information.

• DOE records show that over 250 known or suspected intelligence officers from 27 countries have visited or been assigned to DOE facilities in recent years.

• Foreign collectors pose a significant—and growing—cyberthreat to DOE computer systems. DOE scientists have extensive computer contact with their foreign colleagues and rely heavily on e-mail communications to maintain their dialogue. These interactions, however, allow foreign collectors to elicit information freely and repeatedly. (S NF)

This assessment is a necessary and sound starting point for understanding the dimensions of the threat to DOE's weapons and technology. However, the US Intelligence Community (USIC), working together with DOE, must do more to gain a full understanding of the nature and extent of foreign targeting of DOE's unique scientific knowledge base. The USIC needs to commission follow-on assessments to determine the impact of the loss of scientific and technological knowledge on US national security, regional stability, and economic competitiveness. The USIC also needs to issue specific collection and dissemination requirements to raise the priority of the foreign threat to DOE and to expand the sharing of information within and across agencies. (S NF)

Foreign Collection Against the Department of Energy: The Threat to US Weapons and Technology (C NF)

Introduction (U)

This assessment will focus on the wide range of foreign threats to DOE and the potential loss of classified and sensitive unclassified knowledge of US weapons and technologies. The interagency working group that prepared this assessment reviewed currently available FBI cases and investigations, DOE information, as well as CIA and NSA intelligence reporting, as a basis for judgments. The assessment will highlight the evidence of foreign targeting of DOE, discuss the information foreign collectors find of value, and survey the collection roles of not only foreign intelligence services, but, more important, foreign scientists, academics, engineers, and businessmen. It is organized to examine who the collectors are, what they are collecting, and how they are collecting it. A key portion of this assessment will be its identification of important shortfalls and gaps in our understanding of the foreign threat to DOE and what is required by the USIC to better assess the threat in the future. (C NF)

DOE's reputation as a world leader in science and technology (S&T) makes it a prime target for foreign collection. The working group reviewed several USIC products, including PDD/NSC-35, *Intelligence Priorities*, NACIC's *Annual Report to Congress on Foreign Economic Collection and Industrial Espionage*, the National Security Threat List, and DOE's Sensitive Country List,[1] to help identify which countries already have demonstrated the opportunity, capability, and the intent to target the United States in other areas. In most cases, these countries almost certainly see DOE, with its vast storehouse of expertise, as a potential target for collection of important intelligence on weapons and technology. (S NF)

[1] The Sensitive Country List includes Algeria, China, Cuba, former Soviet republics, India, Iran, Iraq, Israel, Libya, North Korea, Pakistan, Sudan, and Taiwan. (C)

Using these documents as guides, the interagency working group focused on 12 countries and searched available data to assess the specific threat to DOE. These countries are China, Russia, India, Pakistan, Iran, Israel, Taiwan, South Korea, Japan, France, North Korea, and Iraq. The focus on them in this assessment does not mean they are the only countries targeting DOE information. (C NF)

DOE Information Targeted by Foreign Entities (C NF)

The foreign threat is directed at both of DOE's primary areas of responsibility—information related to US nuclear weapons and other areas where DOE exerts scientific leadership. Within those two broad areas, foreign entities have demonstrated a strong interest in *all* categories of information: classified, declassified, and unclassified nuclear information; proprietary information; sensitive unclassified information; and unclassified information. Reporting shows that some countries have used their intelligence services or resources to collect unclassified information. However, due to biases and limitations of intelligence collection and security investigations, we know much more about foreign interest in DOE nuclear information than any other type or classification of information. (S NF)

Nuclear Information—Classified, Declassified, and Unclassified

Foreign collectors of nuclear information are interested in all facets of US capabilities and in past experience in the design of nuclear explosive devices. While the modern US stockpile has tended to coalesce around a fairly narrow set of technical approaches to weapon design, the vast storehouse of information contained in the storage vaults and in the minds of personnel involved in all phases of the US program represents a lucrative target for collectors. (C NF)

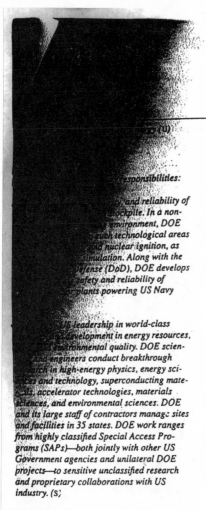

...(U)...

...esponsibilities:

...and reliability of
...ockpile. In a non-
...environment, DOE
...technological areas
...nuclear ignition, as
...mulation. Along with the
...ense (DoD), DOE develops
...fety and reliability of
...ants powering US Navy

...US leadership in world-class
...velopment in energy resources,
...onmental quality. DOE scien-
...engineers conduct breakthrough
...in high-energy physics, energy sci-
...s and technology, superconducting mate-
...ls, accelerator technologies, materials
...ences, and environmental sciences. DOE
and its large staff of contractors manage sites
and facilities in 35 states. DOE work ranges
from highly classified Special Access Programs (SAPs)—both jointly with other US
Government agencies and unilateral DOE
projects—to sensitive unclassified research
and proprietary collaborations with US
industry. (S)

DOE Personnel
DOE is operated by 10,500 Federal employees.
However, the bulk of the actual work force is
made up of approximately 120,000 personnel
working for prime contractors, subcontractors,
and those on support service contracts. Of the
personnel working for DOE as Federal employees or contractors, 66,000 have "Q" security
clearances, meaning they have access to Top
Secret/SCI/Restricted Data material. Restricted

Data (RD) concern the design, manufacture, or
utilization of atomic weapons; the production of
special nuclear material; or the use of special
nuclear material in the production of energy. Of
the remaining personnel at DOE, 39,000 have
"L" security clearances, meaning they have
access to Secret National Security Information,
as well as to Confidential/RD material and
Secret/Formerly Restricted Data material. (U)

DOE's Visitor/Assignee Programs
The number of foreign scientists with access to
DOE facilities has grown significantly in recent
years. In 1998, approximately 25,000 foreign
scientists will visit or are assigned to DOE facilities.* This number is just an estimate, as some
laboratories have been exempted from the
requirement for recordkeeping. Further, as a
whole, DOE does not track foreign visitors from
countries not on DOE's Sensitive Country List—
some of which are identified in this report as targeting DOE. But where DOE records exist, we
know that the number of foreign scientists visiting or assigned to DOE facilities from the list of
sensitive countries has increased over 200 percent from the mid-1980s to the mid-1990s. (S NF)

Counterintelligence Issues at DOE
DOE's goal of maintaining US technological
superiority drives it to constantly seek to
improve its world-class research and development efforts. Recognizing that the United States

* Foreign assignments involve periods of more than
30 days and initially are approved for a two-year
period. Foreign national visits involve periods of less
than 30 days in a given year. Foreign visitors, however, may make several separate visits to a particular
laboratory and also may visit several different laboratories during a year. As a result, the access of a foreign visitor may be greater than that of a foreign
assignee. (C NF)

Overview of the Department of Energy (U) (continued)

does not have a monopoly on cutting-edge scientific research and development, DOE believes that its continued interaction with international scientists is essential. Further, it is intrinsic to their professions for DOE scientists to want their information to be used and visible in the national and international scientific and academic communities. From a CI perspective, however, this creates an inherent tension between diffusion of DOE knowledge for purely scientific advancement and the protection of classified and sensitive[b] unclassified DOE information. (U)

Historically, the effectiveness of the DOE CI program has been undermined by a series of structural and systemic problems, including a lack of programmatic accountability and ineffectual centralized control over CI resources in the field. These problems stymied efforts to assess, understand, and reduce the foreign intelligence threat. PDD/NSC-61 was issued to address these issues and resolve many of the underlying structural deficiencies. CI challenges remain at DOE, but with new authorities and resources given to the reorganized Office of Counterintelligence, DOE hopes to make significant strides toward finding the right balance of openness and protection of national security. (C NF)

[b] A sensitive technology is an unclassified subject identified by DOE that involves information, activities, and/or technologies that are relevant to national security. Disclosure of sensitive subjects has the potential for enhancing nuclear proliferation, divulging militarily critical technologies, or revealing other advanced technologies. Therefore, sensitive subjects require special management oversight, especially prior to release to foreign nationals. Sensitive subjects include nuclear weapons-related information, technologies under export control, certain dual-use technologies, and rapidly advancing technologies judged to have a critical military application. (FOUO)

Countries with advanced nuclear weapons programs—such as Russia, China, Israel, and France—are interested in advanced nuclear weapons designs, testing simulation techniques, and data on the long-term viability of nuclear weapons. Such information can enhance the military utility of nuclear stockpiles and reduce the need for nuclear testing. Listed below are a few examples of such targeting:

• During the period 1984 to 1988, China obtained through espionage the design information on a current US warhead. To obtain this information, the United States conducted tens of nuclear tests. Once obtained, the Chinese were able to accelerate their research and advance their nuclear weapons program well beyond indigenous capabilities.

• Starting in 1985 and as late as 1997, Dr. Peter Lee, who once worked at Los Alamos National Laboratory, provided China with classified information on nuclear weaponry.[2]

• Over the last 10 years, at least 22 of 103 Israeli visitors to Lawrence Livermore National Laboratory were either associated with Israel's nuclear weapons program or involved in research at Lawrence Livermore that could be applied to nuclear weapons development. Israel also benefits from Lawrence Livermore's unclassified test results, which can be used to validate its codes. (S NF)

[2] Lee, a contract DOE employee at Los Alamos, traveled with a group of scientists to China in 1985 at the invitation of a Chinese visitor to his laboratory; Lee's services were needed to translate for the delegation. During his trip, Lee was approached late one night in his hotel room by two State Science and Technology Commission officials who pitched him and secured his cooperation, appealing to his ethnic/cultural ties to China. Lee was convicted in 1997 and later admitted to passing information on nuclear weaponry and antisubmarine warfare. (C NF)

Foreign Visits and Assignments to DOE Labs
1 Oct 97 – 30 Sept 98

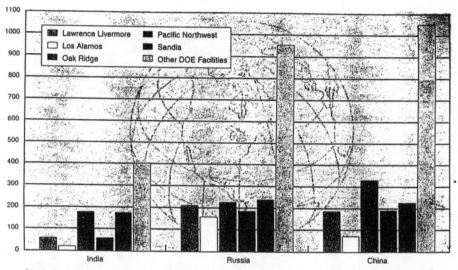

Chart depicts those nations on DOE list of sensitive countries that have a major presence in US.

Secret

Countries with less sophisticated nuclear programs—such as India and Pakistan—are equally interested in US capabilities developed much earlier in the US program,[3] even though many of the technologies are no longer considered state of the art. These countries target current DOE nuclear-related information and also look to early, declassified US approaches to guide their design and production activities. Such information is significant because it can guide foreign efforts to develop or refine nuclear weapons and may lead to proliferation of these weapons:

- Pakistan's two primary nuclear weapons program entities—the Khan Research Laboratories (KRL) and the Pakistan Atomic Energy Commission (PAEC)—may be seeking DOE information. One method is through interaction between KRL and PAEC officials and DOE scientists at international conferences on South Asian arms control and nonproliferation.

- Indian scientists have used unclassified DOE information to advance their understanding of firing system-related technologies. Moreover, Indian nuclear weapons-related technical publications include many references to DOE reports—some dating as far back as the 1970s—which describe technologies the United States considers outdated. (S NF)

Prospective nuclear weapons states—such as Iran, Iraq, and North Korea—are interested in the basic parameters of first-generation nuclear explosives.[4] Once again, much—if not most—of the information that these countries would find useful is declassified or unclassified:

- In 1996 and 1997, Iranian visitors to Lawrence Livermore were involved in discussions of subjects potentially useful to advancing Tehran's nuclear and biological warfare programs.

- The Iraqi program also benefited directly from unclassified DOE publications detailing fissile material development activities. In particular, the United States tested and abandoned electromagnetic isotope separation as inefficient and expensive; the Iraqis, however, chose this as potentially the fastest method to produce fissile material. We also believe that the Iraqi program benefited from inadvertent disclosures of information on high explosives by DOE scientists at a symposium.

- During inspections by the International Atomic Energy Agency (IAEA), a copy of an unclassified Sandia publication relating to high-precision detonations was found in Iraq. (S NF)

Proprietary Information and Sensitive Unclassified Information

Foreign entities also are targeting a wide range of DOE sensitive unclassified[5] information including proprietary collaborations with US industry. In many cases, foreigners have gained access to DOE facilities through lab-to lab agreements,[6] Cooperative Research and Development Agreements[7] (CRADAs), and government-to-government exchanges and treaties. In some cases, these individuals use their access to acquire other sensitive or proprietary information. For example:

- A French scientist—granted unescorted, but unclassified, access to Lawrence Livermore in 1995 under

[3] A study completed by Sandia National Laboratory in mid-1998 examined India's scientific and technical infrastructure to support nuclear weaponization. The report illustrated how Indian scientists have used unclassified DOE information to advance their understanding of nuclear weapon technologies. Examples show the relative ease of obtaining nuclear weapons-related reporting, but also call into question the criteria used for determining which DOE documents are available to the public. The report also suggests that current classification/declassification procedures are inadequate. (S NF)

[4] Topics of potential interest include—but are not limited to—shock strengths required for simple spherical implosion geometries, equations-of-state, the function of various components in an implosion system, estimation of explosive yield, preinitiation issues, and fissile materials specifications. (S NF)

[5] DOE has several types of sensitive unclassified information, including unclassified controlled nuclear information, official use only, naval nuclear propulsion information, export-controlled information, and proprietary information. (C NF)

[6] China and Russia have particularly extensive laboratory-to-laboratory relationships with DOE. (C NF)

[7] CRADAs involve joint research on commercially viable technologies that usually involve US companies but also can involve foreign corporations. Moreover, foreign national employees at the DOE laboratories can and do participate in these CRADAs, sometimes without the knowledge of the US corporations that are a party to them. (C NF)

Secret

a joint agreement between DOE and the French Atomic Energy Commission—has actively collected technical information outside his area of research.

Unclassified Information

Not surprisingly, foreign countries have a voracious appetite for unclassified DOE information. From 1990 to 1994, DOE maintained a sensitive country information logging system (SCILS) that attempted to record unsolicited requests from countries on DOE's sensitive country list for information from DOE weapons laboratories. Despite the weakness of the database, including lax and incomplete reporting from various DOE entities, SCILS documented annually over 10,000 of such unsolicited requests. This database is no longer active but with the advent of the information age, DOE suspects the database has largely been superseded by direct requests to US scientists via e-

At Pacific Northwest National Laboratory, ...re unsolicited requests are still being monitored, some 250 arrive each week by e-mail as opposed to 15 that come by mail. Moreover, some of the information that foreign entities may have requested in writing in the past can now be downloaded off the Internet. (S NF)

The systematic and thorough manner in which unclassified information is often collected gives a sense of its substantial value to foreign entities. Following are two examples:

• A Chinese scientist conducting unclassified work on silicon detectors[x] at Brookhaven National Laboratory was found to be sending dozens of long technical faxes to the Chinese Academy of Sciences

---

[x] Silicon detectors are related to accelerometers, a critical component of ballistic missile guidance systems. (C NF)

(CAS). The information enabled the CAS to duplicate Brookhaven experiments as they were being conducted. (S NF)

Foreign intelligence collectors derive valuable insights or guidance from unclassified information—even apart from the obvious technical value of the information. For example, such information:

• Can be used to spot and assess potential sources. Foreign entities can presume that a DOE scientist who authors an unclassified article on a topic with classified applications may have access to sensitive, proprietary, or classified information.

• Can reduce the need for covert or illicit collection as well as help a service reduce the risk of such activities. Instead of haphazardly approaching numerous sources for a particular piece of classified or sensitive information, a foreign intelligence service can use knowledge of open-source writing, biographies, and collaborations to reasonably ascertain which DOE scientists may have the requisite knowledge or access. (S NF)

The Denial and Deception Angle

While most of the DOE information is targeted for its technical merit, foreign countries also seek the information to enhance their denial and deception (D&D)[9] programs.

In addition, foreign entities also have demonstrated a strong interest in DOE information on the capabilities and limitations of US intelligence verification and collection programs. (S NF)

---

[9] Denial operations are aimed at hiding military weapons development or other sensitive activities from hostile spies or reconnaissance. Deception operations involve attempts to provide information in order to intentionally mislead or misdirect intelligence. Of the countries we believe to be a threat to DOE, an earlier National Intelligence Estimate judged that China and Russia have the most effective D&D programs. In addition, Iran, Iraq, and North Korea—and also India and Pakistan—engage in D&D directed against the United States. (S NF)

DOE Technology and Foreign Denial and Deception (S NF)

Foreign knowledge of how the USIC collects and analyzes information about suspected foreign weapons programs can allow foreign countries to disguise the true nature of their activities. Foreign intelligence collectors appear to have specifically targeted DOE as a prime source for critical information. These examples are among the most significant:

- *China has expressed great interest in Los Alamos papers on how to verify compliance with weapons limitations agreements, including "The Strategic Arms Reduction Treaty and Its Verification" and "Criteria for Monitoring a Chemical Arms Treaty: Implications." A variety of different Chinese institutions made at least 47 requests for these two documents.*

- *India and Pakistan repeatedly have accessed a Sandia document posted on the Internet dealing with satellite imagery analysis. The document contains photographs of India's nuclear test site and details verification information that could aid nations attempting to avoid detection. (S NF OC)*

Foreign Targeting of DOE Facilities, Personnel, and Technologies (C NF)

There is strong evidence of foreign efforts to collect information on DOE facilities, personnel, and technologies. In addition to using their intelligence and security services to target DOE via classic human and technical intelligence means, foreign countries employ a variety of methods to obtain targeted information and materials, both in the United States and overseas. These methods—some of which overlap with those of the intelligence and security services—include the use of: scientific, academic, and commercial exchanges; open-source collection via published journals, conference proceedings, and the Internet; front companies and joint ventures; and exploitation of cultural ties. (S NF)

Known Targeting by Foreign Institutes and Foreign Intelligence Services

Our research provided a wide variety of examples of human and technical approaches, tactics, and methods employed by foreign collectors to tap into DOE's knowledge base. Foreign intelligence services are clearly engaged in targeting DOE. Probably even more significant are the individual foreign scientists and other end users who obtain information and provide the results of their efforts directly back to their home institutions. In these cases, intelligence officers may be relegated to supporting roles. In both categories, it is important to recognize that whether the protected DOE information is collected by a foreign intelligence service or a foreign academic institute, its ultimate recipients are foreign research institutes and defense establishments that will apply this knowledge to their own scientific and technological efforts, some times to the detriment of US national security. (S NF)

In several instances, we have knowledge of specific intelligence collection requirements for DOE-related information levied on or by foreign intelligence services:[10]

- An undated document sent anonymously in 1993 to the US Embassy in Paris and the press listed specific collection requirements by French intelligence on US corporations, government agencies, and US national laboratories. Los Alamos and Lawrence Livermore were listed among the service's top collection priorities.

In addition to evidence of intelligence tasking, our research indicates that some countries place intelligence officers in direct contact with DOE facilities or personnel. This presence represents one of the key components of the threat—opportunity—and is an

indication of the priority assigned to DOE by foreign intelligence collectors. Significantly, DOE information notes that there have been over 250 known or suspected intelligence officers from 27 countries visiting or assigned to various DOE facilities over the last five years alone. Russia and China had the largest intelligence presence with 141 and 37 officers, respectively. (S NF)

Threats From Other Foreign Collectors
The threat posed by traditional foreign intelligence services is only a small portion of the human intelligence threat to DOE. Many others—including foreign scientists, academics, engineers, and businessmen—also collect information even though they may not have been trained or tasked by foreign intelligence services. Some Asian countries, particularly China and Japan, are very adept collectors of scientific and technological information, using nonintelligence organizations and personnel.

- Rather than send its intelligence officers out to recruit knowledgeable sources at facilities such as the national laboratories, China prefers to exploit over time the natural scientist-to-scientist relationships. Chinese scientists nurture relationships with national laboratory counterparts, issuing invitations for them to travel to laboratories and conferences in China.

- Japan is targeting DOE national laboratories for sensitive (dual-use) technologies. Through the Japan External Trade Organization (JETRO), an intelligence-gathering arm of the Japanese Government located in the Japanese Ministry of International Trade and Industry, Japan is targeting US critical technologies, including superconductor-related research and development.

(S NF OC)

In other cases, foreign entities are known to engage in S&T collection activity, and despite the shortage of

---

[10] The paucity of hard information about specific taskings does not mean that foreign intelligence services do not consider DOE a significant target. It could indicate that the USIC often may not have sources positioned to report such information or that some foreign services do not compile specific, formal target lists. For example, some Asian intelligence services, most notably those of China and Taiwan, rely on their collectors in the field to decide what information is of greatest value. (S NF)

specific targeting data, we are highly confident that they are focused on DOE:

- A high percentage of the Iranian students studying hard sciences in the United States are doctoral candidates, and many of them are engaged in research programs at US universities that have contractual research agreements with DOE laboratories. While these students may not have direct access to classified material on critical technologies, some of them are in a position to interact with those who do.

- Israel's military and commercial partnerships with the United States provide a wealth of opportunities for the legitimate Israeli presence at cleared US facilities, including DOE laboratories. Israel routinely exploits legitimate access to acquire restricted and/or classified US S&T information.

- South Korea, particularly the Korea Advanced Energy Research Institute, has a long history of involvement with US DOE facilities, and many of South Korea's nuclear experts have participated in US national laboratory programs.

(S NF)

Targeting of DOE Personnel Abroad

Indigenous intelligence and security services of all the countries we reviewed pose a serious threat to visiting DOE employees and contractors. Some services are more skilled than others, but most employ similar practices: conducting surveillance, using tour guides, prostitutes, and hosts as access agents; searching hotel rooms and laptop computers; and monitoring communications by telephone, e-mail, and fax. Since 1995, DOE debriefing databases reflect several hundred reports by DOE travelers of incidents of CI significance. The following examples underscore the various methods foreign entities employ:

Exploiting Cultural Ties (C NF)

USIC reporting confirms that DOE employees of certain cultural or ethnic backgrounds have been targeted by foreign entities. For example, China, India, Iran, Israel, North Korea, Russia, South Korea, and Taiwan have targeted US Government and/or DOE employees with cultural ties to those countries. Oftentimes, this cultivation process is very subtle and may take many months or years to fully develop. Sometimes, the process is direct and US citizens willingly support the collection efforts of these countries. Other examples:

- *Seoul has openly attempted to attract ethnic Korean scientists to come to Korea to work on developing indigenous industry.*

- *India's defense industry organizations and intelligence services target ethnic Indian scientists and professors as well as Indian students attending US universities to assist in S&T collection.*

- *The Israelis target anyone with access to the classified and sensitive US information they seek, yet they have used common cultural and religious affiliation as a basis to elicit information and also as a basis for potential agent recruitment abroad and in the United States.*

- *The Peter Lee case, cited earlier in this assessment, stands as a good example of China's use of cultural ties to collect successfully. (S NF OC)*

The French intelligence services have a history of targeting visiting officials and businessmen for economic, S&T, and commercial information. French intelligence is particularly adept at collecting information from visitors through surreptitious entry operations, often with help from hotel staffs; these techniques have been employed against DOE travelers.

- The Israeli intelligence services are particularly aggressive in dealing with US officials and scientists within Israel—repeatedly demonstrating their interest in collecting almost any information pertaining to advanced military and civilian technology. DOE personnel who have traveled to Israel have experienced everything from unusual questions to the monitoring of their faxes to outright discovery of surveillance devices in their hotel rooms.

- All US visitors to North Korea are under constant escort and believe all of their faxes are copied. In addition, a DOE scientist reported that his escort asked him to discuss "in private" US and North Korean nuclear weapons complexes.

- Chinese intelligence encourages US scientists to visit China, expediting arrangements to enable Chinese experts to assess and develop these contacts. During the visit, the US target is introduced to several senior officials and receives VIP treatment. The Chinese services' involvement is often not exposed and frequently will not lead to official recruitment of the individual, even though valuable information is obtained. (S NF OC)

DOE has several reports of its personnel being targeted in third countries. For countries that have limited access to DOE facilities and are rarely visited by DOE employees, international conferences may represent major collection opportunities. In other cases, targeting of DOE scientists at international conferences is only one facet of a broader collection program:

- At a conference in Greece, a DOE scientist was approached by an Israeli national who requested any information Lawrence Livermore had concerning radon as an indicator of nuclear activity.

- At a Biological Weapons Convention conference in Vienna in 1995, a Japanese official asked a DOE scientist for information about the capabilities of the Chinese and French to simulate nuclear weapons effects. (S NF)

SIGINT Collection Against DOE
While explicit evidence of foreign SIGINT collection activities against DOE communications is sparse, China, France, India, Israel, Pakistan, Russia, and Taiwan are known to intercept US satellite communications and, in many cases, have extensive capabilities to intercept other communications. The fact that SIGINT is a passive activity that is well protected by its controllers makes it extremely difficult to gather hard evidence about specific foreign SIGINT targets. However, based on the growth of SIGINT activities worldwide and the fact that US technology continues to be a priority target for many intelligence services, we judge that DOE information systems are being intercepted. (S NF)

Secret

access to these very computers as well as remote
access through the Internet. DOE, however, does not
have a robust intrusion detection capability or an adequate monitoring capability to audit how such access
is used. In addition, DOE scientists have extensive
computer contact with their colleagues throughout the
world. One laboratory, for example, reports that its e-
mail traffic exceeds 1 million messages per month.
Since the traffic is virtually unmonitored. DOE is
unable to report how much involves contact with sensitive countries or other foreign entities. (S NF)

The increased access to DOE computers coincides
with an increased capability of foreign entities to
exploit such opportunities. Even technologically and
economically backward countries, such as North
Korea, are acquiring sophisticated computer and telecommunications technologies. Hacker tools, including
password-cracking programs, are widely available at
hacker conferences and via the Internet. Moreover,
these tools have become increasingly user-friendly
over the past five years. Likewise, the capability to use
the Internet to access computer systems has been rapidly proliferating. (S NF)

The threat to DOE information systems is real. The
Computer Incident Advisory Capability, which is
DOE's incident response team providing technical
assistance and information to sites with computer
security incidents, recorded 792 computer security
incidents during the period from October 1997 to June
1998. Of these, 324 involved attacks from systems
located outside the United States. All of these attacks
involved activities intended to gain password files,
probes and scans, as well as actual compromises of
DOE computer systems where the intruders gained
access. Such access included successful root compromise—giving an unauthorized person complete access
and total control to create, view, modify, or execute
any and all information stored on the system. (U)

There is ample information indicating that foreign
entities are attempting to collect restricted or sensitive
information—particularly S&T information—using

Cyberthreat to DOE
The foreign cyberthreat—employing computers to
collect against and/or to attack US information systems—is a growing problem. DOE's high-performance computers give the national laboratories a
greater computational capability than any other facilities in the world. Some visiting foreign nationals have

" The predecessor of the Internet. (U)

computer systems. While little of the available information is specific to DOE, we believe that foreign entities likely direct similar efforts at DOE given the value of its information. Evidence of this targeting includes the following:

most cases, the protections between restricted databases—if any—are far less robust than those protections that keep "outsiders" from gaining access. For example, Russian intelligence has attempted to use insiders to gain access to restricted information on foreign computer networks. (S NF OC)

- US Army Private Eric Jenott passed information on DoD computer systems to a Chinese national who was an exchange student at Oak Ridge. Jenott was arrested in June 1996.

- In the mid-1980s, Russian intelligence used the services of a group of West German hackers to penetrate computers at Lawrence Livermore and Sandia. At Lawrence Berkeley Laboratories, the hackers were able to obtain system-manager privileges.

Foreign efforts to obtain information resident on US computer systems can be greatly aided by "insider" access to the computer systems. Recruited insiders—those with direct access to data or information systems—often provide information or access that allows easier access to, and movement within, databases. In

[12] Foreign activities designed to cause widespread, long-duration damage or denial-of-service to significant portions of critical US information-based infrastructures. (U)

Appendix A

Foreign Country Threats . . . Unique
Approaches, Unique Requirements (C NF)

The following overview highlights the unique approaches of the various
threat countries. More detailed examples of the threat posed by these countries are documented in earlier portions of this assessment, and there is
additional evidence that supports these findings. (C NF)

China

China represents an acute intelligence threat to DOE. It conducts a "full
court press" consisting of massive numbers of collectors of all kinds, in the
United States, in China, and elsewhere abroad. The Chinese have successfully employed a combination of open-source collection, all forms of cyberconnections, elicitation, and espionage to obtain information needed to
advance their weapons program. China is highly reliant on many different
types of technical specialists, scientists, and engineers. China is an
advanced nuclear power, yet its nuclear stockpile is deteriorating. As such,
China has specifically targeted DOE for the collection of technical intelligence related to the design of nuclear weapons, and seeks information relating to stockpile stewardship and reliability. This effort has been very
successful, and Beijing's exploitation of US national laboratories has substantially aided its nuclear weapons program. (S NF)

Russia

Russia presents a formidable intelligence threat to DOE, relying on the legacy of decades of highly calibrated, aggressive, and successful S&T collection against the United States. Russia uses a wide variety of collection
methods and has targeted many DOE facilities.
                                          Russians count heavily on their intelli-
gence services to obtain US nuclear secrets, and also rely on other technical
specialists, scientists, and engineers to target individuals with access to
information on DOE projects. DOE specialists and their information especially are at risk while traveling to Russia, where intelligence and security
services actively target information they possess. As an advanced nuclear
power, Russia primarily seeks US nuclear weapons secrets that involve
state-of-the-art technologies. As its general purpose forces have deteriorated, Russia has become even more dependent on nuclear weapons and its
nuclear capability to underscore its status as a great power. (S NF)

India

India has emerged as a dangerous intelligence threat. India has a well-devel-
oped and aggressive intelligence collection capability to acquire S&T and

Secret

collecting any secret or restricted US Government information—particularly pertaining to advanced military and civilian technology. (S NF)

Taiwan

Taiwan also is an aggressive collector, and its collection program against DOE is a small-scale version of China's. As such, Taiwan's collection program is characterized by ample person-to-person contacts and a substantial intelligence presence in the United States. Taiwan focuses its collection against only two countries of critical importance—the United States and China. Taiwan relies on a diverse and balanced collection effort, with contributions from both intelligence and nonintelligence officials to identify and target DOE sources of S&T information. Taiwan also places significant emphasis on Chinese professional associations in the United States to locate persons and technologies of interest. The DOE national laboratories are targets of Taiwan's S&T collection, with Argonne receiving substantial attention in recent years. (S NF)

South Korea

South Korea has been seeking US S&T and economic information in an increasingly aggressive fashion in the 1990s. Its collection approach features many person-to-person contacts, and the South Koreans also possess a major intelligence presence in the United States. These activities are directed at both US military and civilian targets, and are carried out by a range of South Korean Government entities and private corporations. South Korean intelligence has expanded its role in collection related to nuclear technology during the 1990s. (S NF)

Japan

Japanese collection features the close interaction between business and government and its collection against DOE proceeds accordingly. Unlike the other Asian countries noted in this report, the Japanese do not have a clandestine intelligence collection service. Japan maintains a large, overlapping, assertive information collection program, heavily focused on US S&T and economic information. This program is characterized by collection of massive amounts of open-source information. A portion of this effort appears to be earmarked to collect against DOE technologies. Incidents reported to authorities by cleared US contractors in recent years reveal Japanese intent and opportunities to acquire protected US nuclear information. (S NF)

France

France is a longstanding nontraditional intelligence adversary with a proven record of clandestine collection against US S&T information, both in the United States and in France. The French rely on a wide range of collection approaches, which include many contacts with the national laboratories.

France has a record of exploiting legitimate access to US businesses and government institutions to collect against a specific target or on a target of opportunity. A common French methodology is to seek information beyond the parameters of joint agreements. (S NF)

North Korea and Iraq

North Korea and Iraq have aggressive intelligence programs that place a priority on S&T collection. They have marginal access to DOE facilities in the United States, with very few opportunities for person-to-person collection. As such, they operate abroad to obtain US nuclear technologies and information related to their needs. (S NF)

North Korea has little opportunity to collect against DOE facilities in view of its negligible access and limited resources in the United States. Nonetheless, North Korea has tried to obtain US nuclear-related information or technology from third-country sources. (S NF)

Iraq remains of CI concern because Iraqi intelligence services have continued to pursue S&T information that can aid in strengthening the country's military capabilities. The Iraqi services traditionally have looked to other countries as places to target US technologies, and they rely increasingly on nonofficial cover. (S NF)

SECRET

March 8, 1999

MEMORANDUM FOR: LOUIS J. FREEH
                              DIRECTOR
                              FEDERAL BUREAU OF INVESTIGATION

FROM: THE ATTORNEY GENERAL

SUBJECT: National Security List (U)

The Federal Bureau of Investigation, in conjunction with the Department of Justice and the Department of State, has submitted a proposed National Security List (NSL) for 1999/2000 pursuant to section II.A. of the Attorney General Guidelines for FBI Foreign Intelligence Collection and Counterintelligence Investigations (FCIG). (U)

Based on that submission, I hereby designate the following countries as country threats under the NSL for 1999/2000: Russian Federation, People's Republic of China, Cuba, People's Democratic Republic of Korea (North Korea), Federal Republic of Yugoslavia, Republika Srpska (the Serb-controlled region of Bosnia under the Dayton Accords), Socialist Republic of Vietnam, Syria, Iraq, Iran, Libya, Sudan, and Taiwan. (S)

Also based on the FBI's submission, I hereby designate the following categories of activities as issue threats under the NSL:

1.   **Terrorism** - activities that:

        (1)   involve violent acts dangerous to human life that are a violation of the criminal law of the United States or of any State, or that would be a criminal violation if committed within the jurisdiction of the United States or any State;

Classified by: Frances Fragos Townsend, Counsel for Intelligence Policy,
                   Department of Justice
Reason: 1.5(c)
Declassify on: X1

SECRET

In this secret Justice Department memorandum from 1999, the Clinton administration included Taiwan as one of the counterintelligence priorities for the FBI. Taiwan is among the nations designated as national security threats even though its intelligence-gathering activities are very limited compared to those of the People's Republic of China. (7 pages)

SECRET

(2)   appear to be intended:

    (a)   to intimidate or coerce a civilian population;

    (b)   to influence the policy of a government by intimidation or coercion: or

    (c)   to affect the conduct of a government by assassination or kidnaping; and

(3)   occur totally outside the United States, or transcend national boundaries in terms of the means by which they are accomplished, the persons they appear intended to coerce or intimidate, or the locale in which their perpetrators operate or seek asylum. (U)

2.   **Espionage** - foreign power-sponsored or coordinated intelligence activity directed at the U.S. Government, or U.S. corporations, establishments or persons, which involves the identification, targeting and collection of U.S. national defense information. (U)

3.   **Proliferation** - foreign power-sponsored or coordinated intelligence activity directed at the U.S. Government, or U.S. corporations, establishments or persons, which involves:

    (1)   the proliferation of weapons of mass destruction to include chemical, biological, and nuclear weapons, and delivery systems of those weapons; or

    (2)   the proliferation of advanced conventional weapons. (U)

4.   **Economic Espionage** - foreign power-sponsored or coordinated intelligence activity directed at the U.S. Government, or U.S. corporations, establishments or persons which involves:

    (1)   the unlawful or clandestine targeting or acquisition of sensitive financial, trade, or economic policy information, proprietary economic information, or critical technologies, or

    (2)   the unlawful or clandestine targeting or influencing of sensitive economic

SECRET

policy decisions. (U)

5.   **Targeting the National Information Infrastructure** - foreign power-sponsored or coordinated intelligence activity directed at the U.S. Government, or U.S. corporations, establishments or persons, which involves the targeting of facilities, personnel, information, or computer, cable, satellite or telecommunications systems, which comprise or are associated with the National information infrastructure. The national information infrastructure is the electronic backbone for the storage, processing and communication of information for nearly every sector of U.S. society. Proscribed intelligence activities include:

    (1)   denial or disruption of computer, cable, satellite or telecommunications services;

    (2)   unauthorized monitoring of computer, cable, satellite or telecommunications systems;

    (3)   unauthorized disclosure of proprietary or classified information stored or transmitted through computer, cable, satellite or telecommunications systems;

    (4)   unauthorized modification or destruction of computer programming codes of information, computer network databases, stored information or computer capabilities; or

    (5)   manipulation of computer, cable, satellite or telecommunications services resulting in fraud, financial loss or other federal criminal violations. (U)

6.   **Targeting the U.S. Government** - foreign power-sponsored or coordinated intelligence activity directed at the U.S. Government, or U.S. corporations, establishments or persons, which involves the targeting of government programs, information, or facilities, or the targeting of personnel of:

    (1)   the U.S. intelligence community;

    (2)   the U.S. foreign affairs, economic or financial community; or

    (3)   the U.S. defense establishment and related activities of national preparedness. (U)

7.   **Perception Management** - foreign power-sponsored or coordinated intelligence

SECRET

activity directed at the U. S. Government, or U.S. corporations, establishments or persons, which involves manipulating information, communicating false information, or propagating deceptive information and communications (domestically and internationally), or of U.S. Government officials regarding U.S. policies, ranging from foreign policy to economic strategies. (U)

8.   **Foreign intelligence Activities** - foreign power-sponsored or coordinated intelligence activity conducted in the U.S. or directed against the U.S. Government, or U.S. corporations, establishments, or persons, that is not described by or included in any other issue threat. (U)

The reconsideration and review of these lists should begin no later than March 2000 in order that reapproval may be accomplished before December 1, 2000. (U)

NFIP INVESTIGATIVE PRIORITIES

The National Security Threat List (NSTL) is the FBI's National Security Division's investigative strategy. The strategy is defined by the eight investigative priorities set forth below. It should be noted that while the priorities are of necessity set forth in sequential order, this should not be interpreted as a rigid order of precedence; rather, the list should be looked upon as a collective list of priorities. .

Terrorism: The protection from anti-US activity intended to intimidate or coerce a government, the civilian population, or any segment thereof, in furtherance of political goals conducted by groups or individuals.

Espionage: The protection of the national security of the United States through investigation to detect and thwart espionage activities directed against the United States.

Proliferation: Cooperative investigative efforts directed toward the prevention of unauthorized acquisition, by or on behalf of foreign powers, of technology, information, or materials which could be used in the development, manufacture, or delivery of nuclear or chemical/biological weapons.

Economic Espionage: The protection from foreign power-sponsored or coordinated intelligence activity directed at the US Government, or US corporations, establishments or person, which involves: the unlawful or clandestine targeting or acquisition of sensitive financial, trade or economic policy information, proprietary economic information, or critical technologies; or, the lawful or clandestine targeting or influencing of sensitive economic policy decisions.

Targeting the National Information Infrastructure: The defense mechanism used to detect foreign power-sponsored or coordinated intelligence activity directed at the US Government, or corporations, establishments or persons, which involve the targeting or facilities, personnel, information, computer cable, satellite, or telecommunication systems which comprise, or are associated with the National Information Infrastructure.

Targeting the US Government: This involves foreign power sponsored or coordinated intelligence activity directed at US corporations, establishments, or persons, which involves the targeting of US Government programs, information, facilities, or personnel of: the US Intelligence community (IC); the US foreign affairs, economic or financial community; or, the US defense establishment and related activities of national preparedness. .

Perception Management: Involves protection from foreign power-sponsored or coordinated intelligence activity directed at the US Government, or US corporations, establishments or persons, which involves manipulating information, communicating false information, or propagating deceptive information and communication (domestically or internationally) designed to distort the perception of the public (domestically or internationally) or of US Government officials regarding US officials regarding US policies, ranging from foreign to economic strategies.

Foreign Intelligence Activities: Involves foreign power sponsored or coordinated intelligence activity conducted in the United States or directed against the US Government, or US corporation, establishments, or persons, that is not described by or included in the other issue threats.

NATIONAL SECURITY DIVISION

--INVESTIGATIVE PRIORITIES--

THE NATIONAL SECURITY THREAT LIST (NSTL) is the FBI's National Security Division's investigative strategy. The strategy is defined by eight investigative priorities:

Terrorism

Espionage

Proliferation

Economic Espionage

Targeting the National Information Infrastructure

Targeting the US Government

Perception Management

Foreign Intelligence Activities

These investigative priorities will apply to the activities of all foreign nations, with special attention given to those countries determined to be a strategic national security threat.

SECRET/NOFORN

NSTL COUNTRY THREAT LIST

CUBA

IRAQ

IRAN

LIBYA

NORTH KOREA

PEOPLE'S REPUBLIC OF CHINA (PRC)

RUSSIAN FEDERATION

SUDAN

SYRIA

TAIWAN

VIETNAM

SECRET/NOFORN

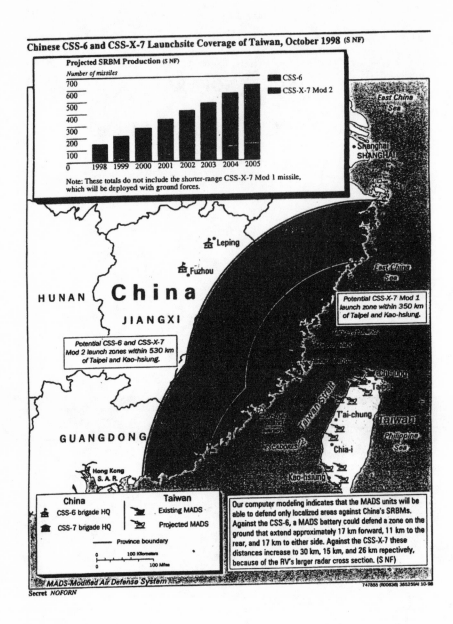

Chinese CSS-6 and CSS-X-7 Launchsite Coverage of Taiwan, October 1998 (S NF)

A secret Defense Intelligence Agency report showing that in the next several years Chinese short-range missile deployments are projected to increase to as many as 650 missiles. China will then be able to blanket Taiwan with missiles. (1 page)

SECRET

NAIC-1030-098B-96
November 1996

China Incrementally Downsizing CSS-2 IRBM Force (S)

The Chinese may be incrementally downsizing their CSS-2 force in areas where China's deployed mobile solid propellant systems such as the CSS-5 Mod 1 and CSS-6 offer adequate target coverage (S-US ONLY)

(S-US and AS, CA, UK ONLY) Analysis of CSS-2 crew training and activity at CSS-2 missile launch complexes (MLCS) and field garrisons (FG) indicates the Chinese may be incrementally downsizing the CSS-2 force. Reduction of the CSS-2 force is probably occurring in areas where the mobile, solid-propellant, CSS-5 Mod 1 (2,150 km), one of the replacement systems for the CSS-2, offers adequate target coverage. In areas where the CSS-2's 3,100 km range

launchers, are believed to still operate the CSS-2, and three of those four LSGS are now candidates for conversion to the CSS-5. The CSS-2's range capability is largely redundant in the 51st army since the CSS-5 Mod 1 can target all of Japan, North and South Korea, and parts of Taiwan from these deployment areas. At Dengshahe FG, also in the 51st army, up to four CSS-2 launchers are active. However, training levels at Dengshahe have dropped over the past few years, from 5 to 8 months per year in the late 1980s to about 4 months per year in the 1990s.

(S-US ONLY) The 52nd army, located in eastern China opposite Taiwan, includes CSS-2 ballistic missiles operated at Lianxiwang. Of the 16 LSGS built at Lianxiwang, up to ten are believed to currently operate the CSS-2. At least two Lianxiwang LSGS are being converted for use with the CSS-5 Mod 1. These factors, plus increasingly low levels of CSS-2 crew training observed at

Fig. 15 (S) Selected CSS-2 Associated Facilities

CSS-2   CSS-5 Mod 1

SECRET

Fig. 14 (S) Chinese CSS-2 and CSS-5 IRBMs

Lianxiwang, indicate the CSS-2 force is being significantly reduced at Lianxiwang. Since no US bases remain in the Philippines, and CSS-6 SRBMs, which can strike Taiwan, are deployed with the 52nd army, the need for the CSS-2 in the 52nd army, as in the 51st army, has significantly diminished. The CSS-2 force at Lianxiwang will probably fall to one launch group (four LSGS) until the system is retired.

capability is required, crew training activities remain robust and the number of deployed launchers likely remains unchanged. Comparison drawings of the CSS-2 and CSS-5 Mod 1 are shown in Figure 14. Launch complexes and facilities of current interest are shown in Figure 15.

(S-US ONLY) In the 51st army, located north of the Korean peninsula, replacement of the CSS-2 with the CSS-5 Mod 1 is well underway. Of the 12 CSS-2 Launch Site Garrisons (LSGS) at Tonghua, only four LSGS, assessed to consist of eight

While the training levels at Dengshahe have decreased, continued training indicates the CSS-2 will be retained there for the near term.

(S-US ONLY) In areas deeper inside China, where longer range is necessary for target coverage, CSS-2 activity levels are relatively high, indicating the missile could remain in service in these regions until new missiles such as the CSS-5 Mod 2 are deployed. Once CSS-5 Mod 1 and Mod 2 deployments are adequately underway, the CSS-2 will likely be removed completely from service, perhaps by 2002.

(S-US ONLY) Four LSGS and one launch complex garrison (LCG) at Jianshui in the 53rd army support the CSS-2, and four LSGS support the CSS-5 Mod 1. Despite 53rd army CSS-5 Mod 1 deployments, however, CSS-2 activity in the 53rd army is still very high, as evidenced by large-scale crew training exercises observed at Kunming this year (See Figure 16) (up to three launch units were in the Kunming training area simultaneously). The reason for this activity is probably related to the CSS-2's maximum range capability. Its range of 3100 km, versus 2150 km for the CSS-5 Mod 1, allows the CSS-2 ballistic missiles at Jianshui to target

Map labels: Tonghua Launch Complex • ; Dengshahe Field Garrison • ; Datong Field Garrison • ; Haiyan Training/Support Facility ; Yidu Field Garrison • ; Lianxiwang • ; CHINA ; Lianxiwang Launch Complex • ; Kunming Training/Support Facility ; Jianshui Launch Complex • ; SECRET

US ONLY

SECRET

A secret report by the U.S. Air Force's National Air Intelligence Center on China's medium-range missile deployments and a report on flight test preparations for a new DF-31 mobile intercontinental ballistic missile. (3 pages)

SECRET

NAIC-1030-098B-96
November 1996

most of India, while the CSS-5 Mod 1 can cover Southeast Asia from the same launch facilities. All eight of the current CSS-2 launchers may remain active in the 53rd army until the CSS-2 is removed from service.

(S-US ONLY) Large-scale CSS-2 training activity involving at least two launch units from Datong FG has also recently been noted at Haiyan training facility in the 56th army, located in central China. Datong FG is an ideal deployment site for the CSS-2 as the site is much less vulnerable to air attack than the coastal areas of the 51st and 52nd armies. From Datong, the CSS-2 can strike targets in India and Russia. Nevertheless, recent demolition activity at Datong indicates that facility is also undergoing conversion. Four barracks have been razed since

late April, two more are in the process of being razed, and a third may be razed as well. Datong will probably continue to operate eight CSS-2 launchers until the CSS-5 Mod 2 enters service.

(S-US ONLY) The CSS-2 order-of-battle, currently 40 refire-capable launchers, will likely decrease in the future. In the 51st and 52nd armies, and at Yidu FG as well, the CSS-2 force is being replaced by the CSS-5 Mod 1. Even in the areas where CSS-2 activity levels are high, it is unlikely the number of deployed launchers will increase, although storage of displaced CSS-2 airframes may occur. Once CSS-5 Mod 1 and Mod 2 deployments are adequately underway, the CSS-2 will likely be removed completely from service, perhaps by 2002.

(S) A video showing typical CSS-2 launch operations is shown in Video 1. A typical fueling operation, also depicted in the video is shown in Figure 17. Preparations for a normal CSS-2 training launch are shown in Figure 18.

CL BY: DCI
DECL ON: E.O. 12951

SECRET-US and AS, CA, UK ONLY

Fig. 16 (S-US and AS, CA, UK ONLY) CSS-2 Training Exercise At Kunming

CL BY: DCI
DECL ON: E.O. 12951

FOR OFFICIAL USE ONLY
Fig. 17 (S) CSS-2 Fueling

(S) This is a VIDEO ARTICLE. In the electronic version of this document available on Intelink, click the left mouse button on the squares at the right for a video of the CSS-2. Classification of video: SECRET.

Video 1

SECRET-US and AS, CA, UK ONLY
Fig. 18 (S) Typical CSS-2 Training

SECRET

NAIC-1030-098B-96
November 1996

Shipping Containers at Wuzhai Suggest the Chinese Are Prepared To Initiate a Flight-Test Cycle for the DF-31 ICBM
(S-US and AS, CA, UK ONLY)

(S-US and AS, UK ONLY) China will probably conduct final assembly of the DF-31 ICBM airframe at Beijing Nanyuan. Two environmentally controlled shipping containers typically used only at Beijing Nanyuan were recently used to transport a probable DF-31 airframe to the Wuzhai Missile and Space Test Center. The missile will later be flight-tested from Wuzhai. Use of these containers suggests final assembly of the DF-31 airframe was conducted at Beijing Nanyuan, since their presence has never been noted at any other final assembly facility. Airframe integration and payload mating will likely be conducted at Wuzhai.

31-associated trainset was identified at Wuzhai rail transfer point (RTP) Northwest. The complement of railcars included two 14-m-long heavy-duty flatcars and a 20-m-long environmental railcar (Figure 13) previously associated with transport of Chinese solid-propellant ballistic missiles. Each flatcar carried a light-toned rectangular container. These containers probably housed portions of the DF-31 ICBM's airframe. The containers are appropriately sized to contain the first stage and second stage/third stage combination of the DF-31 airframe, respectively. The presence of the environmental control railcar is also an indicator that a live DF-31 airframe was housed in the containers.

(S-US and AS, CA, UK ONLY) Other DF-31 activity at Wuzhai also suggests the Chinese are prepared to initiate a flight-test cycle for the DF-31 ICBM. This activity includes the presence of a probable canvas-covered DF-31 ejection test device and a probable DF-31 transporter at the main support facility at Wuzhai. Two cold-launch ejection tests were conducted from the silo at Wuzhai MSTC Pad A6 in October. Construction of the silo at Pad A6, to be used for the initial DF-31 flight tests, has been recently completed, and apparent training at Pad A6 has also recently occurred. Such activity suggests preparations for an integrated DF-31 flight test.

(S-US and AS, CA, UK ONLY) China's two older solid-propellant ballistic missiles, the CSS-5 Mod 1 and CSS-5 Mod 2, undergo final assembly at Nanjing Guided Missile Plant 307 before being shipped by rail to Beijing Nanyuan for airframe integration. These missiles are then shipped by rail from Nanyuan to either the test facility or an operational garrison. It appears, however, that the DF-31 shipping process will be similar to that employed for the CSS-6 short-range ballistic missile (SRBM), wherein Nanjing Guided Missile Plant 307 is bypassed completely. The reason for this change is uncertain at present, but the new procedure will significantly reduce the time required for assembly and checkout by eliminating some transit operations between production and test facilities.

(S-US and AS, CA, UK ONLY) On 6 August, a probable DF-

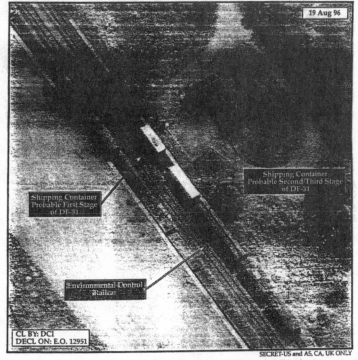

19 Aug 96

Shipping Container Probable Second/Third Stage of DF-31

Shipping Container Probable First Stage of DF-31

Environmental Control Railcar

CL BY: DCI
DECL ON: E.O. 12951

SECRET-US and AS, CA, UK ONLY

Fig. 13 (S-US and AS, CA, UK ONLY) Environmentally Controlled Shipping Containers Associated With the DF-31 ICBM at Wuzhai

SECRET

Force Developments

*Force Structure and
Modernization,
Deployments, Training
and Exercises*

China: Expanded Aerial Refueling Program

(S) Beijing has converted two more B-6/BADGER medium bombers into aerial refueling tankers, bringing its tanker inventory to five. Modifications to the newest airframes indicate China is improving the overwater capability of its tankers. By 1997, Chinese tanker and receiver aircraft probably will be able to perform some long-range escort, air-to-air, and ground-attack missions over the South China Sea or elsewhere in the region.

SECRET

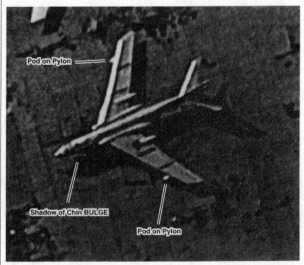

Pod on Pylon

Shadow of Chin BULGE

Pod on Pylon

(S) Newly Converted Chinese B-6D/BADGER Tanker. Confirmation of the fourth and fifth tankers, 6 months after the third was identified, suggests the rate of tanker conversions is increasing.

"These new tanker developments offer strong evidence that the Chinese have begun batch conversion of B-6 bombers to tankers."

(S) The two additional BADGERs were observed on 23 January with underwing pylons for refueling pods at Xian Airframe Plant 172, adjacent to Xian Flight Test Center, where the tanker program has been under development; one BADGER had pods installed. The two newest tankers have prominent ventral chin bulges forward of the nose landing gear. Both have a darker, less reflective paint scheme than the other three Chinese tankers. By 7 February, refueling pods had been installed on four of the five tankers. Previously, only one set of pods was known to exist in China.

This secret report in the Defense Intelligence Agency's Military Intelligence Daily *reveals China's plan to project power far from its shores by extending the reach of its warplanes through the conversion of bombers to aerial refueling jets. (2 pages)*

SECRET

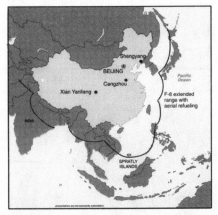

(C) Extending Combat Capability. The combat radius of the F-8-2/FINBACK will increase from about 375 NM to 550 NM, enabling China to conduct combat missions over the South China Sea, near Taiwan, along the Sino-Indian border, and over the East China Sea. An extended-range FINBACK would be able to escort B-6 bombers or the developmental FB-7 during ship interdiction activities.

SECRET

Expanded Tanker Force: A Critical Requirement

(S) The Chinese Air Force has an operational requirement for at least 20 tankers. As many as five could be operational during the next 5 years to support additional regiments of fighters and fighter-bombers. Shenyang Aircraft Corporation has outfitted about 15 new-production F-8-2/FINBACK fighters with refueling probes. The first regiment of roughly 24 FINBACKs could be capable of extended-range missions before 1998. China's late-model F-16-equivalent fighter, the F-10, also is likely to be air refuelable. Steady progress in air refueling will give China a power-projection capability over the South China Sea by the turn of the century.

Comment

(S) These new tanker developments offer strong evidence that the Chinese have begun batch conversion of B-6 bombers to tankers. The ventral bulges on the two new tankers are similar to the chin radome on the Chinese Naval Air Force B-6D strike aircraft, which uses a Chinese copy of the Russian SHORT HORN J-band bombing, navigation, and acquisition radar. Such a system enhances the overwater operational capability of the tanker by allowing it to function as forward air control for strike aircraft on extended missions. In light of this development, the forthcoming FB-7 strike fighter, which will carry the new C-801 air-to-surface cruise missile, could be configured for aerial refueling.

Middle East: General Purpose Forces (Arabian Peninsula) — Part II

(S) Most Arabian Peninsula states are continuing to receive and assimilate new weapons ordered as a consequence of Iraq's invasion of Kuwait. Because of an unstable internal security situation, Bahrain may increase the military's involvement in ensuring domestic order. Qatari forces played no direct role in the "palace coup" last June. Financial constraints will restrict force modernization in that country. The armed forces of the United Arab Emirates are still incorporating modern equipment, but maintenance remains a critical weakness.

PANAMA

Intelligence Overview
TAG Report #070-2000

U.S. CUSTOMS SERVICE
INTELLIGENCE DIVISION
TRENDS ANALYSIS GROUP
May 2000

Portions of a U.S. Customs Service intelligence report discussing China's activities in Panama. The report highlights Hutchison Whampoa's reported ties to the Communist Chinese government as well as Chinese involvement in drug and arms smuggling. (4 pages)

Executive Summary:

This report was written to assist Customs personnel in their duties by providing an overview of Panama and it's potential threats. Statistics contained in this report are concerned with FY98, FY99, and FY00 through May 1 and measure cocaine and heroin seizures with FDIN numbers extracted from TECS.

- Since the U.S. arrested General Manuel Antonio Noriega in December 1989, the country of Panama has experienced political instability, coup attempts, and severe economic difficulties.

- The immediate past president, was unable to stabilize his country, and consequently, drug-trafficking, money laundering, and corruption have continued.

- Panama has made few inroads in the fighting of both narcotics trafficking and money laundering thus far in 2000, due in part to Mireya Moscosos's recent taking over as the country's president and the U.S. withdrawal and turn over of its military bases and the Canal in January 2000.

- Panama's corrupt and ill-trained law enforcement units continue to be overwhelmed by trafficking efforts and are basically ineffective in their struggle.

- Reports show that Panama's drug seizures declined 80% in 1999 from its 1998 seizures and that no major narcotics traffickers or money launderers were arrested.

- Panama remains a major transit country for cocaine and increasingly heroin, due to its proximity to Colombia and other narcotics producing nations and it's apparently inadequate border, airport, and maritime controls.

- Panama's flag air carrier, COPA, has entered into an alliance with Continental Airlines, who now have 49% ownership in the airline. A serious security problem at Tocumen International Airport exists, with internal conspiracies involving ramp and cargo personnel who facilitate narcotic loads.

- The *Colon Free Trade Zone* provides a convenient means for the infusing of narcotics into legitimate cargo or empty containers destined for the U.S. and the laundering of drug money, allowing drug traffickers to co-mingle funds gained from illicit activity with funds from legitimate trade.

- Panama continues to be vulnerable to the threat of money laundering in spite of a 1998 Panamanian Banking Law aimed at strengthening their banking system, and deterring money laundering.

1

Zone, all add to its desirability as a money laundering center. Panama has a relatively large banking sector, with more than 110 domestic and international banks. Intelligence indicates that narcotics traffickers launder significant amounts of drug proceeds through both legitimate and front businesses in the *Colon Free Trade Zone* as well as Panama's banking and offshore sectors. Legitimate companies are also vulnerable to money laundering through the black-market peso exchange, a plot where Colombian peso brokers convert U.S. dollars into clean, usable pesos for drug cartels. They then use the dollars to buy goods that are smuggled into Colombia. In spite of a 1998 Panamanian Banking Law aimed at strengthening their banking system, and deterring money laundering, Panama remains vulnerable to the threat of money laundering. One particular weakness of the relatively new law, is the fact that only narcotics related money laundering is considered a criminal offense and a narcotics trafficking connection must be shown by prosecutors. The Panamanian Banking Laws due not permit the sharing by their police of money laundering information gained from Panamanian financial institutions with other countries.

Panama's Offshore Banking Center

Chinese Involvement in Panama- The Hutchison Whampoa Company, LTD., a Hong Kong based conglomerate, won what has been called, an unfair and corrupt contractual bidding process to develop ports at both the Atlantic and Pacific entrances to the Panama Canal. Its major shareholder, billionaire Li Ka-shing, reportedly has ties with the Red Chinese government. Shen Jueren, the Communist official who heads China Resources, and Li Ka-Shing, owner of Hutchinson Whampoa, are both reportedly partners in a Hong Kong Bank. This company has also established its self as a consolidator of ocean freight containers in Freeport, Bahamas as well.

OFFICIAL USE ONLY

Intelligence sources indicate that Chinese and Russian organized crime factions are active in narcotics, arms, and illegal alien smuggling utilizing Panama as a base of operations. The Chinese population in Panama has grown dramatically in the past five years and the Chinese government maintains an embassy in Panama City.

Narcotics Seizures- Cocaine and heroin seizures from Panama in FY 99 were down 13.4 % from FY98, however FY00 statistics reveal that Panama seizures are on pace for exceeding the FY98 amounts. Of note also are the Heroin seizure figures from FY00 YTD, which show that Heroin seizures have already exceeded FY99 figures and is only one seizure short of FY98's total. The method with the highest total seizures for all three fiscal years is commercial passengers, while commercial sea cargo is second in number of seizures, it was the method that produced the highest amounts in seizures. For FY00 YTD, JFK Airport and Mail Facility have produced the most total seizures with 15, Miami Airport, Seaport, Mail Facility and FEDEX Facility produced the second highest with 12, and Houston's Intercontinental Airport is third with seven seizures. Also of note, are the two significant seizures made in Charleston Seaport, one of 967 lbs. of cocaine and a second of 3,083 lbs. of marijuana.

~~SECRET NOFORN~~ *unclas*

DCSINT
USARSO
INTELLIGENCE UPDATE

Period of Report: 22 - 24 April 1998

Information contained in this summary is initial reporting of items pertinent to the USARSO
AOI/AOR

CURRENT DEPLOYMENTS

PANAMA

● CHINA AWAITS U.S. DEPARTURE (U) 221333Z APR 98

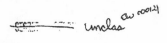 *unclas* *aw 0001y*

PANAMA

- China Awaits U.S. Departure (U)

— (U) According to a DIA Intelligence Information Report, Li Ka Shing, the owner of Hutchison
Whampoa Ltd. (HW) and Cheung Kong Holdings Ltd. (CK), is planning to take control of Panama
Canal operations when the U.S. transfers it to Panama in Dec 99.

— (U) Li is directly connected to Beijing and is willing to use his business influence to further the aims
of the Chinese government. He has been positioning his son, Victor Li, to replace him in certain CK and
HW operations such as HW's Hong Kong International Terminals (HIT).

— (U) Due to a decline in raw materials from within China, freight rates dropping due to excess tonnage
in the market, and the current Asian financial crisis, corporate revenues should decline. Consequently,
China is looking to expand into new markets. (DIA, 221333Z APR 98)

(C) Analyst Comment: Li's interest in the canal is not only strategic, but also a means for outside
financial opportunities for the Chinese Government. China, the canal's third largest user, consequently
has a significant amount of influence. If China were to assume control of the canal operations it would
have to abide by the neutrality requirements of the Torrijos-Carter treaties.

~~SECRET NOFORN~~ *unclas aw 0004y*

*These two declassified Pentagon intelligence reports reveal the Chinese threat to the Panama
Canal—contradicting the Clinton administration's public claims that a Chinese presence in the
canal poses no danger. (4 pages)*

SECRET//X1   ~~UNCLASSIFIED~~

Intelligence Assessment

26 October 1999

Panama: People's Republic of China Interests and Activities (U)

(S) The Ports of Balboa (Pacific) and Cristobal (Atlantic) were leased for 25 years, with an option to exercise 25 years, to the Panama Ports Company (PPC). There is no direct ownership between the People's Republic of China (PRC), PPC or its parent company Hutchison Whampoa.

(C) Summary: The PPC is a subsidiary of Hong Kong-based Hutchison Whampoa

(C) Discussion: The PPC's contract includes tug boats operations, ship repair, and pilot services within ports facilities. Hutchison Whampoa also may plan to lease a limited portion of Rodman Naval station as well as some storage space at the reverted Albrook Air Station. Neither Hutchison nor PPC are involved directly with day-to-day operations of the Panama Canal at this time.

(S) Any potential threat posed by the presence of a pro-Chinese corporate entity in the Panama Canal zone is indirect. It is unlikely that PPC officials or employees would overtly sabotage or damage the canal on orders from Beijing, as it would be contrary to their own financial interests and would undoubtedly elicit an immediate response from the US and the international community.

SECRET//X1   ~~UNCLASSIFIED~~

SUBJ (b)(1) sec 1.3 (c)

5 USC 552 (b)(1) See 15(c)

SECRET//X1   UNCLASSIFIED

(U) Hutchison Whampoa's owner, Hong Kong tycoon Li Ka-Shing, has extensive business ties in Beijing and has compelling financial reasons to maintain a good relationship with China's leadership.

(S) Economic influence equals political leverage and in some Latin American countries PRC and Taiwan competition for influence is running head-to-head. Currently, 16 of the 30 countries worldwide which diplomatically recognize Taiwan are located in Latin America.

SECRET//X1   UNCLASSIFIED

SECRET//X1   UNCLASSIFIED

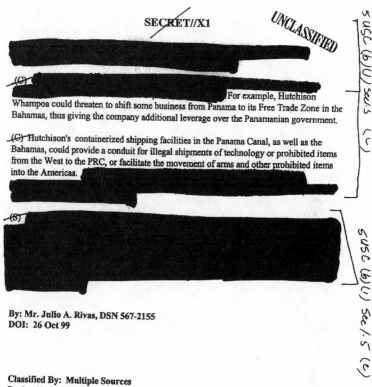

(C)

For example, Hutchison Whampoa could threaten to shift some business from Panama to its Free Trade Zone in the Bahamas, thus giving the company additional leverage over the Panamanian government.

(C) Hutchison's containerized shipping facilities in the Panama Canal, as well as the Bahamas, could provide a conduit for illegal shipments of technology or prohibited items from the West to the PRC, or facilitate the movement of arms and other prohibited items into the Americas.

(S)

5 USC (b)(1) Sec/.5 (c)

5 USC (b)(1) Sec/.5 (c)

By: Mr. Julio A. Rivas, DSN 567-2155
DOI: 26 Oct 99

Classified By: Multiple Sources
Declassify On: X1
Coordinated with: USDAO Panama City
Sources:

SECRET//X1   UNCLASSIFIED

CHINA: **Jiang's Position Remains Unconsolidated (S NF)**

Communist Party General Secretary Jiang Zemin appears to have weathered criticism of his Taiwan policies but remains unable to parlay his appointment as Deng Xiaoping's chosen successor into the paramount position. The US Embassy reports that rivals are trying to limit his power as next fall's 15th Party Congress nears.

press reports say National People's Congress Chairman Qiao Shi has been openly critical of Jiang's Taiwan policy and key appointments and

(S NF OC)

In addition, Jiang has been unable to assert his authority in areas he should be able to control after seven years as party General Secretary, six as Central Military Commission chairman, and three as President.

deposed Beijing party secretary and former Politburo member Chen Xitong, whose corruption investigation Jiang spearheaded, will not be brought to trial.

military leaders, some of whom Jiang promoted, last summer attacked Jiang's policy toward Taiwan as too lenient.

— Jiang is still resorting to Deng's theories to provide legitimacy to the Communist Party, suggesting an inability to claim Deng's mantle on his own.

(S NF OC)

Jiang's inability to consolidate his power means he will remain focused on domestic issues and is unlikely to initiate any steps to improve relations with the US or Taiwan that could spark internal criticism. Rather, he will pursue less controversial activities—such as his recent African tour—to build his own and China's international stature. (S NF) *-CIA, DIA-*

A report from the CIA's National Intelligence Daily *analyzing Chinese President Jiang Zemin's efforts to consolidate power. (2 pages)*

China: Jiang's Rivals for Influence (U)

Li Peng 67	Premier; member, Politburo Standing Committee	Maintains tactical alliance with Jiang when collective leadership faces threat, such as economic downturn, but working to undercut Jiang's authority behind the scenes . . . has criticized Jiang as too soft on Taiwan, US issues.
Qiao Shi 71	Chairman, National People's Congress; member, Politburo Standing Committee	Frequently identified in press, other reporting as Jiang's chief rival . . . criticizes Jiang's policies in private, seldom makes obligatory references to him in public speeches . . . attempting to strengthen influence of NPC to boost own political standing . . . past behavior suggests more likely to act as "kingmaker" for another challenger than to take on Jiang directly.
Zhu Rongji 67	Vice Premier; member, Politburo Standing Committee	Has maintained low profile in recent months but had past disagreements with Jiang over economic policy . . . still frequently cited as likely to hold higher office in future.
Li Ruihuan 61	Chairman, Chinese People's Political Consultative Conference; member, Politburo Standing Committee	Largely sidelined in recent years, but support would add prestige to a Jiang challenger . . . associated with group of Dengist reformers critical of Jiang's performance . . . has input on Taiwan, Hong Kong policy decisions.
Tian Jiyun 66	Vice Chairman, National People's Congress; member, Politburo	Has backed Qiao Shi's efforts to bolster influence of NPC, probably shares his views on Jiang . . . associated with Dengist reformers.
Yang Shangkun 89	Former President	Charged by Deng Xiaoping to support Jiang but has criticized some of Jiang's decisions, according to a variety of reporting . . . often rumored in Hong Kong media to be planning direct challenge . . . probably seeks acknowledgment of preeminent stature among elders after Deng . . . has been courted by Jiang in attempts to ensure his backing.
Wan Li 79	Former Chairman, National People's Congress	Rumored to be among group of Jiang opponents criticizing his handling of Taiwan affairs . . . also disagreed with Jiang on some corruption cases, according to press reports . . . among most active of party elders . . . has been associated with Qiao Shi, Tian Jiyun, other Dengist reformers.

352629PM5 5-96

**At the request of the Central Intelligence Agency,
the publisher has withdrawn a classified report that
was to have appeared on this page.**

Summary of a highly-classified National Security Agency report showing how China was able to predict the start of the 1991 Persian Gulf War by intercepting military communications in the region from its listening posts in western China. (2 pages)

At the request of the Central Intelligence Agency,
the publisher has withdrawn a classified report that
was to have appeared on this page.

SECRET   ░CRET
                          NATIONAL SECURITY COUNCIL
                            WASHINGTON, D.C. 20504
                               March 12, 1998

MEMORANDUM FOR MIKE HAMEL/JOHN NORRIS, OVP
               JOHN HOLUM, STATE/T
               ROBERT EINHORN, STATE/PM
               SUSAN SHIRK, STATE/EAP
               MELINDA KIMBLE, STATE/OES
               TED WARNER, DEFENSE
               MARC BERKOWITZ, DEFENSE
               KEITH CALHOUN-SENGHOR, COMMERCE
               CATHERINE NOVELLI, USTR
               JEFFERY HOFGARD, OSTP
               NORM WULF, ACDA
               ROBERT DIEKER, JCS
               JOHN SHOEMARKER, NASA

SUBJECT: China Missile Proposal

The attached paper proposes elements of a missile deal with
China, to be presented during U/S Holum's trip to China March
25-26. In essence, we would offer to expand commercial and
scientific space cooperation with China (in limited areas) if
China meets our conditions for joining the MTCR and controlling
its missile-related exports to Iran, Pakistan, etc. (Note that
Article 10 of the draft NASA-SSTCC Agreement for Scientific
Cooperation in the Areas of Earth Observation, Environment, and
Climate Change has been largely deleted.)

Please provide your comments and clearance to me by COB Tuesday,
March 17. Thanks.

                              Gary Samore
                              Special Assistant to the President
                                and Senior Director for
                                Nonproliferation and Export Controls

cc: Sandy Kristoff/Jeff Bader

SECRET   ░SECRET

A proposal by White House National Security Council proliferation specialist Gary Samore that
would have allowed China to gain access to missile technology in exchange for agreeing not to
sell missile technology to rogue states. The plan was never implemented after it became public.
(3 pages)

ELEMENTS OF THE CHINA MISSILE DEAL

Following are the elements of a missile deal that would be
proposed to China during Bob Einhorn's expert-level talks in
China March 23-24 and U/S Holum's "Global Security" discussions
in China March 25-26. In presenting the package, we would
propose to complete the elements in time to be announced during
the President's trip to China later this year.

What China Does:

1. Establishes effective MTCR export controls, and "catch-all"
controls on items destined for MTCR-class missile programs.

- This meets one of the MTCR's two substantive requirements
  for Chinese membership. It would require China to adhere
  to the current MTCR Guidelines and Annex, and to
  incorporate them into China's export control system.
  "Catch-all" is not an MTCR requirement, but is needed to
  deter circumvention of MTCR controls and to enforce
  limits on Iran [see below].

2. Does not transfer MTCR-controlled equipment and technology
to Category I (MTCR-class) missile programs in any non-MTCR
country, including Egypt, Indonesia, Iran, Libya, Pakistan,
Syria, Turkey, etc.

- This meets the second of the MTCR's two substantive
  requirements.

3. Does not assist ground-to-ground missile programs in Iran.

- This would cover all ground-to-ground ballistic and
  cruise missiles, even those below MTCR thresholds, and
  would include B610/8610/CSS-8, NP-110, and Shahab-series
  missiles.

What the U.S. Does:

1. Support Chinese MTCR membership, upon implementation of 1 and
2 above.

- This would provide China with political prestige, the
  ability to shape future MTCR decisions, substantial
  protection from future U.S. missile sanctions, and would

expedite somewhat the consideration of MTCR-controlled U.S.
exports to China.

2. Conclude NASA-SSTCC Agreement for Scientific Cooperation in
the Areas of Earth Observation, Environment, and Climate Change
Research. (See attached.)

- We would table the draft umbrella agreement during the
  talks, noting its conclusion would be dependent on a
  missile deal. (NOTE: Regardless of whether we reach a
  missile deal, we would proceed with the space projects
  that were agreed in the context of the Jiang visit.)

3. Issue blanket Presidential waiver of Tiananmen Square
sanctions to cover all future commercial satellite launches.

- Such waivers currently are issued case-by-case. Under a
  blanket waiver, we would continue to review case-by-case
  the export licenses required to launch U.S. satellites on
  Chinese boosters.

4. Increase number of permitted commercial space-launches.

- We would amend the existing Commercial Space Launch
  Agreement to increase the launch quota. We would also
  make clear to the Chinese that, as a practical matter, a
  lack of progress on the missile issue would prevent us
  form increasing launch quotas and could even endanger the
  existing quota.

3

The Honorable J. Dennis Hastert
Speaker of the House
  of Representatives
Washington D.C. 20515

SUBJECT: CDA Request from the Intelligence Authorization
          Act for Fiscal Year 1998/Section 308 re Intelligence
          Activities of the People's Republic of China

Dear Mr. Speaker:

     This report responds to Section 308 of the Intelligence
Authorization Act for Fiscal Year 1998 which directed that the
DCI and the Director/FBI provide an annual unclassified report
to Congress on the intelligence activities of the People's
Republic of China directed against or affecting the interests
of the United States. Also, as specified in Section 308, this
report has been produced in consultation with other appropriate
federal agencies. The classified version of this report was
forwarded to the Committee on 19 August 1999.

     The information provided in this report does not
incorporate or contain any Foreign Intelligence Surveillance
Act (FISA), grand jury, or federal criminal investigative
information. Additionally, as you are aware, CIA and FBI have
provided information in testimony before the Senate Select
Committee on Intelligence, the House Government Reform and
Oversight Committee, and the Senate Governmental Affairs
Committee on Chinese activities to influence the US political
process.

     An original of this letter is also being sent to House
Minority Leader Gephardt, along with the Senate Majority and
Minority Leaders, the Chairman and Vice Chairman of the
Senate Select Committee on Intelligence, and the Chairman
and Ranking Democratic Member of the House Permanent Select
Committee on Intelligence.

An unclassified FBI-CIA report on Chinese intelligence activities. The report states, "Penetrating the U.S. intelligence community is a key objective of the Chinese." (7 pages)

The Honorable J. Dennis Hastert

    If you have any further questions regarding this
issue, please do not hesitate to call.

Sincerely,

George J. Tenet
Director of Central Intelligence

Louis J. Freeh
Director, Federal Bureau
of Investigation

Enclosure

UNCLASSIFIED

SUBJECT: Report to Congress on Chinese Espionage Activities
           Against the United States

Background

   The "*Intelligence Authorization Act for Fiscal Year 1998*,"
Section 308, requires that the Director of Central Intelligence
and the Director of the Federal Bureau of Investigation, jointly
and in consultation with the heads of other appropriate federal
agencies, prepare and transmit to Congress a report on the
intelligence activities of the People's Republic of China (PRC)
directed against or affecting the interests of the United States.
This is the second annual submission of that report.

Overview of the Threat

   Beijing's national security priorities include maintaining
internal stability, gathering science and technology information
to advance China's economic development, and monitoring as well
as influencing developments related to Taiwan and worldwide
perceptions of China.   Its foreign intelligence collection goals
include gathering information about key players and developments
in countries that might affect China's interests.   Penetrating
the U.S. intelligence community is a key objective of the
Chinese.

   Due to its limited resources, much of China's intelligence
collection in 1998 continued to be accomplished by a network of
nonprofessional individuals and organizations acting outside the
direction and control of the intelligence services.   Nonintelligence organizations—such as private companies, research
institutes, and defense facilities—conduct independent and
uncoordinated collection activities to acquire sensitive
information and technology.   The Chinese intelligence services
have a long history of using Chinese students studying abroad to
collect information, either formally for those services or
informally for their home-based research institutes or
universities.   Many Chinese students in U.S. graduate schools are
studying hard sciences and are able to collect a wide variety of
information that is of value to China's efforts to ascend the
technology ladder.

   Because the Chinese consider themselves to be in a
developmental "catch-up" situation, their collection program
tends to have a comparatively broad scope.   Chinese collectors
target information and technology on anything of value to China,

UNCLASSIFIED

which leads then to seek to collect open-source information as well as restricted/proprietary and classified information.

China's intelligence infrastructure includes a variety of government entities. The following are assumed to have directed resources in 1998 to collection activities targeted at the United States:

- The Ministry of State Security (MSS) is responsible for civilian collection of foreign intelligence and for counterintelligence operations in China and abroad.

- The Military Intelligence Department of the People's Liberation Army General Staff (MID/PLA or Second Department) collects military and technological information and foreign intelligence.

- The Liaison Department a unit in the PLA's General Political Department, collects intelligence on Taiwan.

Foreign Intelligence Collection

Political Espionage: Beijing continues to view the United States as one of its major targets for political collection. It focuses on the foreign policies and intentions of the United States as well as information on U.S. leaders and sensitive bi- or multi-lateral negotiations.

Military Espionage: As the most advanced military power with respect to equipment and strategic capabilities, the United States continues to be the MID/PLA's primary target. Military intelligence collection against the United States is primarily conducted by military attachés assigned to the Defense Attaché's Office in the Chinese Embassy in Washington and the Military Staff Committee at the United Nations in New York City. For the most part, attachés openly collect information from Western publications as well as from their contacts in accordance with MID/PLA directives. Nonetheless, since 1987 the FBI and the U.S. Customs Service have detected and interdicted at least two MID/PLA clandestine collection operations in the United States.

Chinese attempts to obtain U.S. military and military-related technology—reflecting recognition of the overwhelming technological superiority enjoyed by the Western alliance in the Gulf War and Kosovo—have increased since the early 1990s. Other topics of interest to the MID/PLA are Sino-U.S. relations, U.S. military operations overseas, and the sale of U.S. military technology to Taiwan.

2

Recent FBI Case: The sentencing of Dr. Peter H. Lee on
26 March 1998 brought a close to an important FBI case that had
its origins in the 1980s. Lee, who had pleaded guilty the
previous December to espionage charges for transmitting
classified national defense information to the PRC, had admitted
to sharing classified information with Chinese scientists during
lectures he gave in the PRC in 1985 and 1997. Lee was also
charged with making false statements to a government agency when
he denied giving technical talks to the Chinese. Lee received a
suspended five-year prison term, one year of incarceration, three
years of supervised probation, a $20,000 fine, and 3,000 hours of
community service.

Economic Espionage: In 1998 China's collection of open
source, sensitive, and restricted proprietary/trade secret U.S.
technology and economic information, particularly advanced
civilian, military, dual-use and bio-technology, remained a
priority. China's official collectors of economic intelligence
prefer to use collection methods that are low-key and
nonthreatening. For example, the MSS, operating both in the
United States and in China, tries to collect proprietary or
sensitive U.S. information and technology in small increments,
involving a large number of people for an extended period of
time.

The MSS is particularly active against U.S. businessmen and
other Westerners inside China, where MSS officers can be
aggressive. Because most Chinese share a common cultural and
historical background, Chinese leaders refer to all individuals
of Chinese ancestry as "overseas" Chinese. When approaching an
individual of Chinese origin, the Chinese intelligence services
attempt to secure his or her cooperation by playing on this
shared ancestry.

The MSS and the MID/PLA play only a small part in China's
overall S&T collection process. Some of the thousands of Chinese
students, scientists, researchers, and other visitors to the
United States also gather information, working mostly for the
benefit of government-controlled, end-user organizations and
other scientific bureaus, research institutes, and enterprises.
The MSS, when requested, assists these institutions by matching
their information needs with assets the service has developed in
the United States or elsewhere.

Chinese nationals working abroad lawfully gather most S&T
and economic intelligence through open sources, such as U.S.
university libraries, research institutions, the Internet, and

3

unclassified databases, providing the Chinese Government with highly valued, yet unclassified information.

PRC scientists, through mutually beneficial scientific exchange programs, gather S&T information through U.S. national laboratories. Programs to enhance cooperation between the two countries have created an atmosphere of informational exchange, creating vulnerabilities in safeguarding U.S. technical intelligence. These vulnerabilities emphasize the significant difficulty the United States encounters in detecting PRC espionage activity.

Political Influence Activities

China continues to devote attention to building political influence in the United States. The increased emphasis dates from the June 1995 visit of Taiwan President Lee Teng-hui—a visit that caused Chinese leaders to redirect resources towards gaining a better understanding of Congress and greater political influence in the United States. The same year, Chinese leaders created the Central Leading Group for U.S. Congressional Affairs to oversee the task of increasing support for Chinese objectives.

Much like the rest of the world, the Chinese Government continues to seek influence in Congress through various means, including inviting Congressional members to visit the PRC, lobbying ethnic Chinese voters and prominent U.S. citizens, and engaging U.S. business interests to weigh in on issues of mutual concern.

Use of Commercial Entities for Intelligence Operations

During the past 20 years, China has established a notable intelligence capability in the United States through its commercial presence.

China's commercial entities play a significant role in its pursuit of proprietary/trade secret U.S. technology. The vast majority of Chinese commercial entities in the United States are legitimate companies; however, some are a platform for intelligence collection activities. Although a commercial entity may not be directly involved in the acquisition of information/technology, it may provide cover for both professional and non-professional intelligence collectors. Professional collectors are usually affiliated with one of China's intelligence services, while non-professionals usually collect for themselves. These collectors enter the United States to gather sensitive and/or restricted proprietary/trade secret

4

information or to act as a liaison to consumers of intelligence back in China.

The primary targets from which China seeks to acquire sensitive and restricted proprietary/trade secret U.S. technology are the U.S. Government, private U.S. corporations, academic institutes, laboratories, as well as persons involved in sensitive and/or restricted work. These operations are usually low-key and singular in nature, thus creating a significant counterintelligence dilemma for the FBI.

Propaganda and Perception Management

China primarily uses government-owned or government-controlled press to ensure its views on policy issues are heard in the United States. For example, Wen Wei Po, which appears as a periodic supplement to Chinese-language newspapers published in the United States, is a favored outlet for reaching ethnic Chinese audiences, whose perspectives in turn can influence the broader public's views of China.

TOP SECRET UMBRA GAMMA

At the request of the National Security Agency, the publisher has withdrawn a top secret report that was to have appeared on this page.

A top secret report in the National Security Agency's Sigint Digest *on China's sale of a chemical weapons factory to Iran. (2 pages)*

TOP SECRET UMBRA GAMMA

At the request of the National Security Agency, the publisher has withdrawn a top secret report that was to have appeared on this page.

**At the request of the National Security Agency,
the publisher has withdrawn a top secret report that
was to have appeared on this page.**

*A top secret National Security Agency report revealing how the Chinese are helping Iran develop
its missile program. (1 page)*

EAST ASIA *(continued)*

China: **Possible Missile-Related Delivery to Syria**

China Precision Machinery Import-Export Corporation—China's premier missile sales firm—delivered what probably is military-related cargo to Syria early this month, according to special intelligence. Though the exact nature of the equipment, described as special and dangerous, remains unclear, *the involvement of CPMIEC and the Syrian end user suggests the shipments are missile related.*

the cargo was destined for the Scientific Studies and Research Center, which is responsible for Syria's ballistic missile, weapons-of-mass-destruction, and advanced conventional weapons programs.

— SSRC runs Syria's Scud C ballistic missile production program and an upgrade program for antiship missiles. Moreover, in recent years it has sought and received assistance for each of the projects from CPMIEC

China: **Seeking Advanced US Defense Technology**

a Chinese firm has illicitly obtained sophisticated US-made millimeter-wave traveling wave tubes, power transmission devices that can be used in a variety of military applications, including airborne missile seeking and fire-control radars, targeting systems, and navigation pods.

— *The Chinese will most likely try to duplicate the technology in the power transmission tubes.* They have reportedly tried—with little success—to produce similar tubes in the past; their efforts have included joint ventures with the Russians.

The cost of the tubes—obtained in the Philippines—increased fourfold to $80,000 each because of the illegal nature of the transaction, *but there is high military and commercial demand for this equipment.*

A top secret CIA report on China's weapons sales, including a delivery of missile-related cargo to Syria. (1 page)

ACKNOWLEDGMENTS

Many people helped me with this book. Some cannot be named because they would face retribution from a U.S. government seemingly more intent on covering up questionable policies and pursuing "leaks" of information than protecting national security from threats, such as those posed by aggressive foreign intelligence services. I view these people in the intelligence, military, and national security communities as heroes. They had the courage to expose, often by providing documentary evidence, Chinese activities and U.S. initiatives and policies that were disastrous for America's national security and the post–Cold War balance of power.

A special note of thanks goes to the *Washington Times*. The *Times* was founded in 1982, toward the end of the Cold War, by the Reverend and Mrs. Sun Myung Moon. It has been unceasing in its coverage of communism and its anti-human policies. The *Times* has continued to play an important role in highlighting the growing threat to the United States from a People's Republic of China that, despite reforms, remains anti-democratic and firmly communist.

In particular, I want to thank several *Times* editors for their support, namely Editor-in-Chief Wesley Pruden, Managing Editor William E. Giles, Deputy Managing Editor Francis B. Coombs, Jr., and National Editor Ken Hanner. My *Times* colleagues Rowan Scarborough and Jerry Seper also provided valuable help.

I want to thank the Social Philosophy and Policy Center at Bowling Green State University for helping me as a media fellow with this project. Jeffrey Paul and Fred D. Miller, Jr., were especially helpful.

I am grateful to Larry Klayman and Tom Fitton of Judicial Watch for their help with Freedom of Information Act searches that produced valuable intelligence reports on Chinese activities in Panama. Scott Wheeler of *American Investigator* deserves praise for getting a copy of the FBI's secret National Security Threat List.

Others who helped include David Braaten, Robert Morton, Dan Fefferman, Constantine Menges, Al Santoli, I. C. Smith, Stephen Engelberg, William C. Triplett II, Edward Timperlake, Michael Ledeen, Richard Fisher, and Christoph Wilkening.

INDEX